Margaret Mellon
Hay-on-Wye
27.9.87.

HYPNOSIS
A Gateway to Better Health

Dr Brian Roet

HYPNOSIS

A Gateway to Better Health

WEIDENFELD AND NICOLSON · LONDON

Published in Great Britain by
George Weidenfeld & Nicolson Limited
91 Clapham High Street
London SW4 7TA

ISBN 0 297 78813 2

Printed in Great Britain at
The Bath Press, Avon

Illustrations by Elizabeth Dawnay

*To Danielle, Sophie and
Brownie the donkey
from whom I learnt so much whilst trying to teach*

Contents

Contents

Foreword by Claire Rayner

This book could be the most important you have ever read. It offers, for those who are willing to take the time to read it and to open their minds to what it has to say, the answers to a great many of the fears and phobias, pains and pressures of the life you lead. Do you smoke and wish you didn't? Eat too much and would rather not? Feel shy, full of tension, short of self-confidence, aggressive, angry and tearful? Have trouble in dealing with your lover, your spouse, your children, your boss? Have chronic pains, headaches and bellyaches and sleeplessness which have plagued you for years and which no doctor seems able to relieve?

The answers to all these problems are here. *But only if you want to find them.*

The most illuminating thing that emerges from reading these pages is that to a considerable extent we all choose to be what we are: unhappy or happy, successful or disastrous, liked or disliked ... it's all in our own hands – or rather our heads. Inside every one of us there is the capacity to live our lives as they were surely meant to be lived – giving us and the people with whom we deal, pleasure. One of the most useful keys to finding and releasing that capacity is hypnosis. There is nothing mysterious or dangerous or dubious about it at all. It is, as Dr Brian Roet explains with wit, charm and a great deal of common sense, simply an all-purpose tool that can be used to improve our lives.

I take a great deal of personal pleasure in the existence of this book. As one who deals with a great many appeals from people who need such a tool as hypnosis to help them solve their dilemmas, I find it very gratifying that the suggestion I dropped into Dr Roet's lap, in my kitchen one dark winter afternoon a year or so back, has borne such splendid fruit. I knew Dr Roet had the knowledge that would help people to be happier. What I couldn't know was whether he could get the necessary information across in a way that would make it easy to understand and possible to use.

Well, I know now. He most definitely can. His pages are full of fun, information, and real people and their problems, as well as theories about how to cope. I found reflections of myself in many of the examples he quotes here and so will you.

9

I do hope you're one of the people who will one day tell everyone that you once read a book that changed your life, rather than one of those who throw aside every aid they are offered and say despondently, 'Nothing can help me …'. For people like that, sadly, there are no answers, because they don't really want them. But if you are open-minded and truly want to help yourself be happier and healthier, this is the book to help you do it.

Acknowledgements

I would like to thank Des and Claire Rayner for creating the idea for this book. Lorraine, for her remarkable ability to decipher a doctor's illegible handwriting and convert Aussie slang into the Queen's English. Gill, for helping compile enormous amounts of written material. Liz, for her visualisation of my ideas into coherent diagrams. Bernard Oliver and Lucy Hamson for their help and tireless work to further the use of hypnosis in medicine and dentistry. And, last but not least, all the patients who have shown me, in their own way, how to understand difficulties and to appreciate limitations.

'. . . but where does this gateway lead?'

'To a pathway.'

'Is this a pathway I should venture on?'

'That is up to you. Consider how you may be if you remain stationary.'

'Can you describe this pathway?'

'No, it is different for everyone. It will twist and turn, soar over mountains, plunge into ravines. It is as full of adventure and challenge, hope and disappointment as life itself. The choice is yours.'

Introduction

*There are many people to whom the crucial problems of their
lives never get presented in terms they can understand.*

The word hypnosis has a long history associated with mumbo-jumbo,
the occult and power-controlling mystery men. Because of this, many
people fear its use and will avoid the concept of being hypnotised at
all costs.

This book is written to remove the myths and misconceptions surrounding hypnosis, and to present it as it really is – a natural phenomenon
occurring to us many times a day.

It is a day-dream state in which we relax, drift away and make use
of the resources of our unconscious minds. In a trance or dream-like
state we can view our problems from a distance, remove tension and
present optimistic alternatives to ourselves. By using this method it is
possible to get off the merry-go-round which occurs when we try with
our conscious mind to solve unconscious puzzles.

Many of the problems, and illnesses for which we seek help, either
from friends, therapists or doctors, contain a large psychological element.
It may well be this element which keeps the problem going long after
one would expect it to be resolved. Understanding and altering the psychological component, provides a simple and brief way to overcome
the troublesome situation.

In this book I would like to explore ways in which you, with your
specific problems and your unique resources, can learn to use hypnosis
to provide a new way to deal with what may be a very frustrating difficulty.

Imagine being in a room of your house and smelling a very unpleasant
smell. Every time you enter the room you are upset by the smell. You
can't enjoy music, reading or the television as your mind keeps wandering
and wondering what is causing the smell. You clean the room thoroughly,
searching for the source of the problem. You empty the cupboards and
wash the curtains. You shampoo the carpet. But still the smell persists.
As time goes on frustration and anger are added to your problem. It
seems the harder you try the worse you feel.

A friend visits you and you tell him about your problem. He helps you search. With his different view of things he goes out of the room and looks in the cupboard under the stairs. He returns triumphant, holding a bag containing fish which has been left there by mistake months before.

Instantly you feel better and over the next few days the smell goes and you learn to enjoy your room and all the things you can do in it.

Often we try to solve our problems by looking in the wrong place. Instead, you can learn to use hypnosis to find the source of the smell. I can assure you that there is no fear, no lack of control, no talking about things you don't wish to.

This book is the beginning. If you find it interesting you might like to listen to the tape (see page 14). In this way you can move another step along the pathway to having some positive influence over your problems. If you find the tape useful you might like to learn more from a competent therapist (see page 255). In reality all the learning is about something which you already know, but don't know you know. It is just that the pace and stresses of life direct you towards 'doing' and 'trying' rather than 'relaxing' and 'being'.

You will benefit most by approaching this book with an open mind. If you read expecting to criticise, or find scientific evidence, you may have great success as I'm sure there are unproven statements. But the success you will have will not help you to find the peaceful relaxation which may be of much greater benefit.

By reducing tension the body and mind function in a much more natural, healthy way. A car performs better and lasts longer if you drive with your foot off the brake unless it is required. Stress in daily life may be putting the brake on the way your body and mind function. Allowing a few minutes a day for self-hypnosis may release that brake and allow you to enjoy more fully the many aspects of life available to you.

It is important to read this book in the sequence it has been written and not immediately turn to the hypnosis section. Just as a large piece of cake is better digested in small mouthfuls, this book will be of more use if read one chapter at a time. Allow time for the thoughts and teachings to be digested before moving on. Perhaps one chapter a night may be an appropriate caloric intake for your specific diet.

It is set out as advice on how to get out of a maze. In order to achieve the simplest, quickest and most satisfactory solution, an understanding of the different aspects of the problem is essential.

The first section gives an overview of aspects which may be involved in the problem and its maintenance.

The second section describes how our self-imposed restrictions play a major role in preventing us from finding different openings in the maze. Previous beliefs and indoctrination make us blind to the possibilities available, and an understanding of these may be essential if we are ever to get out of the dead ends we continually find ourselves in.

The third section helps to provide alternative choices to the ones we are unsuccessfully using. No answers are given but the fact that different openings in the maze become apparent provides hope for the future.

The fourth section is an explanation of hypnosis and how it may be the thread linking the inside world of the unconscious mind to the outside world of reality. This thread can provide a recognisable route out of the maze.

The fifth section describes the partnership between mind and body and discusses essential aspects necessary to understand health problems.

The sixth section analyses some specific illnesses – dead ends in the maze – and the role of hypnosis in dealing with these.

The final section provides a discussion about some common queries concerning hypnosis.

Self-hypnosis is of greatest use when you have a full knowledge of the problem and your involvement in maintaining it. By reading through the sections in order, I hope you will gain this knowledge and therefore benefit most from the daydream state we call hypnosis.

Hypnosis is not a cure all, it is not an instant piece of magic that will change your life in a few days. It is just a small ingredient, like the drop of oil that changes an irritating squeaky door into a silent one. But if the door is warped and the hinges rusty, no amount of oil is going to help.

I suggest you all know about hypnosis already. As a child staring out of the classroom window daydreaming, you were in a trance. But adults have forbidden such wasteful pastimes and so they have been discarded as useless. I maintain that relearning to daydream will provide many benefits.

It is important that you accept, as I do, that you already possess all that is required to help your situation. It is often very easy to understand and help your friends in need. I hope this book may prove useful in enabling you to help your very best friend – yourself.

PART ONE
Opening the Gate

1 Dealing with Life

The power of memories and expectations is such that for
most human beings the past and the future are not as real,
but more real than the present.
ALAN W. WATTS, *The Wisdom of Insecurity*

Life can be looked on as a card game of chance. Our 'opponents' may
be many and varied, recognised and unrecognised, from the past, present
or future. Often once one hand has been won the challenge is on again.
It often seems as if our 'opponents' hold all the good cards, they are
in control of the game while we are constantly fighting a losing battle,
trying to build up the bank while the chips are dwindling.

How can you improve your game? Some people are better card players
than others. They seem constantly to win or minimise their losses. Perhaps
they are just lucky or perhaps they know something we don't. There
may be a few tips that could be useful in the game of life. We can discard
some cards to improve our hand. One thing in our favour is that we
are the dealers of our own cards. Some have been dealt to us when
we were growing up but perhaps we can learn to adjust them, to hold
on to the right ones and discard those no longer useful.

This may seem too far-fetched, too removed from the 'real' problems
of life. Of course, life isn't a card game. As my headmaster once said
to me, 'Brian – life is real and life is earnest.' He said it with such intent,
I imagine it was how Moses delivered the commandments.

Life is what you make it. And if you make it real and earnest it will
be so. Firstly one must know the rules of the game. To join a poker
school and believe your knowledge of snap will get you through, is
courting disaster. The majority of us still use mechanisms and tactics
we learnt when we were very young to deal with adult problems.

How many of us resort to the 'snap' level of a temper tantrum when
things go wrong? It worked when we were three – we got Mum angry
and received attention, so we still keep using it long after Mum has
gone. Can you imagine what reaction there would be in the poker school
if two similar cards are discarded and you put your hand over them

and say 'snap', looking eagerly into the tense faces of cigar-smoking card sharps?

So learning the appropriate rules is the first step in dealing with life. These are *here and now* rules, not rules from the past or other people's rules.

A woman in her forties came to see me with a multitude of problems. Life was getting too much for her. She wasn't dealing well in the game and seemed to be a constant loser. She was bored, depressed, lonely, 'couldn't cope', no-one respected or understood her, her family used her, etc. etc.

Her husband came home from work, sat down to read the paper and called out for a drink. She provided this, and when he was ready she served the meal she'd prepared, waiting on him hand and foot. He didn't talk to her much except to give her directions and commands.

They made love (if you could call it that) when he wanted to. She got up before him to give him tea in bed, ran his shower, prepared his clothes, etc. etc. When I asked why she did this she replied, 'Mother said I must look after my husband – it's my duty.'

When I asked her what did she think of this, she burst into tears and complained bitterly of her slave-like life. When I again asked her why didn't she stop doing this she repeated Mother's rule, 'Thou shalt look after thy husband as a duty.'

She was playing the game by someone else's rules. They were not her rules for the here and now. They were Mother's rules from the past (and possibly not even hers but her mother's rules) and with this woman they were inappropriate to her beliefs.

We spent some time forming some up-to-date rules, more appropriate to her belief system. We both realised there might be some difficulty with her husband's response to the new rules but she was prepared for the time it might take for the changes to occur.

She didn't believe (in her rules) that she needed to get up earlier to get her husband's tea in bed or run his shower and she decided to discard this card in her hand. She agreed to try some other gentle changes over the next few weeks and report back.

She had a struggle over the next few months as her husband had got used to 'Mother's rules' but in time a compromise was achieved with more communication, understanding and up-to-date rules to the game.

2 *The Hidden Commander*

Theirs not to reason why
Theirs but to do or die
Into the valley of death
Rode the six hundred.
ALFRED LORD TENNYSON,
The Charge of the Light Brigade

In the Crimean War in 1854 the Battle of Balaklava was fought. During the battle Lord Cardigan commanded the British. He was situated on a hill overlooking two valleys. He directed his troops from this vantage point to charge into one valley. He couldn't see that at the end of that valley were Russian soldiers with cannons at the ready. The troops below him could see that they were riding into the 'valley of death' but, as good soldiers, they obeyed the command irrespective of their knowledge, and proceeded to their destruction.

'Theirs not to reason why.' No questions allowed. It wouldn't be right and proper. The commander is in command and if the troops questioned his decision where would they be? In some cases this is the correct attitude; in other cases it is disastrous.

In the Charge of the Light Brigade the well-trained troops ignored *their* knowledge and followed the Commander. So it is in life for most of us. We ignore the evidence and present-day facts and follow a hidden commander from inside our minds. We pay deference to a higher authority and if a choice has to be made we follow its directions. I will give you an example of the hidden commander who, like General Cardigan, may not have been in a suitable position to advise.

Julian is thirty-five. He is a computer operator and he thinks of himself as being pretty worthless. He needs reassurance about most of the things he does; he never feels he is good enough or competent enough, quick enough or careful enough. He has steadily received promotion but at all times doubts his ability. The present-day facts are that he is a competent and useful worker, but his hidden commander working on previous experience keeps telling him he is no good.

He visited me suffering from sleeplessness, despondency and

depression. He was 'not getting much out of life'. He was not married, has had few and unsuccessful relationships which, when he told me about them, he ended with the comment, 'she is too good for me'.

In order to find out where his hidden commander created the belief that he was worthless, we used hypnosis. In a trance Julian went back to situations where his parents continually criticised him. He was never good enough to please them. If he got 80 per cent at maths, they said he should have got 90 per cent. If he made 50 runs at cricket, why wasn't it 100?

He recalled a time when, giving the wrong answer to a question in class, he was dragged in front of his laughing schoolmates and ridiculed. His hidden commander was receiving lots of intelligence work (not so intelligent) to reach the conclusion that he was worthless.

As he grew up Julian developed many talents in different areas, but always failed to accept that he had these abilities. People would show their recognition of him with jobs, friendships, etc. but he was always sent down the wrong valley by his advisory expert, who was years out of date.

His commander, who recognised the terrible humiliation little Julian had experienced in that class and with his father, decided to protect him from further pain. The tactic was 'In order to avoid pain from humiliation, humiliate yourself first. In order to avoid the pain of failure, don't attempt anything, then no criticism can occur.'

It sounds feasible, but as he grew up he found he was also criticising himself for not doing anything. He didn't know of the commander's existence and had no communication with him. He didn't question the orders but followed them blindly, irrespective of the evidence presented to him.

I suggest we learn to take control from the hidden commander, that we act on present day evidence. Perhaps I'm suggesting a mutiny on a ship which is continually being directed onto the rocks.

All our experiences in growing come from trial and error, not from advice. We learn to crawl our own way in our own time. We make mistakes and learn from these mistakes. We pull ourselves up on a chair leg and see the world differently. We fall and cry then try again, eventually making the change from a baby to a toddler. We still have the ability to crawl but find it more exciting or adventurous to walk. If, when we had just fallen, we decided it was too painful to try again and allowed our commander to protect us, think of how much we would miss. It may be a little safer, a little less painful, but how limiting to go through life crawling everywhere. So it is with many other aspects of life where we obey protective orders from inside, even if they are contrary to conscious beliefs.

I ask many of my patients if they learnt to ride a bike when they were young. Some say they started, fell off and grazed their knees and didn't continue. Often these people continue this protective mechanism through many other aspects of their lives. They can't swim, don't drive, don't form relationships, still live with their parents even though they may be over 30, are negative and lack confidence.

I do not wish to generalise about people, but if we continue to avoid the pain of experience we also may be avoiding a lot of other things life has to offer.

It would take a very strong soldier, I suppose, to refuse to ride into the valley of death. So perhaps it is very difficult to refuse the inner directions that differ from your present knowledge.

How do you know if you are responding to the hidden commander and that it is contrary to your understanding of how it would be sensible to behave?

If you find you 'can't do things' which you believe you are capable of doing or wish to do, ask yourself, 'Why am I unable to do these things? What is preventing me? Is it due to my present ability or an assessment that occurred some time ago?'

If you say to yourself, 'I'd love to do that but I just can't', and what you are seeking is reasonable, it is more than likely that the part of you saying, 'I can't' is basing its direction on false information from the past. It seems to me that trial and error learning is the main way we make progress; not giving this a chance may not allow you to explore many potentials you have.

My mother was a keen golfer and my father said he would like to have a round of golf with her one day. He had never played before.

On the allotted day he, understandably, spent most of his time in the rough, missing the ball and see-sawing across the fairway. At the end of the round, in order to give him some encouragement, my mother said, 'You play quite well, you should have some lessons.' My father was greatly disturbed as he had been having lessons secretly for six months. He never played golf again and claimed it was a useless game trying to hit a silly little white ball into a hole. Some time later when we could discuss it unemotionally, he said he really would like to have continued, but the humiliation of that first game was too much to go through.

Quite understandable, but because he gave up after one round, he missed the opportunity he might have had to enjoy the pleasures (and frustrations) of golf. Maybe if he had tried a few times and learnt that what looks so easy is very difficult to most of us, he may have persisted. Many golfers have the initial problem he had, they spend years trying to correct slices, replace divots, putt properly, but many gain great pleasure from what the game offers even if it is only the fresh air and exercise.

So it is on the golf course of life. If we can learn from our mistakes, we can eventually have a reasonable round with an occasional birdie to compensate for five shots in the bunker.

I would like to pass on some advice I received from a golf professional, after I'd studied many books and talked to lots of people about my terrible golf. I was always in the rough, digging in the undergrowth, cursing and swearing and embarrassed by holding up my partner with a crowd on the previous tee waiting to hit off. When my partner drove off, the fairway looked like the tarmac of an airport. When I drove off it had miraculously changed to a narrow country lane.

The professional said to me, 'I'll give you three pieces of advice, (1) Practice, (2) Practice, (3) Practice.' May I give the same advice. Reading a book, theorising, will never make any difference in itself. Putting theories or suggestions into practice will help you to learn how to learn. I will guarantee you will make mistakes and have failures. These are very useful learning experiences.

Growing up can be defined as learning from experiences. If we don't learn from our experiences – good and bad – we would still be doing the same thing, the same way, as we did when we were children. In fact under stress we sometimes return to childhood responses and have tantrums, cry and behave as we did under similar stress at a much younger age.

Each experience is stored in the unconscious mind to help us avoid making the same mistake again and again. We learn not only from our own experience but those of our parents who direct us from their experiences. So gradually we build up a 'bank of learning experiences' and in time of need revert immediately to this reserve without thinking about it, just as a soldier is trained to react without question in times of war. Some experiences have much more effect on us than others. Those which cause guilt or fear may loom large in the 'bank' and present themselves immediately a similar situation occurs.

Trixie was a woman of forty when she came to see me. She had an unnatural fear of men. When she was five she was molested in a park. A most unpleasant and terrifying experience with associated fear, guilt, anger and sadness which were stored in her mind with no avenue for release. She was perplexed by the events and feelings surrounding that time and had partly forgotten them when I saw her. She grew up as a normal teenage fun-loving girl, but was always wary of boyfriends and understandably didn't date much.

Some years ago she met a very nice, quiet protective man and after a long courtship they were married. She loved, respected and trusted him and apart from some difficulties with sex, their marriage was a very happy one.

Two years ago she began to develop a generalised fear of men. If she was in a room on her own and a man came in she began to tremble and sweat, her heart raced and she had to leave the room. If she was walking down the street and a man came the other way she would cross the road. It seemed to be getting worse. If she was with her husband she felt fine but when he was not there she became nervous. It seemed to me that the hidden commander was in control, still protecting her from something which happened many years ago.

This is how the hidden commander becomes part of us. A situation causes us difficulty when we are young, makes us develop advisory mechanisms. These may be reasonable, helpful and protective but as we grow we no longer need such support.

Trixie was not reacting to the situation as it existed in the present. She still exhibited the intense fears she had acquired when she was five. In order to help her we needed to deal with the hidden commander during hypnosis and direct it to 'go off duty' as it was no longer necessary. In this way she learnt to see men from an adult point of view with their strengths and faults and to decide for herself how to react.

I call it the hidden commander because the motivating force for a particular behaviour is hidden from the conscious mind. This is where hypnosis is useful in making us aware of what is driving us. Fighting inappropriate but powerful internal directions by saying, 'It's silly but I can't change, it's not my fault, I'm hopeless,' doesn't usually help.

What often happens is that we experience repeated failures 'to wrest control' from the hidden commander and these failures reinforce the belief that we cannot behave differently. Instead of its power getting less as we grow older it takes control more and more. New fears reinforce the original ones and our ability to change or to explore the possibility of change diminishes.

Jonathon had problems driving which had grown worse over the years. He became more and more nervous every time he got behind the wheel. As his work required him to drive he was in danger of losing his job. In all other aspects of his life he was in control, happy and carefree, but gradually his fear of driving began to alter his nature. He drank more than usual, snapped at his wife more and argued with his partners at work. He could not understand what was happening. He was a good driver, had never had an accident, and used to love driving his BMW, but recently just the thought of it made him nervous.

I talked to him about the hidden commander being in control and it appeared its aim was to prevent him driving. He had no idea why this should be.

Using hypnosis we went back to the first time he had been nervous about driving three years before. He had been to a party and was very drunk. Driving home he nearly had a head-on collision. He had completely forgotten this and after the trance remembered it as if through the alcoholic haze he was experiencing at that time. His recent attempts to minimise his fear by having a few more drinks were understandably making matters worse, as his hidden commander was attempting to protect him from his previous drink-driving experience.

He made a commitment consciously and also in a trance to the hidden commander that he would not drink and drive and that he would drive carefully. An agreement was reached between the two that the anxiety would decrease if he kept to his commitment. Over the following weeks he felt much better and his fears subsided. I believe if he does drink and drive the commander, no longer quite so hidden, will begin to exert its influence again.

If you ever go to a local tennis court and watch people play, you may notice the strange way some people serve. The gyrations and distortions that occur in order to get the ball over the net are an interesting example of the learning process. If we could video such a serve and observe it in slow motion there would be a number of separate movements, one following the other. Often the first movement is countered by the second and the explanation for this is that in learning to play, different pieces of advice have been tried. When one piece of advice has failed, instead of discarding it, another piece of advice has been included to counterbalance the first.

Some tennis players go to such extremes to incorporate all the techniques they have learned that the end result is laughable. I suppose one can win a point by making one's opponent weak with laughter but there must be better ways of winning.

If our tennis player realised that trying to solve an initial problem by adding compensatory mechanisms was not working, perhaps he or she could start again and learn a straight and simple way to serve.

We do something similar in life when we continue to incorporate 'failed learning' in our attitudes and activities. We devise many complicated ways of compensating for unhelpful inner commands and so tend to make life more difficult.

The fact that the tennis courts are full of wildly gyrating servers may indicate how difficult it is to return to a simple straightforward way of play. Or it may indicate that people are unaware that an alternative is available.

Another example of alternative ways of doing things is apparent when we try and work out how to use a new appliance. After purchase we hurry home, anxious to see how it works (it being anything from a can opener to a video). Unwrapping it and plugging it in (if necessary) we tend to try all the knobs and do what we feel is correct to 'get it going'. In my case, after a long frustrating time of failure, cursing and blaming the manufacturer, I may ring up a friend and ask 'how to work the damned thing'.

Often the explanation is relatively simple and, when I check, is neatly stated in the instructions. The motto I now use is, 'When all else fails read the instructions.'

An acquaintance of mine complained that the photos I took were always much better than his. His were blurred, under-exposed, grey and barely decipherable. They had been this way for three years, in fact since he had bought his camera. He was thinking of buying a new one but couldn't afford it. I asked him to show me the camera and he had the lens set for what would have been suitable for the Sahara Desert at noon. I asked him why he chose this setting and he said, 'I didnt think of moving it, it was like that when I bought it.' We both looked at the instructions which stated simply and clearly how to alter the setting to suit the subject. If he had learnt from his first failed film and either asked advice or read the instructions, his three years of exasperation and grey films would not have occurred.

A very famous hypnotherapist in America called Dr Milton Erickson told a story of when he was fourteen years old. He saved his pocket money for a month in order to buy a record. He needed $5 and by the end of the month he had just the right amount. He very proudly walked to the record shop, chose the record but when he went to pay he realised he had lost his $5. He said, 'That was a great experience for me. That lost $5 has probably saved me thousands by now. I learnt to be very careful and make sure I looked after my hard-earned money very well.'

Another story, from a different storyteller, called 'The Enlightenment Ceremony', is also relevant.

In India there was a very wise guru who sat under a banyan tree. People came from far and wide to talk with him and some came to be enlightened. He would talk with them a while, then lead them to a large disused aeroplane hangar situated nearby. There was a door at one end which had no handle on the inside. He would explain, 'I will escort you to that door, let you in and close the door. As it has no inside handle you cannot come out that way. At the other end of the building is a door which you can easily open and when you do, you will be enlightened.

'I must advise you that the building is full of one thousand of your worst fears. You will be very frightened when you get inside so I have two pieces of advice I want you to think of at all times.

'Firstly realise that the thousand fears are all of your own creation. Secondly you will only be able to achieve enlightenment if you keep moving. If you stop and remain still it is impossible for you to reach the other end, so whatever you do keep moving.'

PART TWO
Self-imposed Restrictions

3 An Attitude towards Attitudes

> Things are neither good or bad but thinking makes them so.
> SHAKESPEARE, *Hamlet*

> As you go through life make this your goal,
> Keep your eye upon the doughnut and not upon the hole.
> DOUGHNUT CAFE, MELBOURNE

Shakespeare in the sixteenth century was able to state succinctly what is still applicable today. The way we view life, the different attitudes we have towards events and our feelings about them, often bear little relation to the events themselves.

How often in a group is one person constantly complaining while the rest are enjoying themselves? And often this 'bad apple' attitude infiltrates the group so that soon everyone is agreeing with the fault-finder. Some people wear what I call the 'dark glasses of negativity'. Whatever happens they see a negative side to it and concentrate on that aspect. Pessimists *may* be happy being unhappy, but many of them miss out on so much of life. Often the attempt to rectify things is directed at the event or situation itself, when in fact it is the negative attitude which is causing the problem. The 'thinking' of Shakespeare's quote influences the situation in a way which results in a 'feeling' which may be positive or negative (see figure overleaf).

For example,

A: Rita is invited to the pictures.
B: She says to herself, 'It will be a lousy film, he will be late picking me up, I haven't got a dress to wear.'
C: She feels so bad she refuses to go.

Joe wanted to borrow a ladder from his neighbour. As he walked across the lawn he said to himself, 'I bet he won't lend me the ladder.

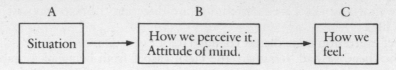

He's a stingy so-and-so: I remember asking for his lawn mower two years ago and he said it wasn't working. I've noticed how he keeps things locked up so I don't pinch them. What a rotten fellow he is.'

When he reaches his neighbour's door, he rings the bell and when it is opened he shouts to the astonished man, 'You can keep your rotten ladder, I don't want it anyway.'

Many people, due to the experiences they had growing up, develop defensive negative attitudes, forever minimising the benefits and maximising the difficulties in any situation past, present or future. The continued discussion about *the event* (often unchangeable) serves no purpose. A look at *attitudes* would provide more fertile ground for improvement.

Dealing with (B), the attitude of mind, by using hypnosis often improves things in a simple and less abrasive way than by conscious criticism.

Reframing is a term used to describe a way of obtaining a different point of view. It is a powerful and simple way of altering feelings related to attitudes. There is a positive or negative viewpoint in most situations. If people take the negative viewpoint and are not content with the feeling associated with this, then reframing – pointing out the positive view – in hypnosis, may dramatically alter how they feel. The following examples may illustrate this better.

A woman had an obsession with cleaning her carpets. She had a pink carpet with a deep pile and if anyone walked on it footprints appeared. This upset her, and she was continually vacuuming the carpet to keep it smooth.

When the children came home from school they were ordered to take off their shoes but even this didn't stop the footprints. She became more and more obsessed, worried, tense and anxious. The carpet became the constant topic of discussion and argument in the family.

After some months she was persuaded to seek help and went to a therapist who asked her some questions.

'Close your eyes and imagine your carpet pink and fluffy with not a footprint on it. How do you feel?'

She smiled and said, 'I feel wonderful.'

'Now imagine yourself sitting in a chair in the middle of the room surrounded by the pink expanse of virgin carpet.'

'Yes, it really feels good.'

'Now realise that this means none of your family or loved ones can come near you. You are isolated and are directing them to stay out of your life.'

Her expression immediately changed to one of sadness.

The therapist had 'reframed' the clean carpet from being pleasurable to being unpleasurable. By so doing the woman's view of things changed. No longer was she happy with a fluffy unmarked carpet as it meant she was isolated. In fact the footprints on the carpet now represented a happy home and her need to vacuum instantly disappeared.

A forty-year-old man worked for a merchant bank and was constantly under stress. Six months prior to visiting me he had an attack of tachycardia (rapid heartrate) which made him feel faint, and he thought he might die. His father had died of a heart attack and he began to worry that it might happen to him, too.

A week later he had another bout of tachycardia and went to see his local doctor. He was understandably very anxious. He had a cardiograph, which was normal, and was reassured there was nothing to worry about. He continued to have bouts of tachycardia lasting 5–10 minutes. He felt faint and lay down until they stopped. He was prescribed some tablets but the attacks continued. A month later, when he was in an important business meeting, another bout of tachycardia started and didn't stop when he lay down. An ambulance was called and he was taken to hospital, many more tests were performed and his tablets increased.

By this time a vicious cycle had been set up: the fear of an attack liberated adrenaline which caused the attack. It was a self-fulfilling prophecy (see below).

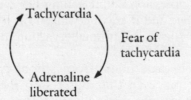

When he left hospital he went on holiday for a few weeks and things seemed to settle down. Soon after his return to work, where the backlog was immense, he had some more attacks and came to see me.

I explained what was happening and taught him relaxation and self-hypnosis. He was asked to practise these three times a day for ten minutes. I also explained that the tachycardia was an important sign from his body that he was under too much stress. In fact, I said, I would be very concerned if he was stressed and did *not* have tachycardia; this would mean his warning system was not working and he may do damage to his heart.

In this way I was reframing his bouts of tachycardia as being beneficial rather than something to fear. I took considerable care and patience to explain this to him and in order to test his relaxation I requested him to bring on an attack by thinking of a stressful situation and then to get rid of it by relaxing. I helped him do this a few times in the surgery and directed him to practise starting and stopping the attacks three to four times a day.

When I saw him the next week he was quite upset. 'I'm really worried, doctor, I can't bring on an attack. I've tried and tried and it just won't happen. Does that mean my heart is being injured?' I reassured him that his relaxation must have been successful in lowering the level of stress and this was preventing the attacks. I smiled to myself at the complete change in attitude helped by reframing and relaxation. This man, who was initially terrified of having an attack of tachycardia, was now upset because he couldn't.

Over a period of weeks he had occasional attacks which he coped with by relaxing, and gradually we were able to reduce his medication. He continued to do self-hypnosis three times a day and learnt other ways of identifying and dealing with the stress of his job.

I am not suggesting that all cases of tachycardia can be treated in this way and it is important to have medical tests to rule out any underlying heart condition which may indicate other forms of treatment.

The beauty of the altered state of hypnosis is that the reframed proposition may be put to the person in a relaxed state and a different attitude about things is created. This feeling then helps to look at future experiences from a different, more positive, point of view.

We tell ourselves negative things.
We listen to ourselves
and believe our statements to be facts.
In following these facts
we feel bad.
It is just as simple
to tell ourselves positive things,
so when we believe and follow them we feel better.

Often what we do or think about a problem is what keeps it going. Just as the worry of the man with the tachycardia kept his problem going so it is in many situations. By thinking about what you do with a problem and by altering your attitude in a reframing manner, it may be possible to prevent keeping the problem going.

A woman came to see me suffering from general anxiety and tension. She was always on edge, snapped at everyone, couldn't sleep and was generally miserable. She had remarried a year previously and had a teenage daughter from her first marriage. Her new husband and her daughter were continually arguing and she acted as referee. She had feelings of guilt, anger, sorrow and divided loyalties and these continual arguments were getting on her nerves. She was extremely upset as she described these nightly bouts. Most nights she went to bed in tears with the arguments from both sides ringing in her ears.

I taught her self-hypnosis and enabled her to feel a relaxed drifting feeling of strolling in a garden. She enjoyed this and said she would practise it at home.

Two weeks later she returned saying the relaxation was of some benefit, but she still was very upset by the disagreements between her husband and daughter. I asked her to go into a trance so she would be more receptive to what I had to say. She did this quite easily and I talked to her about her husband and daughter.

'Your husband and daughter have their own way of seeing things, their own way of getting to know each other. I imagine it's very difficult for both of them to smooth down the rough edges they each possess. Each has learnt about life their own way and have been thrown together with no real option or chance to adjust.

'Imagine that each time they try to get to know each other in their own way by discussing things, you step in and stop them, telling them they are wrong to behave that way. As they both love you they respect your wishes, even if it is against their own way of integrating. They are prepared to stay apart just to please you; they will stop their discussions as they know it upsets you.'

As she sat with her eyes closed, I observed many alterations in her breathing, skin colour and head nodding and I believe she was readjusting to the alteration of 'arguments' to 'discussions'. In this way her role of referee was reframed as a role of keeping her husband and daughter apart.

I inferred that perhaps she was prolonging their process of integration by her interference and suggested that when she heard raised voices she should go to bed and listen to music and let them 'get on with it'. When she opened her eyes she said, 'Do you really believe I'm prolonging the problem?'

'I don't know,' I replied. 'But perhaps it would be worth keeping out of it for a few weeks and see what happens. Perhaps while they are discussing things you can do some self-hypnosis.'

She managed to 'keep out of it' for a few weeks and noticed that things didn't get any worse. If anything, they were a little better. She realised that her interference only upset her and decided to continue doing her relaxation whenever they 'discussed' things.

In time the household settled down to a situation of tranquillity and arguments, but she no longer took the role as 'peace keeper' and was able to accept arguments as a part of everyday life. Her sleeping and general tension improved. Some time later she confessed that she quite enjoyed it when they shouted at each other. 'I go and do some self-hypnosis. I feel they are getting to know each other much better with their discussion,' she said.

If you are continually struggling with a problem and any attempted alteration of the 'facts' doesn't seem to help, look at your attitude or role in the problem. Perhaps this is playing a part in maintaining it and change in this area may help find a solution. Keep in mind Hamlet's words to Rosencrantz, 'Things are neither good or bad but thinking makes them so.'

4 *The Book of Shoulds*

Nobody can give you better advice than yourself.
CICERO

There are many famous and important books which have affected civilisation through the ages. The Book of Kells, The Bible, Das Kapital, Mein Kampf, The Talmud and Koran just to name a few.

All of them have had a powerful and long-term effect on how civilisations behaved, and lived their lives.

In modern times a relatively unknown code of conduct is fulfilling the same role for a large proportion of the western world. You may be following it to a major or minor degree, and at the same time may be completely unaware of its existence.

This code is used in every aspect of life and there are devotees who follow it to the letter. Its commandments are never questioned and are adhered to in spite of overwhelming evidence against them. I am referring, of course, to the little known but often quoted *Book of Shoulds*. Its companion the *Book of Shouldn'ts* and the relative size of each volume varies from person to person.

In the Jewish religion The Talmud is the book on which Jewish law and tradition are based. The history of this book goes back long before Christ and students of the Talmud, the Hasidim, spend years studying it.

Different interpretations are discussed and examined over the years so that no Jew can be unaware of his or her duties and obligations.

Not so with the *Book of Shoulds*. Its authority is never questioned, never challenged yet we obey it as easily as we do a policeman directing the traffic.

How many times a day do we say 'I should do this', 'You shouldn't say that'? Every day I hear people refer to hundreds of shoulds with no real basis or authority. The inference when we say or think 'I should' or 'I shouldn't', is that someone, sometime directed us to behave in a certain way. Let us take an example.

When I was a young boy my mother, in her wisdom, said to me when

I dropped a piece of wood and nearly hit my toe, 'Don't drop anything heavy on your toe, Brian, or you'll get lockjaw.' I had no idea what 'lockjaw' was, but it seemed very serious and very dangerous by the look on my mother's face. From that day on anything above the weight of a feather landing within a yard of my feet, immediately caused me to clutch my face in case the dreaded 'lockjaw' occurred. I developed a commandment from The Book of Shoulds (in this case written by my mother) 'Thou should not drop something on thy toe or lockjaw will develop.'

For years that dictum haunted me. I never analysed, questioned or doubted my mother's authority.

Later on, in medical school, to my embarrassment, I quoted this edict from the *Book of Shoulds* to a Professor and some other students. It was only then that the authority was questioned. During a discussion which pleased my smirking fellow students no end, I found out where my mother had received her information. She was talking about tetanus. This disease causes severe spasm of the muscles (including those of the jaw) and can be fatal. It is caused by an organism which grows in dirty wounds. She must have been told that this had occurred when something had fallen on someone's toe. The disease can be caused by *any* wound in any part of the body. Dropping something on my foot was not a necessary requirement for tetanus.

People limit themselves enormously by saying 'I should' or 'I shouldn't' without questioning 'Why?', or 'Who said so?' or 'When did they say so?'

'When I get up to speak in public I'm very nervous and I shouldn't be.'

Who said so? What were their qualifications? When did they say that and to whom? These are questions never asked of the *Book of Shoulds*. If the Hasidim spend a lifetime analysing the book on which they base their rules, surely we can spend a little time questioning ours.

How often do you say to yourself 'I shouldn't do that' and stop doing it without any understanding of why you shouldn't behave like that. Most likely the edict was instilled many years previously, by a well-intentioned parent. In order to direct little Johnny to behave in a suitable manner, to suit the parents or society, the *Book of Shoulds* is created. The authors of many of these commandments may have had them instilled by *their* parents.

But instilled they certainly are, often by repetition until the rules are firmly planted in the back of the mind. And there they remain, unexamined as a reminder of how things should be said, done, felt.

And so they stay buried there, ready to be referred to when an appropriate situation arises. As we grow older, more are added, either by others or by ourselves as protective devices against the adult world. Never questioned, never updated but strictly adhered to, the rules create a narrow, twisting pathway following archaic directions and resisting the influence of personal experiences or feelings.

I'll demonstrate how contorted we can become by following the *Book of Shoulds*.

Peter is a thirty-two-year-old architect who came to see me in Australia. He had no confidence in himself because in his early life his parents continually put him down. His father left his mother when he was very young. He didn't believe he was worthy of 'playing a leading part' in life but that he was cast to play a role on the sidelines.

He had been living with a thirty-eight-year-old woman, Liz, and was concerned and upset by the arrangement. He liked her a lot but didn't love her. He didn't want to hurt her by going out with other girls or leaving her. They didn't sleep together but it was a reasonably friendly relationship.

I asked him if he showed her any signs of the affection he obviously had for her, such as taking her out to dinner, giving her flowers or telling her he liked her.

His reply astounded me: 'I do like her and I would like to give her flowers occasionally but I *shouldn't do that* or she will be upset when I leave.'

He had been living with Liz for *five years* and was constantly in conflict between what he wished to do but believed he 'shouldn't'.

He had been taught: 'Thou shalt never hurt a girl by telling her you like her and then leaving her.' His mother, obviously and naturally upset by the departure of her husband, had drummed it into her son that a woman should not be betrayed by affection which would not be permanent.

Peter had fixed this in the back of his mind and during the five year relationship wih Liz, whenever he felt like expressing his feelings of happiness with her the *Book of Shouldn'ts* boomed down from the past and he held his tongue.

When Peter and I analysed how this had come about he appreciated it did not apply to his present relationship in the same way as it applied to his mother all those years ago.

Often the *Book of Shoulds* makes commonsense and is appropriate to the present situation. In order to make the most of it the following points may be helpful.

When you next catch yourself saying or thinking 'I should or shouldn't' or 'they should or shouldn't' ask a number of questions:

'Why shouldn't they?'

'Do I believe *now* in *this situation* that they shouldn't?'

'Who is it that says they shouldn't?'

'Do I respect whoever said it?'

'Should' infers that the decision is not one's own. If it is applicable it can be replaced by other words which give the speaker or thinker responsibility for the comment. So 'I should go and see her' becomes 'I want to go and see her', 'They shouldn't say that' to 'I don't like them saying that because . . . .'

If we buy a new washing machine and it is accompanied by an instruction manual from an outdated model, we may expect problems when following the instructions. We may become confused, make mistakes and end up frustrated.

The instruction manual, if appropriate to the machine, will provide a basis for achieving the desired results. So wouldn't it be preferable to update our 'instruction manual' to suit our abilities and beliefs?

Hence by updating the *Book of Shoulds* we transfer responsibility from some figure in the past to ourselves in the present. Making our own decisions about our thoughts, feelings, behaviour, allows us so much more freedom to act. We develop more confidence in ourselves and reliance on our own beliefs and decisions.

5 Labelling

The biggest block to any man's success is in his head.

One way to be sure that you will go round in circles rather than forward in life, is to use the 'negative labelling' technique. This requires much perseverance and determination. Against all positive forces you cling steadfastly to your negative label, afraid of what lies outside.

The negative label is one we hear frequently. In case you don't understand what I mean by negative labels, I refer to the way people describe themselves – in a negative way – to deal with situations for which they do not want to accept responsibility. An obvious example is *The Worrier*.

'Mrs Jones, you seem to be very upset by the fact that little Suzie got a splinter in her finger last week?' 'Oh yes, Doctor. I'm just a born worrier.'

Just think how protective, as well as punishing, negative labels can be, like a portcullis that automatically comes down when anything larger than a grasshopper moves on the other side of the moat.

The negative label implies an inability to change. It says, 'I would act differently if I could, but as I'm a born worrier it's out of my control.'

Others say, 'I know I'm fat and I hate being 25 stone but I'm *just a pig*.' 'Yes, I know I should do some exercise but I've always been a *lazy sod*.' 'You tell me it would help if I spent some time on myself but that would mean I'm selfish.'

I'd like to discuss how labels develop, how they may have been of use at one time but are restrictive. Let us take a look at some of the labels people hang around their necks and repeat to themselves consciously and unconsciously. Studying how they came about, what role they play in the present, how they limit the wearer, and how they can be removed or modified will be an interesting exercise.

The label follows a pattern of internal dialogue which was at one stage a protective, comforting, punishing or excusing one. The internal dialogue is usually in the form '. . . but I'm a . . . .' Some of the more common labels are :

... but I'm just a fat pig.
but I'm not worthy of receiving that.
but I'm not capable of saying that.
but I'm too shy to ask that.
but I haven't got the confidence to demand that.
but I'm just a loser (failure, sufferer, etc.).

These labels came about when someone explained our behaviour by using one.

'No wonder you can't lose weight, you're just a fat pig.' The next time this person overeats she repeats the words to herself as a reason or excuse for her action. Repetition eventually convinces her of its truth so she unhappily continues through life, wearing the label without question.

One of the saddest labels is the *unselfish* one. The owner at some stage may have been praised for helping someone, 'Oh, what a lovely child, she's so unselfish that she goes to help Mrs Smith every day.' This praise makes the child feel good, so she heads along the unselfish road propelled by praise and perhaps some criticism, 'Oh, Suzie, don't be so selfish, thinking of yourself before poor old Mrs Smith.'

Gradually the unselfish label is moulded to fit Suzie perfectly, like a chastity belt, ensuring she doesn't have any 'selfish' pleasure. Owners of this label feel guilty if they have five minutes to themselves a day. They assume a martyr-like outlook on life: *their* life is worthless and they must suffer by spending all their waking moments on their husband, job, children, church, charities, neighbours etc. etc.; no minute of the day is for them.

The reason negative labels are limiting is because they are beyond logic or challenge, they are inflexible in the varying situations which make up daily life. If Suzie could help people the *majority* of the time and spend *some* time on herself, the physical or mental problems she may have, could be minimised.

Self-punishment results from failures, which commonly occur. 'Because *I'm just a fat pig* I'll be overweight, unhappy, lonely, laughed at, and lack confidence.' All painful sequels which may be due to underlying guilt from thoughts, feelings or actions in childhood.

The protective role is useful as a barrier to any questioning of or responsibility for the wearer's actions. The 'I'm just too shy' label protects the person from risk-taking and progressing into new situations. It may have developed from past fears or pain which occurred in an exploring situation.

The steps required to modify or remove a negative label are as follows:

1. Recognise that you are wearing a label. This is done by noticing how you avoid situations, or feel limited in relationships.
2. Study the ways the label is being maintained by internal dialogue

(self-talk) or by explanations of failures to do, say or succeed in things.

3. Ask friends or family if they recognise the label you feel you are wearing.
4. Analyse the benefits and restrictions it is bringing you.
5. Cast your mind back to when it was first applied and by whom and for what reasons.
6. Remember times you acted contrary to the label.
7. Catch yourself applying the label during the day. Try and act differently to avoid the stereotyped self-description.
8. Gradually replace the label with either a *more positive* one or be flexible and have no label at all.

Tom was a thirty-five-year-old chemist's assistant. He still lived with his parents and his life was pretty gloomy. He came to see me for problems due to lack of sleep, but the conversation soon came around to his loneliness and lack of female companionship.

He very seldom went out and if he did it was to drink at the pub with 'the boys'. He longed to have a steady girl-friend, but repeated to me (and himself) his label . . . 'but I'm just no good with girls'.

He had experienced some embarrassing situations in his early twenties (as most young men do) and had developed his 'no good with girls' label after being rejected at a dance on a few occasions.

As the label fitted closer and closer, he repeated the message 'I'm no good with girls' every time he went out. When he did approach girls, he quickly let them know he was 'no good', so they accepted his message.

When we discussed the possibilities of meeting someone, he kept inferring that it was 'no good', he'd never be any good and there was nothing that could be done.

Of the numerous alternatives available to him he found reasons why none could help him in his predicament. The fact that he was pleasant, personable, reasonably handsome and caring, were all negated by his label. His terror of finding someone who initially liked him and then found out that he 'was no good with women', prevented him from taking the first step out of his hiding place behind the label.

6 *The Worrier*

Only one kind of worry is proper, to worry because you
worry so much.
Don't worry about tomorrow, who knows what will befall
you today?
JEWISH SAYINGS

As we grow, many of us assume an image of ourselves. I have referred
to this in the 'labelling' chapter. A very common self-description which
we constantly meet in all situations is *The Worrier*.

I'm sure you know someone who would fit this category, who is constantly concerned about all or some of his life. When solutions occur
to his problems he may worry about not worrying. He answers any
criticism by 'but I'm just a born worrier' to end any further discussion.

We all have had worries about things in the past, present or future.
These feelings occupy a proportion of our lives and are necessary, to
some degree, to ensure we carry out our commitments. We can worry
about the past, 'Why did it happen to me?' We can worry about the
present, 'It's not fair that I haven't got a Rolls Royce', or the future,
'I'm really concerned that Johnny won't pass his exams next year.'

But the *real* worrier gets an honours degree in all three categories.

Mrs Johnson, a sixty-year-old grandmother, got a scholarship on her
worrying ability. She continually complained about her lot in life. Words
like 'It's not fair', 'Why does it always happen to me', 'What have I done
to deserve this', were bandied about with not so gay abandon.

She confided in me she was a worrier and that she *had* to worry about
the family as *no-one else did*. On further questioning her family included
every relation in existence all over the world. She had about two hundred
in her 'family', from distant aunts on their last legs to second cousins
twice removed. Because of this large family there was always some mishap
or other for her to worry about.

'Why are you feeling down today?' I would inadvertently ask, too
late to realise I'd fallen into the trap.

'Because I just heard little Johnny has fallen and cut his leg.' Little
Johnny turned out to be a distant relative living in Canada, but due

to her vast network of contact via 'phone, mail, courier and smoke signal she had learned of the mishap. She daily received a flood of information, mainly negative, about her 'family's' circumstances and had food for worry to last a lifetime. Maybe her worry label was in some way of benefit to her – she saw her role as a worrier and may have believed she was worthless without that. The fact that she was continually ill, unhappy and taking tablets led me to believe there may have been some other role she could play. But the worry label was tattooed into her skin and would not be removed. I wonder now, as 'her family' must have doubled since I last saw her, whether she has installed a computer to record all the tragedies coming in.

There is a showman's saying, 'Yer pays yer money and yer takes yer chances.' I think this philosophy applies to those who call themselves worriers. If you choose and accept unquestioningly the worry label, then you have little choice as to the outcome. The woman above in paying her money for a worry label felt lousy. If she had been amenable to the possibility of change I would have pointed out a few alternatives.

1. To accept her worrying as a great way of receiving daily communication from a lot of people. Lots of people like to be worried over, and she had gathered a horde who were happy to despatch their problems to her. She could continue this, but grade the amount of worry, to relate to the closeness of the relative. Surely she could learn to worry more for a grandchild than a distant second cousin.
2. If she considered she only had a certain quantity of worry available she could keep some for herself, then dispense the rest according to priority. But each day she should spend some of her worry allowance on herself. This meant she was to spend time on herself to prevent the 'worry bank' being overdrawn.
3. It might be useful to have some input of 'non-worry' to balance the output of worry. To notice some nice things happening to her relatives so her thoughts might be balanced. For example, 'Little Johnny twisted his ankle but he got very good grades at school.'

If she has to continue being a worrier there are a few pointers as to how to be a 'better worrier'. The worriers have an all-pervasive feeling, like a dark cloud, hanging over them at all times, draining energy and adding a negative tinge to all inputs and outputs occurring during the day and night. Any thought, situation or experience triggers off the 'worry feeling'.

The *steps to better worrying* are to divide your worries into:

1. Those that you can do *something* about today.
2. Those that you can do *nothing* about today.

I suggest to worriers that they have a 'worry diary' to get into the habit of improving their worry technique. It is important to designate half an hour once or twice a day as a 'worry period' to concentrate on their worries. This time is to be spent *only* on worrying and if worries creep up during the day they are to be relegated to those times. Any pleasant or non-worrying thoughts are not allowed during these times.

During this half hour the worries are analysed and put into the two above categories. For those in group (1) a commitment is made to do *something* during the day towards helping that situation. Those in group (2) are written down for the next day in the diary to see if they become group (1). The majority of worries that people concern themselves with are those that nothing can be done about at present, either because they are in the past or are in no way under the control of the worrier.

In this way the worries are at least brought under some sort of control, rather than dominating every thought and move.

Just as self-limiting labels restrict the way we use our abilities, so do self-limiting phrases which we say to ourselves or accept from others. Becoming aware of these phrases is a start to dealing with the bind they keep us in.

A very tired, bedraggled woman of fifty, named Pat, came to see me complaining of backaches which had persisted on and off for five years. She had seen many doctors and had many tests but there was no explanation for her backaches.

As she looked about seventy I assumed she had experienced more than her fair share of stress and suffering. She told me a tale of woe. Her husband Arthur was a dominant businessman who believed a woman's role was in the kitchen, looking after the children and tidying up after him. He had no understanding that she was a person in her own right with beliefs, needs, etc. that required fulfilling. They had a twenty-two-year-old daughter, Sue and a twenty-six-year-old son, John.

When Sue was fifteen and still at school, she became pregnant, and after lots of discussion and anxiety, baby Paul was born. It was decided that the best way out of a difficult situation was for Pat and Arthur to adopt Paul, which they did. So Pat started on a new round of nappies and baby feeding just when she was looking forward to a life for herself. She quite happily accepted this role and made the best of the limitations it caused. At times when she complained of the difficulties Arthur would say, 'but she's your daughter', which was a statement against which any discussion was useless.

Three years ago Sue left to live with a married man. Paul was four and growing up into a lovely little boy. Sue had a little girl but was soon deserted by her recently acquired boyfriend. As soon as he left, Sue began dropping in on her Mum and leaving the baby for her to mind while she went out. She would call in at any hour without notice with the baby to be looked after. Pat objected, but her objections were quashed with the 'she's your daughter' routine. So Pat was required to remain at home in case Sue dropped the baby in to be minded. When she did, the baby behaved as most babes do, leaving a trail of disarray behind her. Pat tried desperately to gain some support from Arthur about changing her role as continuous nursemaid, but he would have none of it. In his eyes, Pat should exist only for the family, not for herself, and Pat was accepting this role even though both her body and mind were rejecting it. The backaches were signs of the tension she was under. During the interview, when I suggested she might take some control in her life, and decide when and how she would like to see her daughter and when she could arrange time for herself, she looked at me through tear-filled eyes and said, 'I can't do that, she's my daughter, I can't not be there.'

She was limiting any thought of change by this phrase which kept cropping up again and again in her mind. Over a number of sessions she realised she had 'got herself into a corner' by this phrase and we began the long and arduous task of regaining her self-respect. There was massive resistance by everyone in the family to her not being available for her daughter at all times. She was re-labelled as 'unloving, unkind, selfish, mad' and I was included in the abuse that was thrown around. She is gradually paving the way for herself by gaining some confidence, and the slight twinkle I catch in her eye amongst all those lines of woe on her face, gives me hope that one day she will have more self-esteem.

If the restricting phrases have become so embedded over the years that shining a logical light into the darkness doesn't provide any illumination, then hypnosis may be a useful adjunct to supportive therapy and will enable the growth of self-confidence as well as an alteration in the self-restrictive phrases.

I sometimes hear the phrase, 'I just can't cope' or 'I won't be able to cope', in relation to discussions about the patient's difficulties and ways of dealing with them. I wonder what it means to 'not cope'? My mind wanders to people breaking furniture, sitting in a corner crying, going to mental institutions. For each person this phrase means a different thing and is a fear in the back (or front) of the mind that something terrible will happen due to events beyond their control. A woman I saw with two teenage sons, a busy husband, a job and a large house to look after, came to see me with signs of tension. She looked very weary and explained that she'd been depressed and weepy for months. 'If this feeling continues I just won't be able to cope,' she said as tears welled up.

During the first session she told me how her day was divided into doing things for her husband, work, the children and the house and she had no time for herself. Any spare time was used for charitable work in the local neighbourhood and for the church. She got up at 7 a.m. and went to bed exhausted at midnight. Her sleep was poor although she was very tired.

When I asked her what would happen if she didn't cope, she looked perplexed and, after thinking for a while, said, 'I wouldn't be able to perform my duties properly. I'd probably cry a lot and stay in bed more.'

I commented that perhaps that may not be such a bad thing for a while. It would enable other household members to be involved in the running of the house. I suggested she 'not cope' for the next two weeks and report how it went.

She came back two weeks later stating she couldn't do that as it wouldn't be fair on the others; she had a duty as a wife and mother. I agreed, but suggested she also had a duty to herself and that her performance as mother and wife was hampered by her being constantly drained.

We had a long discussion about her lifestyle and that perhaps the 'not coping' feeling was a message to spend time on herself. I asked her if she would bring her husband and sons on the next visit. She was very anxious about that suggestion and resisted it strongly on the grounds that *they* would never come as it was *her* problem.

When she was about to leave she said, 'Oh well, I suppose there is nothing you can do to help me.' She walked out of the door to continue in a lifestyle which was exacting such a heavy toll.

7 Time and Timing

Time is.
Too slow for those who wait.
Too swift for those who fear.
Too long for those who grieve.
Too short for those who rejoice.

Time and timing are very important factors to take into account in any aspect of life. We all have our own internal clocks which provide us with a way of judging time. Often after setting the alarm to wake early our internal alarm clock wakes us beforehand.

Problems may occur, when some people's internal clocks are set at a different rate to others. That is, some people require longer than others to do things – their metronome is set at a slower rate. This causes complications and disappointments in relationships for no apparent reason.

This 'time' factor may be compared to a catalyst in a chemical reaction. For some reactions the chemical change will not occur without the presence of a substance which does not take part in the reaction but allows it to proceed. This can be represented as follows,

$$X + Y \xrightarrow{\text{catalyst}} Z$$

where the catalyst is necessary in certain amounts, to allow change to occur.

So it is in things we do; the catalyst (time) is important for the results we desire. Taking into account other people's time sequences will allow an understanding of any failure in the transaction (reaction) occurring. In any relationship, achievement, change, or acceptance, the time factor is hidden in the equation.

John likes to get things done. Anything around the house or at work that needs doing is tackled very soon after it is noticed. His actions, speech, thoughts are rapid. He eats quickly, talks quickly and is efficient in most aspects of his life.

His wife Joan is much slower. She likes to think about things, and believes they will take longer than they actually do. She is often late, as she doesn't notice time passing and claims things will be fixed all in their own good time.

John and Joan have many problems in their relationship which seem to relate directly to their different timing devices, and their failure to recognise and appreciate that both of them are correct in their own way. Often John would say Joan was 'wrong' and he was 'right' when in fact they are just 'different'.

It is as if a metronome in the brain dictates the rapidity or otherwise of the music played in the mind. Each speed has its benefits and downfalls; being able to vary the metronome according to the situation allows flexibility. The conductor of the orchestra using his baton dictates the timing to the musicians playing; some symphonies are slower and others faster, some have both slow and fast parts in the one piece of music. A conductor who could only conduct music at a certain pace would soon be out of a job.

The recognition that people take varying periods of time to do things, will allow easier communication and improve relationships. The healing process, changing ability, and acceptance of a situation, all take time and this varies from person to person. If this time factor is ignored the whole process may be blocked, just as the removal of the catalyst stops chemical change.

My own personal timing is very fast. I like to do things immediately, require rapid changes and will keep at things like a ferret until they do. For many years I failed to appreciate that many patients had slower internal clocks. We would agree on a possible solution to a problem and when I saw the patient a week later, I'd eagerly ask if they had reached the solution. When they hadn't (which was most times) I believed we had failed to do something, so I would alter the attempted solution. Had I allowed for the patient's own timing, which may have required a month to make the change, all would have been well.

My interference prematurely added a negative attitude to our attempted solution, the patient became disillusioned and failure generally resulted. I found it very difficult to appreciate that what would take me a week takes other people a month. I injected all sorts of negative thoughts such as – he is not motivated, doesn't want to change, is incapable, etc. etc., hence applying the 'You are wrong, I am right principle' which destroyed any rapport we may have built up.

Now it is astounding to see the relief on people's faces when I ask them to take their own time to decide what to do. Removal of pressure on someone to perform is a major factor in allowing them to achieve what they desire. 'More haste less speed' makes a great deal of sense. In modern society there is pressure to perform within time limits in all areas of life: work, home, sport, leisure, holidays, etc. In hypnosis I often say, 'Things will take time, *your own time*,' which helps the patient to feel comfortable in approaching the tasks he has undertaken.

I learnt about timing from my donkey Brownie. He was a delightful two-month-old long-haired foal when I bought him. His brown hair covered his eyes like an Old English Sheepdog, and anyone who has seen donkey foals will understand when I say I fell in love with him at first sight.

He was transferred by horse-float to my small farm and put in a paddock on his own. He was initially very frightened by the journey so I understood when he kept his distance as I approached on that first day.

The next day I went into the paddock with two large red apples and walked towards him with hands outstretched. To my dismay, as I walked forward he walked backwards, always keeping a distance of ten yards between us. If I moved faster forwards, he moved faster backwards, if I stopped, he stopped, what seemed like a thousand miles separating me from my new love. We moved around the paddock like this for an hour. To an observer it must have seemed like a strange square dance, moving forward, stopping, moving backwards.

After an hour I was exasperated and exhausted. How could he do this to me? I love him and have apples to show it. What if I can never get close to him? My friends were right, I should never have got a donkey, they are stupid. What can I do with him, no-one will buy him. In tears I went inside to worry about the dreadful mistake I'd made.

The next day I took a bucket of apples and carrots – having seen a picture of a donkey trying to reach a carrot on a stick. The previous day's square dance was repeated and all the time the brown eyes seemed to taunt me through the long hair.

I turned the bucket upside down, looked away from Brownie and sat down to ponder my (and his) fate. After a few minutes I felt a warm breath on my neck and the softest of muzzles nestling into my shoulder. I jumped up with joy and thrust out an apple of appreciation, only to see Brownie retreat ten yards, winking at me from a safe distance.

It took a while for me to realise that Brownie's timing was different from mine. Where I needed seconds, he needed minutes to gain the security to make contact. I didn't realise the inherent caution he had for survival.

As it slowly – much too slowly – dawned on me that Brownie and I could get on well if I recognised his internal clock, I began to act appropriately. I waited for him to come to me, moved slowly and did things gradually. We became the best of friends and developed a deep trust which lasted many years. I felt sad at all the negative thoughts I had had about him in failing to appreciate his natural protective timing. Now when I meet patients who act slowly I think of Brownie and the pleasure we had after I had understood his internal metronome.

Maggie, who lives in Scotland, has a problem swallowing food. For years she had tests, X-rays, treatment and no real (that is no organic) cause was found. She is 60, married with three daughters and six grandchildren. She looks after everyone else before herself.

I was called in to see if stress was playing a role in her problem. It certainly was and, in order to understand it I listened to her account of her daily activities. In between describing what she did she made comments like 'because I'm so slow', or 'I'm just too slow to do it efficiently'.

Her day was crammed with activities from 6.30, when she got up (she didn't sleep well so was awake at 4 a.m.), until she went to bed at midnight. Shopping, meetings, family's needs, friends' needs, charities were all squashed into the day. Her explanation was accompanied by her observation of how slow she was.

When I talked about her 'slowness' she remarked how efficient her mother had been. 'She always did things so quickly, got things done so easily without taking nearly as much time as I do.'

So Maggie had it implanted in her mind that her mother's timing was normal, hence she was abnormal and 'slow'. For fifty years she had tried to prove she wasn't slow, by crowding so much into her day that people wouldn't notice her slowness. She was often late, because she did so much, so her friends thought that she *was* slow. I tried to help her recognise her own metronome speed and accept it. She was not 'slow'. She may have been slower than her mother, but had she accepted her own timing and speed I believe her swallowing problems may not have occurred. She certainly would have been less stressed and anxious.

After a number of visits she did realise she had her own timing and accepted her pace as normal. Her swallowing improved and she enjoyed eating meals for the first time in years.

But the network of pressures she had allowed to build up around her gradually made inroads into her commitment to go at her own pace. She gradually slipped back into her earlier 'I'm too slow' attitude. Her swallowing problems returned as if her body was saying to her, 'I can't swallow that rubbish you are telling yourself about your timing.'

'There is no time like the present', is a saying with a lot of truth in it. We *are* living in the present and people who live in the past or the future are leading a life of fantasy. As you read this the time will change from future to present to past – like traffic lights changing colours.

Taking in all that the present has to offer enables us to live a life of reality. Some appropriate quotes are 'Life is what happens while you are planning for the future', or 'Today is the real thing not a dress rehearsal for tomorrow'. The past does have a bearing on how we approach the present but allowing it to dominate us is like running a race looking backwards at where we have been.

Hypnosis is very useful in allowing the past to drift back into the past. It can cut the anchor rope which is holding back the progress of the ship. In a trance one can learn to put the past into perspective. Hypnosis is also a powerful force in altering time ratios and making the internal metronome more flexible. Past experiences that may be unpleasant can be remembered to the fast metronome, so they have less time for impact, pleasant ones slowed down to be enjoyed and appreciated.

If only people would remove the 'if only' attitude they have, regarding how the past has affected them, they may live nearer the present. The past is gone, is unchangeable and 'if only' attitudes have no reality content. We can make use of past events as learning experiences and thus provide the fertiliser for growth however bad it smells.

People apply artificial timing attitudes to changes. 'Doctor, I know it will take a long time for me to get better.' This may or may not be so, but that attitude will ensure it takes a long time. Some situations which have caused problems for years may be altered in weeks.

I have seen patients with chronic pain for ten years improve in weeks or months or years. The time taken was not related to the length of the disease but to the motivation or attitude of the patient. The time it takes to change depends on the person and those around him accepting his change.

Talking of time, patients often say, 'Seeing me for an hour is such a long time. I normally only have ten minutes with my doctor.' I understand the great difficulties in general practice in making time for patients, but to the patient whose problem has beset him for years, an hour is not a long time. The time that is required should be dictated by the diseases, not by the doctor's surgery hours.

It is hard to believe that a problem which has affected a person or family for years can be satisfactorily helped in ten minutes. The patient requires time to be listened to and understood. I realise that I am not offering a solution to doctors who can only allow a few minutes per patient because of their heavy work load. However, I believe that if it could be arranged, it would save time in the long run as visits to the surgery would be less frequent, once the requirements of the illness are understood. At present what we are forced to do is to arrange time suitable to the *system* rather than the patient.

One of the major contributions I make to patients getting better is to offer them *time*. Any other factor involved is secondary to this and, in my opinion, if we could distribute time, rather than pills, illnesses may not be so chronic.

Another major problem is that *people do not spend time on themselves*. I ask every patient 'How much time do you spend on yourself each day?' The answer varies from 'none' to 'a few minutes in the bath'. I believe the body and mind require time spent on them each day: time to relax and time for exercise. I have a great deal of difficulty convincing people that ten to fifteen minutes a day relaxing will be of great benefit. Most would prefer to take a pill or do *anything* rather than spend time on themselves.

The attitude that it's a waste, selfish, useless etc. is most common, that time spent on anything else is more valuable. But many symptoms are caused by people not spending enough time on themselves.

'I can't *find* the time doctor, I've got too many things to do.' Time is something you *make*, not find. It's amazing the changes that occur to illness, personality, confidence and ability to cope by just spending ten to fifteen minutes a day doing a relaxation exercise.

The mind is a finely tuned machine which is on the go all the time. Lubricating the machinery by relaxing a few minutes a day allows it to work much more efficiently, and prevents any malfunction in the form of illness or pain, sleeplessness or anxiety.

PART THREE
Choices

8 The Game of Responsibility

There's always an easy solution to every human problem
– neat, plausible and wrong.

Over the years of working with people and struggling with their problems, I have devised a game which I call the Game of Responsibility (see diagram). I would like to explain this game, in the hope that it may help you understand any situation you are in.

The game is one we are all involved in, like it or not, with the many situations that arise as life progresses. One of three choices has to be made, and we (knowingly or not) accept responsibility for our choice.

The three alternatives are:

1. Accept the situation for a period of time.
2. Change the situation or your attitude to it.
3. Avoid either accepting or changing the situation.

Looking at diagram 1 (overleaf) it can be seen that by choosing to (1) accept or (2) change, you will achieve a winning position. Actually making a change may cause you to realise that the initial situation was preferable, and because of this learning experience, you may return to it with acceptance. What I am saying is that if you don't like the situation and decide to change it, you may find the alternative worse and return to the initial situation but with more peace of mind.

I am not advocating 'change for change's sake', but suggesting that if a situation is not suitable or not acceptable then change is a possible alternative. The decision to *accept* or *change* involves struggles, doubts, risks, failures and a gradual growing process. We need to struggle with negative doubts which beset us at every turn in the road. In order to keep going, the question 'Why not?' may be preferable to 'Why?' when an alternative arises. We are likely to receive criticism, offers of advice and antagonism if we choose either of these two pathways. But as Elbert Hubbard said, 'To escape criticism – do nothing, say nothing, *be nothing*.'

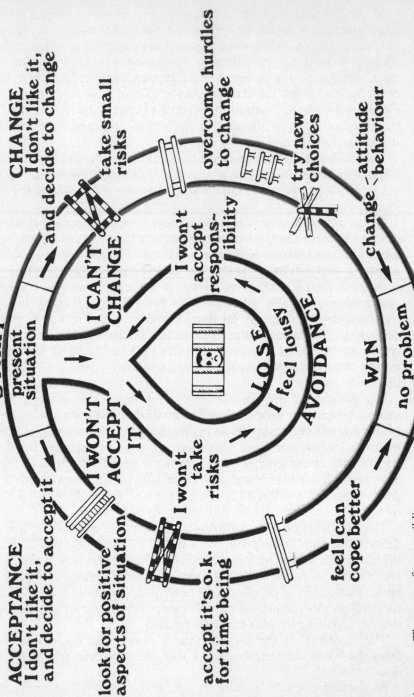

Diagram 1   The game of responsiblity

Many times we will feel we should have stayed where we were, will feel alone and wonder where we are going. Mistakes will occur; the chance to make mistakes is much greater in progress than when stationary. Time is an essential ingredient on these pathways. It often takes longer than we expect or hope for, and so we question the decision to change or to accept things for the time being. There is usually an element of *hope* mixed with the frustration, hope of a better alternative in the future, the so-called light at the end of the tunnel (the pessimists would say it is an oncoming train).

Risk-taking is often necessary if the pathway to *change* has been chosen. Risks that seem enormous at the time but negligible after the event, occur all along the way. One way of gaining is by taking the risk of losing.

The *acceptance* pathway may seem more appealing to the less adventurous, but in reality may be more difficult to maintain. Looking for positive aspects of a situation (reframing) can be very rewarding and lead to a greater understanding of the mechanisms and relationships involved. It takes a lot of courage to accept a situation which has previously appeared unacceptable. One needs to *really* feel comfortable with it *for the time being* which may be days, weeks or months, and to quell the doubts which will continue to arise. An interesting fact is that people choosing the acceptance pathway often end up changing the situation for the better by removing the tension and anxiety which was previously involved.

The pathway of *avoidance* is the most common one which a therapist meets. It means the problem hasn't been dealt with satisfactorily. Responsibility has not been taken to accept or change the situation. It is a circular pathway leading nowhere. This merry-go-round is familiar to all of us. Its lubrication and energy comes from the non-decisions, fears, reasons 'why not to', self-blame and self-doubt. The path is strewn with 'I can't' and 'I won't'. Every time an obstacle is reached, forward motion is blocked by inertia.

The signposts on this pathway are frustration, despair, lack of confidence, blaming ('It isn't fair, why me?'), a lack of learning and a host of other negative and painful feelings. The movement may appear stationary but it is in fact circular. The same negative feelings and events, the same reactions from people continue to recur. The only thing that moves forward on this pathway is *time*. It moves on and on and the realisation that life is passing by adds to the frustration.

The 'avoiders' fit the picture that 'a clever man reaps some benefit from the worst catastrophe, and a fool can turn even good luck to his disadvantage.'

So the big question is how to get off the treadmill of avoidance on to either the acceptance or change pathways.

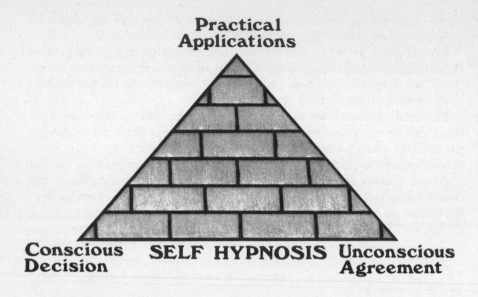

Practical Applications

Conscious Decision   **SELF HYPNOSIS**   **Unconscious Agreement**

Diagram 2   Three points for construction of acceptance or change

The first step is to recognise that you are on the circular pathway of avoidance. The next step is to take responsibility for yourself being there. Don't blame events, people, the weather, your birth sign. Remember, the game is called responsibility and a 'Why me?' attitude is ignoring that responsibility. The next decision to make is that you do not want to continue on the treadmill any longer. Once this decision is made, the alternatives of change or acceptance can be considered, not necessarily as ideal, but preferable to the avoidance one.

If *acceptance for the time being* is chosen then enumerating all the positive, learning factors involved is of importance in order to *really* accept the situation. Giving other people the benefit of the doubt, attempting to understand their actions in a tolerant way, looking at the negative input *you* have been adding to the situation, and making a commitment to temporarily alter this, are all useful suggestions. Make a time by which you will re-assess your acceptance decision.

Change may occur just by the decision to change. The optimistic attitude associated with change is often noted by others. Remember, others change as you do. Hypnosis may be a useful help in providing the energy and insights to get off the roundabout onto a firmer track. A build-up in self-esteem and self-confidence, (always run down in the avoidance circle), may rapidly occur using self-hypnosis, to tap the abundance of willpower stored in the back of our minds.

By using self-hypnosis daily a new perspective to the problem may be seen and positive thoughts and feelings replace barren, negative sensations (see diagram 2). These positive emotions provide energy for the new course we have decided upon.

The small decisions we make, chances we take and mistakes we learn from, can be compared to the small bursts of energy required to change the orbit of a satellite in space. The satellite may have been in the same orbit around the earth for a long time, but just a short burst of energy from the rockets may make a difference of thousands of miles to the overall direction it takes in the future. So it is with our lifestyles and the pathways we choose. Just small bursts of energy may make all the difference. Mistakes are a fact of life. It's our response to them that counts.

9 Choices

It does not take much strength to do things but it requires
great strength to decide on what to do.
It is always safe to assume, not that the old way is wrong,
but that there may be a better way.

When we are confronted by a problem or difficulty in any aspect of
our daily life, we often entangle ourselves in a multitude of irrelevant
thoughts which make a solution to the problem unlikely. We pile on
layer upon layer of 'what if ...s?' 'Why can't I work this out myself?'
'What will they think if I do this?' which distracts us from the core
of the problem and adds to it.

On analysis of many people's problems and their efforts to cut through
the maze of distractions which compound the issue, I have found a five
step direction plan which has proved to be a useful guide (not a solution)
to keep in mind when attempting to deal with the difficulty.

The guide is like a compass, used to point you in the right direction,
but it is no more than a framework and its use will depend on the multitude
of factors involved in the problem and the personalities of those concerned.

Here are the steps to take:

1. State the problem you are having in its most basic form – the
   real crux of what is worrying you. In mathematics it is called the
   lowest common denominator. Eliminate the frills around the problem.
2. List all the possible alternatives available to deal with the problem.
   It is important to make the list long and varied with some absurd
   and humorous items.
3. Decide which of the choices – one or more – *you* want. That is,
   the choice or choices you feel are most appropriate to the problem,
   irrespective of the difficulty in achieving them.
4. Work out how to achieve these choices by
   a) asking yourself what to *actually* do (actions not theories) to
      achieve this choice. The choice must be related to actions *you*

do, not what you hope someone else will do.

    b) Analyse the things, thoughts, feelings, people that have prevented you from using these choices previously.

5. Make a commitment to put into practice, within a period of time and for a period of time, the choice or choices you decide on.

It sounds simple, but I'm sure you will find difficulties in using the framework: often irrelevant thoughts and emotions cause detours which lead to the same dead end. It is not necessary to solve the *whole* problem in the first try. Any new thoughts, ideas or proposals which help deal with a small aspect of the stalemate are useful.

Let us take an example: one presented to me by someone who was really concerned and upset by a constantly recurring situation. John had many difficulties in life, stemming from his lack of confidence and inability to accept his thoughts and feelings as legitimate – either to him or anyone else. He had a relationship with Jill for six months which was fraught with doubts, indecisions and lack of communication. He was feeling overpowered by Jill and unable to state his needs in the relationship. I asked him to tell me one *specific* problem that was worrying him, something he was having difficulty in resolving.

He told me: 'I stay with Jill each weekend at her house. We sleep in her double bed together. She tosses and turns and takes all the room in the bed. I stay perched on the edge all night and can't sleep. It concerns me because this is how the relationship is in many other areas.'

He felt like pushing her over onto her side but his mind got caught up in moral values: his rights, how she would react, whether it would spoil the relationship. His mind went round in circles throughout the long dark night. In the morning, when the dawn chorus heralded the end of his misery, he was angry, frustrated and irritable. These feelings continued throughout the day, without ever being communicated to the more rested but perplexed Jill.

So John and I went through the five steps of the framework.

1. State the problem in its most basic form. 'I want a good night's sleep when I stay at Jill's house.'

2. List all the possible alternatives available – a list as long as possible, including humorous and absurd items. John came up with:

    a) Move Jill.

    b) Remain uncomfortable.

    c) Get out of bed and sleep on the couch.

    d) Push her onto the floor.

    e) Never go there again.

    f) Bring a sleeping bag.

    g) Wake her up and talk about it.

    h) Take two sleeping tablets.

     i) Read all night.
     j) Get up and go to other side of bed.
     k) Discuss it with Jill before bed.

3. John decided he wanted choice (a) to move Jill and (k) to discuss the problem before bed.
4. What did he need to do to achieve this?
   a) To physically and gently move Jill to the other side of the bed.
      To discuss with her his difficulties at some appropriate time before bed.
   b) What had been preventing him from doing this before? During this discussion we removed a myriad of illogicalities, guilt feelings and anticipated problems, which had been revolving in his head and immobilising him. He also realised that he could discuss it with her so that a row would be averted, a row being his greatest fear, making him feel terrible and wanting to run away.
5. He made a commitment to discuss it with Jill during the next week and hopefully to get an agreement to move her if it recurred the following weekend.

Apart from the laughs gained in the choice list, John seemed to have the problem and the solution more within his grasp. He said he now could see it as an isolated problem which he felt he could deal with, rather than an emotional challenge too overpowering to tackle.

By setting out the difficulty in this semi-formal way and arguing the pros and cons, John began to see how he'd magnified a problem which to most people would have been just a passing thought.

I once explained this framework to a patient who went home to put it into practice but came back stumped. 'I couldn't get to first base. I couldn't get the problem to any lower denominator than "I'm fat". From there on, all I came up with was to diet etc. which is what I've been trying for years.'

So we talked about it some more:

DOCTOR: Your problem is 'I am fat', is that right?
PATIENT: Yes and I don't like being fat.
DOCTOR: What do you feel when you are fat?
PATIENT: I feel bad.
DOCTOR: Bad?
PATIENT: I feel unattractive.
DOCTOR: To whom?
PATIENT: To others.
DOCTOR: Which others?
PATIENT: My parents, friends.
DOCTOR: How do you know they find you unattractive?

PATIENT: Well, no-one has actually told me, it's an assumption. I also believe men won't find me attractive.

DOCTOR: So losing weight would help you to feel more attractive and happier?

PATIENT: Well, as a matter of fact when I lose weight I notice my girl-friends are jealous and that makes me unhappy.

DOCTOR: Have they told you that?

PATIENT: No, but I assume they are jealous when they try and upset my diet.

DOCTOR: Jealous of your success or jealous you will steal their husbands?

PATIENT: I'm not sure, I think the former. My friends have always found me comfortable and non-threatening. When I lose weight this relationship may alter.

DOCTOR: So we have travelled a long way from your initial problem of 'I am fat'. Now we can see the problem lies in the belief that your friendships are dependent on your weight.

PATIENT: (*Nodding head slowly and looking doubtful*) Yes I suppose you could say that.

DOCTOR: OK. Let's have that in its simplest form.

PATIENT: I think my friends won't like me if I'm thin.

DOCTOR: Is that a problem?

PATIENT: Yes it is.

DOCTOR: OK. Let's put that in the framework. What alternatives are available to deal with this?

PATIENT: You mean being silly as well as serious.

DOCTOR: Yes.

PATIENT: OK. 1. have no friends.
                 2. stay fat and accept it.
                 3. lose weight and see what happens.
                 4. talk to my friends about my beliefs.

DOCTOR: Which one or more would you choose?

PATIENT: I would choose (3) and (4).

DOCTOR: Do you know what to do to achieve these choices?

PATIENT: Yes.

DOCTOR: How long do you need to put these into practice?

PATIENT: By the time I see you next – in three weeks.

This illustrates how 'dissecting' the problem into pieces enables us to deal with it much more easily, just as it is easier to digest steak when it is cut into small pieces.

In making use of this framework it is important to note:

1. There are many solutions to any problem.
2. The solution you are at present using, which you find unsatisfactory, may or may not be the best one available.
3. Avoid continuing to underestimate your own ability, strength or confidence in trying something new.

4. Try not to approach change with a negative outlook. If John said to Jill: 'I'm sure you would be annoyed if I tried to move you while you were asleep,' the response might well be 'Yes', as he had phrased the question in such a way that 'Yes' was a much easier answer to give than 'No'.

5. Try these steps on a *small* difficulty first and gain confidence in using the framework.

6. The list of alternatives is very important. Many innovative ideas in commerce and industry have come about by 'ridiculous' suggestions. The nucleus of these suggestions is then modified to shed some new light on the problem.

7. Looking at what has prevented you using the choices previously, note what role *you* play in the difficulties and what role other people or events play. Often we say 'I can't do that because she will do this,' when in fact she may not.
   Don't be put off trying a new choice because of what *may* happen – it often doesn't.

8. Make the commitment so that you really mean to put it into action. This book is written as a practical book, its value is not utilised if on reading what I've just written you put the book down with a yawn, saying to yourself, 'He makes sense, I must try that sometime.' 'Sometime' may be too late.

There's a story about a man who was repeatedly having car accidents. He took more driving lessons but he was still involved in collisons. He bought a different, more powerful, car with the same result. Someone suggested he have his eyes tested. It was found that he was colour blind. When he looked at red he saw green and vice versa. No wonder he was having so much trouble!

There was nothing that could be done for his eyes so he had to learn that whenever he saw green he should remember it was red, and with red remember it was green. As he made this adjustment he had no more accidents. It was very difficult at first but he was gradually able to train himself to stop at the (his) green light and to proceed at the (his) red light.

Diagram 3 illustrates how we block choices by telling ourselves not to proceed for various reasons. The problem with this method is that we always end up on the easy path, the same old way but one that is going in the wrong direction.

We need to adjust like the driver in the story above. When we feel guilty and say we can't proceed it is like seeing the green light as red and we should adjust to move forward not back. There is no guarantee it will work but we know from experience proceeding along the easy path *doesn't* work.

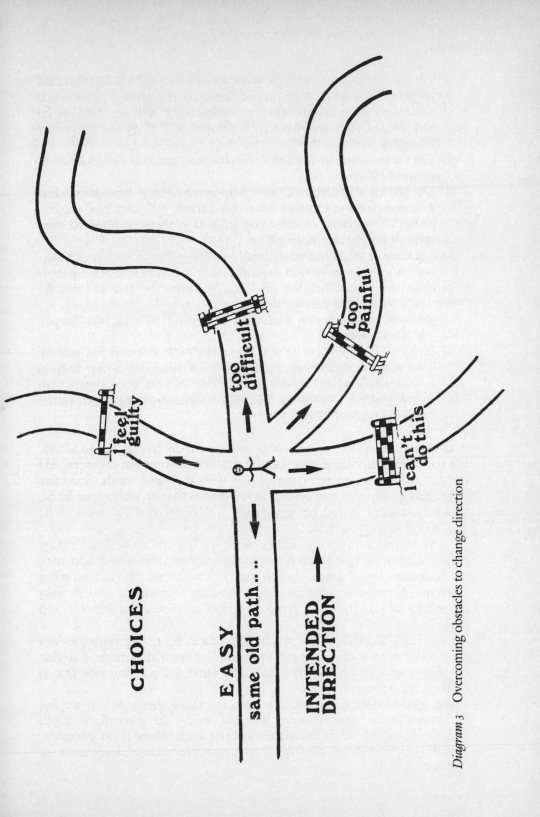

CHOICES

EASY
same old path...

INTENDED DIRECTION

I feel guilty

too difficult

too painful

I can't do this

Diagram 3   Overcoming obstacles to change direction

So, in future, if you stop doing something, or saying something, because you find it too hard, too painful or you feel guilty, try to proceed as if your red light is really green and note the result. If it works then you will use it again; if it doesn't work you have an up-to-date reason for not doing something. In order to know if it is a useful method or not, give it time and have a *positive* attitude. We can all fail if we really put our minds to it.

A woman was complaining about her relationship with her son-in-law. When he behaved in an abominable way, she would have liked to have told him off, 'But I can't,' she told me, 'because it will upset my daughter.'

She had followed this 'red light' of 'I can't' for some years and it wasn't working. I asked her when she next told herself the red 'I can't' to interpret it as a green 'I can'. She found it very difficult to even think of doing this. After a lot of discussion, she realised that it wasn't the end of the world if an argument occurred, or if he didn't like her so much, and she agreed at the next opportunity to 'give it a try'.

Some weeks later at a restaurant he was very rude to the waiter and she overcame her 'can't' and expressed her anger. An argument ensued and the meal was finished in silence, but somehow she felt very good. She couldn't explain it but a feeling of relief came over her. Their relationship didn't improve much, but she learnt she could speak her mind and, as a result, felt much better.

10 *Choice not Chance*

Many are stubborn in pursuit of the path they have
chosen, few in pursuit of the goal.
NIETZSCHE

I was recently given a present of a small glass tube containing five Mexican jumping beans. They were described as 'the perfect household pet – no mess, no feeding, all that is required is to keep them warm and they will entertain for months.' They lived up to their reputation. For the next two months they rattled in their glass vial or jumped about in amazing ways when placed on a table in the sun.

The Mexican jumping bean is a bean in which a moth has laid an egg. The egg hatches into a caterpillar which lives inside the bean. When the bean drops off a tree onto the ground in the hot sun of Mexico, the caterpillar attaches itself to one end inside the bean, curls up, then springs back causing the bean to move or jump. In this random way it hopes to get out of the sun into the cooler shade where eventually it will turn into a moth.

Watching these beans jump around on the table with the hopeless belief that they will get into the shade reminded me of the way people deal with situations. They apply actions in a random way and, like the beans, from time to time succeed. But what a difficult way of moving from A to B.

Hopefully we have developed greater skills than the poor caterpillar springing away inside his shell. The fact that the species exists is proof that its method works but there must be an easier way. *People do the best they can with the choices available*. One way of helping is to provide more choices.

What I would like to write about are ways in which we can improve our choice-making abilities. We may look at life as a series of choices. By not making a choice we are making a choice. From the moment we wake until we go to sleep we are confronted by decisions, some easy to make, others more difficult. When to get up, what to eat, wear, say, all provide us with alternatives; often we fulfil these without thinking but the options are always there.

In any situation where difficulties arise it is preferable to have alternative ways of dealing with them than to have one fixed line of action. Just the availability of choices helps us to have more confidence, more power, feel more comfortable. We often restrict ourselves in the belief that we have no alternative to our behaviour except the one way we act. This restriction poses problems of its own. To be flexible is a great asset in dealing with the variety of situations which confront us continually; in other words to give ourselves more choices.

We can create more choices by removing restrictions and becoming more aware of our potential. Being aware that there is an alternative enables us to look for it. If the thought in the back of our mind is 'there may be a better way', then the possibility of an improved option allows an alternative.

If we remove self-imposed rules, this automatically allows more freedom. A woman came to me and one of her complaints was the difficulties she was having in her marriage. Her husband never apologised even if he had made an obvious mistake, or failed in some situation. When I asked her why, she replied, 'He believes that to apologise is a sign of weakness.' This rule her husband was using was not only incorrect, but it limited him from a choice which would have pleased his wife and hence improved their relationship. We create so many incorrect self-imposed rules that restrict our choices. I once saw a sign hanging on the wall of an office saying, 'In our business there are no rules except this one.'

False logic and self-fulfilling prophecies

We often use *false logic* to restrict our choices. 'If I do *this*, then *that* will happen.' If you have a *negative* attitude you will actually create the negative outcome you predict. This is called a 'self-fulfilling prophecy' and is very common.

Someone going for their driving test with the attitude 'It's too difficult, everyone fails, because I'm so nervous I'll fail', will be quite correct. He will fail, not because he is incompetent but because he is following the negative route he is directing himself along. He is fulfilling the prophecy he is making. This then reinforces his belief that he is no good so the situation keeps repeating itself. These self-fulfilling prophecies may be in the 'self-talk' of the mind or discussed openly.

Ted was a prison worker from Scotland and he had been in London three years. He was very lonely and shy. He wasn't keen on his job but there didn't seem too many jobs available so he stuck at it. He didn't complain, or let anyone know he was sad and lonely in the big city.

One day at a meeting of prison officers he suddenly developed a panic attack. He started to shake, his heart was racing and he felt faint. He didn't want anyone to notice and so he concentrated on concealing his feelings. The meeting was a discussion about a juvenile delinquent on probation, who had mugged an old woman. He'd never been so relieved than when the meeting finished and he could stagger out. His panic attack went unnoticed and he crept home exhausted and threw himself on his bed.

His mind then started to question what had happened. Why had he had the panic attack? Was it the meeting, all those people? Was it talking about the youth mugging the old woman? His mind went round and round. He tossed and turned 'til 3 a.m.

Insidiously, his fear started. What if it happens at the next meeting? What if it happens when a mugging is next discussed? If he got the panics again and it was noticed they'd think he was mad. He'd lose his job, be on the dole. In lonely London, it would be a nightmare. And so the ruminations went on hour after hour, day after day, night after night. He then became *sure* it would happen at the next meeting. He missed the meeting on a pretext that he was busy. Then his worst fears eventuated. At the following meeting he felt the panic come on. The more he tried not to let it show the worse it became. His panics got worse. His fear of meetings got worse. He became more isolated, lonely and unhappy.

Ted was fulfilling a self-fulfilling prophecy. By prophesying that something would happen and being afraid of it happening, he actually created the event. An initial event for no apparent reason can start a self-fulfilling prophecy which can perpetuate the worst fears.

How often does a golfer who says to himself, 'On this hole I always slice into the rough', end up searching for his ball amongst the trees for the next twenty minutes. In Ted's case it may or may not be relevant why he had the first panic attack. If he had looked upon it as an isolated incident it may never have occurred again. But he tried to link it with something to explain it. And with his base of unhappiness this link took hold to create the fear of it happening again in meetings. His ruminations nourished this fear which formed a basis for its recurrence.

Talking logically and on a conscious level to Ted, I didn't make much headway as he had experienced these terrible feelings and they were *real*. So we did some self-hypnosis and Ted imagined what would have happened in the meeting if he didn't try and hide the panic attacks – if he let his teeth chatter and his body shake.

In the trance he found it wasn't a great problem to let people know he didn't feel too good. In fact it led in his mind to discussing with them other problems he had, about the job and living in London. He felt reasonably calm and relaxed as he discussed the feelings and pictures he had in his trance state, and even thought the panic attacks were a useful way for him to start to explain his feelings to others around him.

When he came out of the trance he still had many doubts about how he could put those thoughts into action, but he agreed that if he had a panic attack at the next meeting he wouldn't try to hide it.

As soon as he realised the panic attacks were no real problem, they stopped. They were being kept going by his fear of them happening. Ted's problem wasn't panic attacks – it was fear of panic attacks. Once he'd overcome the fear the momentum pushing them along stopped.

If you have numerous negative, self-fulfilling prophecies occurring in your life you are limiting your choices and opportunities immensely. Any positive possibilities are ignored as they do not fit in with the negative belief system.

Another form of false logic is when one event follows another and is believed to be caused by it. I will explain with an amusing tale from the Australian outback in the last century. Kerosene lamps were being used in all the homesteads and numerous accidents and explosions occurred. Two men in a horse and buggy drove around the countryside with a guaranteed solution to the problem. If you purchased three coloured beads (at great expense), one yellow, one green and one red, placed them in the kerosene lamp and filled it to the top with kerosene, no explosions would occur. They did a roaring trade in beads for many months, until someone discovered that just filling the lamp with kerosene without the beads was equally successful.

How often does something happen which we believe was caused by a previous event when, in fact, the two events were totally unrelated?

Another difficulty is that we see the world through our own eyes and often believe others see it the same way. So when we offer what we think is logical advice it may not be understood or useful to the person we are trying to help.

This was well illustrated on a radio programme I heard whilst driving home from work one day. The programme was about the difficulties in detecting autistic children early enough to be able to help them. A very simple method had been devised. An autistic child and a normal child watched a brief puppet show. The show consisted of a girl (Sue) coming on stage and putting a box of chocolates on a table then leaving the stage. Another girl (Mary) came on stage and put the chocolates under the bed.

The two children were asked these questions:

1. When Sue comes back, where *will* she look for the chocolates?
2. Where *should* she look for them?

The normal child responded, 'She *will* look on the table but she *should* look under the bed.' The autistic child said, 'She *will* look under the bed and she *should* look under the bed.'

The autistic child believed *everyone* saw the world as he did, so he believed everyone would know what he knew. I think we all have a little of that attitude and especially so in doctor/patient relationships. Many therapists, including myself, find it very difficult to understand why patients behave in a certain way because *we* wouldn't behave that way with our knowledge. We lose sight of the fact that because of their very different experiences in life they do not see things the same way that we, with medical training, do. I think we all have a little of the attitude 'because I know it therefore I assume you know it' when communicating with other people.

Often we limit our choices by following the belief, 'If it doesn't work, do it harder, longer and louder and it will work then.' This prescription may be successful when climbing Mount Everest but in my experience has minimal application to life's average problems. A common example of this doctrine is in parent/child conflicts. On the 'battlegrounds' of these relationships, at the dinner table, bed time, tidying the room, etc., gaining control by 'doing it harder, louder and longer' greatly restricts the possibility of any alternatives.

Little Johnny won't go to bed at 7 p.m. as directed by Mum. Mum gets annoyed as each night a battle occurs. She uses logic in the following way:

1. Johnny must go to bed by 7 p.m.
2. If he doesn't he will be tired and jumpy tomorrow.
3. If I force him he will protest so I must force him harder and louder and longer.
4. If I can't force him I'll smack him.
5. If that doesn't work I'll stop his pocket money.
6. If that doesn't work I'll lock him in his room.
7. If this doesn't work we must punish him more until he goes to bed on time.

This is an exaggerated version of what is familiar in most homes at some stage or other. The fact that there may be a more successful alternative is lost as 'the battle of Johnny's bed time' escalates, with other factors, such as saving face, maintaining authority, etc. entering the fray.

I am not going to offer an ideal answer to this problem but I would like to quote another case which may illustrate possible alternatives.

Little Suzie, aged six, was always very slow to get dressed in the morning. This infuriated her working mother who was always late. Her mother escalated the battle to the screaming, smacking stage, which seemed to delay things more because of the tears that flowed. Whilst discussing the problem with me, it was obvious that tensions and frustrations were growing with each morning battle. I suggested that, to avoid the battle, she talk lovingly and seriously to Suzie when she went to bed, stating that if she was not dressed by the right time in the morning she would be dropped off at school in her pyjamas. The mother was horrified at the prospect but agreed to put it into practice.

Suzie was put into the car in her pyjamas when she was late the next morning and her wails of anguish were enough for Mum to extract a promise that it would never happen again if she went back and got dressed, and it hasn't. Thinking 'there must be a better way' may enable a more appropriate formula to be created than the 'more of the same' non-choice.

There is a saying that may be useful to remember when you find yourself escalating a battle. 'If it is not working try something different.' There is no guarantee that the 'something different' will work, but it is very likely that continually escalating a non-working method will produce failure.

'*Be flexible*' is a very wise motto and the eastern philosophy of bending against force rather than meeting force with force has a lot to commend it. A touching old Chinese parable illustrates this much more succinctly than I can. It is the story of the fir tree and the bamboo.

A large proud fir tree growing in the forest next to a clump of bamboo was continually berating the bamboo for its weakness. 'Why aren't you tall and straight like me, king of the trees? Everyone looks up to me. I grow proud and strong every year while you bend and bow down to any wind that blows. Why don't you have some backbone and withstand the pressures?'

The bamboo said nothing but rustled as it swayed in the breeze.

All through the summer and autumn the fir tree talked about its strength and power. Winter came and the winds grew strong. The bamboo bent double in front of the wind. The fir tree, standing erect and straight, scorned the lowly bamboo until a strong gust tugged at a branch, breaking it. As the wind continued more branches cracked and broke under the strain.

Then the snow fell, heavy snow day after day. The snow slid to the ground from the bamboo stem as it bent. The fir branches, stiff and immobile, were weighed down by the heavy snow and broke under the stress.

When spring arrived the bamboo grew new green leaves and was its same old self, rustling in the breeze. The fir tree was a sad and sorry sight. Branches broken and torn, bare wood exposed, the lovely, lofty symmetry lost. No longer did he praise his proud rigidity. 'Why wasn't I supple and flexible like you, bamboo, so I could weather the elements and look forward to the beauty of spring?'

Life presents us with ups and downs. The more flexible we are the more we can survive the pressures with the least damage. Being fixed in attitude or belief is good sometimes but very limiting at other times. Feeling comfortable and going with a situation is not a sign of weakness – it may well be a sign of strength.

Having choices is the first necessity; using them satisfactorily is the second. Some people find the multitude of choices which surrounds them creates a problem which I call the 'disease of choices'. Being constantly bombarded by alternatives may be immobilising and cause great stress.

I was once staying with a friend who said, 'Brian, would you go to the shops and get some bread for us?'

'Sure,' I said, 'What sort do you want?'

'Oh, a sliced loaf will be OK.'

As I prepared to leave he said, 'Do you like brown bread or white?'

'Brown suits me fine.'

'I think rolls are nice, don't you?' he called out as I was leaving. I returned to finalise what I should buy.

'What do you want me to get?' I queried.

'Well, I'm not sure, do you think rolls would be better than sliced bread?'

'Yes, they would be nice, how many do you want?'

'Well, there are only the two of us so get four.'

'OK. Be back in a minute.'

'Perhaps you should get an extra one just in case.'

'OK.'

As I closed the door and walked down the stairs I suspected I would hear more about the bread. The door opened and he called out, 'Don't you think a crusty loaf would be nice?'

I walked back up the stairs to discuss this momentous decision further.

'I really don't mind, by the time I get there the shop will be closed.'

'You don't need to get so upset, I'm just trying to please you. Don't you like crusty bread? I just thought you would prefer it to the plain old sliced loaf. Get what you want, I don't care.'

'I'll see what's there, leave it to me,' I said, trying to pacify him.

As I strolled down the street, the window opened and I faintly heard, 'Don't you think a French loaf would be nice?'

My friend had 'the disease of choices'; every decision was a torment to him, what tie to wear, which route to take, what time to go, etc. etc. So just having choices does not necessarily provide peace of mind.

If you are in conflict because you do not know which decision to make, I have a helpful hint. A conflict implies that two or more choices are present and you are not sure which one to follow. You can decide A or you can decide B. Every time you think of doing A, many reasons crop up for doing B. I suggest you have *three* alternatives:

Choices

1. Decide A.
2. Decide B.
3. Decide *not* to decide for a period of time.

This last choice enables the conflict to be *temporarily* resolved. At a future date a review of the conflict may enable an easy choice to be made, due to altered factors that have occurred with time. Often deciding not to decide is the best decision. Often we may be confused by internal conflicting advice from the past and the present (see diagram 4).

In order to use the available choices to the best advantage, put some into practice and learn from the experience. It seems the only way we learn is from our own experience and if we have had painful experiences in the past we may not be prepared to try that choice again, although it may now be safe and preferable to the ones we are using.

Most people who have difficulty dealing with life's problems have choices available to them but fear prevents them being used. I attempt to persuade them to try and learn, rather than refrain from trying and hence avoid learning. Of numerous journeys to the countryside, the most enjoyable were those when I became lost and discovered things I never would have found had I remained on the motorways. The known tracks may be the safest but they may also be the most limiting.

Trying something different often achieves results when the obvious has failed. The things which seem opposite to what appears logical may work when logical attempts fail – this is called *paradoxical* thinking.

A group of people were under siege in a castle on top of a hill. The besieging troops had been camped at the bottom of the hill for months. Food in the castle was running low. The troops below were bored and frustrated and wanted to go back to their homes.

After six months of siege, the commander of the garrison in the castle asked how much food was left. He was told, 'One ox and a bag of corn.'

'Kill the ox, slit open its belly, fill it with the corn and sew it up,' was the order.

When this was done the commander said, 'Now throw it over the battlements to the enemy below.'

The people in the garrison were horrified – their last remnant of food thrown to the enemy – but they obeyed.

When the commander of the troops below was brought the ox stuffed with corn, he assumed there was food remaining for many more months, and called his troops off. The people in the castle were saved.

A young couple were on the verge of divorce. They argued about anything and everything, their lives were one long argument. The husband, who claimed he really loved his wife and did not want to lose her, asked me for some advice.

Diagram 4 Confused by conflicting advice

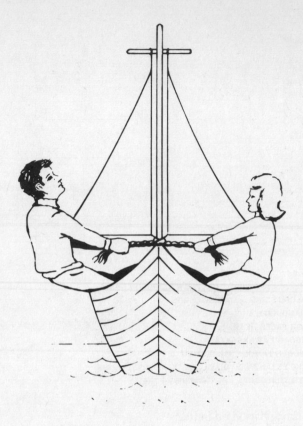

Diagram 5   Steadying the boat

The choice that he had made was to contest his wife on everything. This wasn't working so we discussed choices he had not thought of or which he felt would be of no use. I tried to think of an alternative choice diametrically opposed to what he had been using.

I discussed with him a diagram (see diagram 5) in a book I had. In the boat, husband and wife are leaning as far out as possible to keep the boat stable. As one moved further out the other would do the same to prevent the boat tipping over.

I asked him what would happen if one leaned in towards the other. He replied that either the boat would tip over or the other person would have to move in to keep the balance. He got the picture.

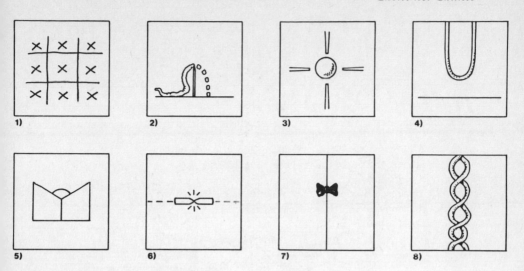

1) NOUGHTS & CROSSES PLAYED BY EXTREMELY STUBBORN PEOPLE
2) DETERMINED WORM CROSSING A RAZOR BLADE
3) CRISIS IN THE BILLIARD HALL
4) FIREMAN'S POLE FOR FALSE ALARMS
5) WIFE'S VIEW OF HUSBAND AT BREAKFAST
6) DUEL BETWEEN 2 WORLD FAMOUS MARKSMEN
7) MAN IN DINNER JACKET STANDING TOO CLOSE TO FRONT OF LIFT
8) 2 SNAKES WHO BOTH THINK THEY ARE CLIMBING A TREE

Diagram 6   Imagination unlimited

Whenever you are stuck in a situation, one way of getting out of it is to study the methods you have been using and try some lateral thinking to create an alternative which may seem absurd but, by its very absurdity, may succeed. The only limit to this method is your creative ability and the more you try the more creative you will become.

Children are often more able to think laterally about things. This is illustrated by the interpretation of the doodles in diagram 6 by a girl of seven.

If you approach problems and decisions as challenges rather than defeats you may be amazed at the simplicity of the solutions you achieve.

11 The Dice Man

All life is a gamble, a risk-taking exercise. Those who
take no risks take the biggest gamble of all.

The race is not always to the swift, nor the battle to
the strong – but that's the way to bet!
DAMON RUNYON

Some years ago a book called *The Dice Man* was published. The story
is about a man who wanted more adventure in his life and decided to
make a list of what he would like to do each day and to throw a dice
to decide. He made a pact with himself that he must obey the number
which came up. He ended up in all sorts of adventures and troubles,
but discovered he could do a lot more things than he believed he could
do.

I have found this a useful 'game' to encourage people to come out
of their self-restricting cocoons. Jennifer Jones, a quiet self-effacing
woman of fifty, was finding life boring and unattractive. She wouldn't
say boo to a goose and was forever finding reasons for not standing
up for herself. If she bought something and the salesman gave her the
wrong change she was too timid to correct him for fear of a confrontation.

She related numerous tales in her early life when she was 'put down'
by a strict, uncompromising father and had continued to put herself
down in a similar way ever since.

We chatted away for an hour and I consistently attempted to suggest
that perhaps it would be OK to express her feelings in this or that situation. She, equally consistently, explained how she wouldn't choose to
do it that way in case she upset someone.

I asked her if she would be prepared to enter into a game of chance.
She initially refused point blank but, after I explained the dice man principle, I noted a gleam in her eye and I believe a seed of daring may have
been sown.

At the next visit she brought up the subject of the dice man principle
and asked more about it. 'It's very simple,' I said. 'You write a list of
new choices and number them 1 to 6. They must be choices you *will*

do so don't make them too daring. Perhaps you may try a new lipstick, or a new hairdresser or walk a different way to work, or engage in a conversation with the bus driver. Nothing too radical. You throw the dice in the morning and whatever number comes up you follow the directions appropriate to that number.'

She seemed very hesitant. However, after some discussion, we worked out six very minor choices for her to follow. She agreed to write a new list every morning (which could contain some of the old choices not performed) and to throw the dice and carry out the commitment.

She seemed nervous and excited as she left with an outsize dice I'd lent her for the week. I wondered if she would carry out her intentions and how daring her choices would be.

Next week she was thrilled to report that she had done some new things. They were pretty minor by average standards but major for her. What was more important she was enjoying the game and also learning that the difficulties she'd anticipated did not actually occur.

Each week Jennifer would come to report how the dice had fallen for her. Some weeks were more exciting than others but I noticed the choices she was writing down were becoming more positive – for her, more daring. Sometimes she said she hadn't been able to follow the choice stated and I admonished her that the only rule was the necessity to 'obey the dice'.

Over the next few months Jennifer gradually gained more confidence and, on some occasions, did two or more of the choices on the day even though the dice had only directed her to follow one.

This game helps to take away the responsibility of thinking about all the pros and cons of doing something positive. For people who lack confidence it enables them to start on the road to building up their confidence after it has been shattered by previous experience. It is important to start with trivial choices so the carrying out of them is not too great a burden and the learning experience of exploring life's activities can be made in easy stages. Jennifer kept my oversize dice on her mantelpiece and it was a constant reminder to her of the choices and chances everyone goes through in life.

12 Movement

The restless man mounts his horse and rides off furiously
in every direction.
C.G. JUNG

One must not confuse movement with progress.

Often we think of ourselves as 'in a rut', going nowhere, doing the same old thing day after day, missing out. This may be with reference to ourselves or in a relationship. In order to be able to understand what is happening, I have tried to describe some of the situations we find ourselves in, so that we can assess our progress. I refer to this as a classification of different forms of movement.

1. FORWARD MOVEMENT

This is the aim of most people in dealing with problems. To state the intended aim and steadily move towards it, noting signs of progress along the way. Examples of forward movement can be illustrated thus:

Someone smoking forty cigarettes a day decides to stop over a period of a month. Each week he notes he has cut down by ten cigarettes a day and at the end of the month has stopped completely. Over the next few months he resists the urge to smoke and maintains the role of 'non-smoker'.

A couple argue vehemently whenever they go driving. The wife constantly complains he drives too fast, the husband maintains she nags him too much. After a very heated argument on the way to a party which ruins the night for both of them, they have a discussion about the problem. He agrees to drive more slowly, she agrees not to criticise. Over the next month, only on one occasion does an argument start, and it stops abruptly when they realise what is happening. This is progress in a *forward direction*.

84

2. STATIONARY

This occurs when the situation does not change in spite of resolutions towards forward progress. The problem remains unchanged, the same end point being reached again and again, associated with feelings of frustration and comments such as 'I'm going nowhere'. This may occur over weeks, months and years and whatever intentions are made or alterations occur the result always seems to be the same.

Little Johnny aged eleven is always leaving his clothes on the floor. In spite of repeated requests, threats and bribes, there is no change. Mum, in desperation, increases the threats, bribes and punishments but the clothes remain tossed on the floor after Johnny gets undressed. As time goes on, although the situation is stationary, to Mum it seems to be getting worse.

The longer a situation is stationary the more necessary a different approach is required. Either try a new approach or accept the situation is unchangeable for the time being. So with little Johnny an alternative approach may be to leave the clothes there accumulating day after day until he can no longer find his bed, due to the debris on the floor, or accept that little children do leave their clothes on the floor and he will grow out of it in time.

Often the annoyance and frustration of one person in the system helps to provide the energy to keep it stationary.

In a psychiatric hospital one patient for many months was causing a lot of trouble by hiding towels in his room. Instead of giving the towel to be washed each day he would hide it in a cupboard. Occasionally he would take someone else's towel to hoard along with his own.

The administration heard about this, the patient was reprimanded and the towels removed. A week later the situation was unchanged and the missing towels were again found in his room.

A doctor volunteered to see if he could help alter this stationary state, which was causing much gossip in the café and a lot of bureaucratic discussion in the corridors. He went to visit the patient as a friend, sat down and talked to him for a while then, in a low whisper, said 'I hear you like keeping towels, is that right?'

The patient, nervously fearing a reprimand, looked to see that there was no-one around and slowly nodded his head.

'I know where I can get some, do you want them?' asked the doctor.

'Yes please,' said the highly delighted patient.

The next day the doctor arrived in the morning with twenty towels and surreptitiously gave them to the patient warning him not to tell anyone. That afternoon he arrived with thirty more.

The next morning he came with fifty towels and another fifty in the afternoon. Soon there was no room for the patient to sit, stand or sleep in his room and he started giving them to the cleaner when he arrived. The patient after a while asked the doctor not to bring any more towels and asked if he could help give them all back as he was sick of the sight of them.

So forward progress was achieved from a stationary position by what may appear to be controversial means.

3. THE DEAD END

In this situation progress has started in a forward motion but stopped before the goal has been reached. This may just be due to the fact that more time is required. Many a failure has occurred because the people involved have not allowed enough time for their methods to work, a temporary halt has been interpreted as a failure.

A couple who were continually arguing about the husband's drinking problem, came to see me. The wife was fed up with him drinking three quarters of a bottle of whisky each night. Constant bickering 'sent him to the bottle' more and more and, in an endeavour to overcome the problem, they sought my help. He worked very hard as an engineer and 'needed a drink' when he came home. She didn't want him to start, as her father had been an alcoholic and she worried that he was going the same way. After some discussion, a general agreement was made that he could have three whiskies a night and she wasn't to comment.

When I saw them two weeks later they were arguing as vehemently as ever. It turned out that he had stuck to his three whiskies a night for the first week, but on a bad night the following week he had more than his quota. She had immediately berated him for failing, he swore at her for nagging and went back to his three quarters of a bottle per night.

Had she been able to accept that progress was occurring and that a temporary hiccup (no pun intended) had occurred, the situation may have proceeded, but it was brought to a dead end by her fear of it getting worse.

As progress is being made before a dead end (cf. stationary), benefit may be gained by observing two things. (1) – what progress was being made? (2) – what caused the dead end? Sometimes just a gesture or comment halts the progress and pushes someone back into a feeling of failure and hence reversion to previous behaviour. Sometimes the fear of a halt creates it.

This often happens when one partner is struggling to change and needs praise or recognition for any minimal progress to sustain the improvement. The other partner may be tired, disgruntled or feels praise may stop progress so doesn't respond accordingly. The person attempting to change does some 'mind-reading' and interprets the lack of praise as disapproval and says to himself 'sod it all' and a dead end results.

4. MERRY-GO-ROUND

This is a very common form of motion. A continual movement at a tangent to the proposed intended direction. Sometimes there is forward movement but just as it is felt progress is being made you realise you are back where you started. (See *Avoidance* in Game of Responsibility).

This is a most infuriating course as movement does not seem to be related to the effort expended; often different advice received adds to the problem rather than helping to solve it. Someone moving in this circular manner has a feeling of 'I've been here before', or 'They said the same thing to me the last time.'

The merry-go-round situation does not show progress so much as variation, in what appears to be an arbitrary manner. Like the facetious comment, 'When the Communist revolution occurs things will be different. Not better but different.'

A patient of mine was very shy and never went out. She was depressed and unhappy about constantly remaining inside and said she desperately needed companionship.

I suggested to her that one option may be to think about her hobbies, likes or pastimes and contact a group who shared them. She could concentrate on her hobby and enjoy that with the possibility of meeting someone with similar interests.

She enjoyed photography and agreed to 'phone a photographic society with a view to joining it, or going on one of their photographic outings. Next week when I saw her she said she had rung someone in a photographic club and was told he would ring back. As he had not done so she had bemoaned the fact that the world was against her and done nothing more. We agreed it was bad manners that he hadn't returned her call but as she was the one seeking some benefit perhaps she could have tried again.

The following week she said she had spoken to the chap and there was an outing the next Saturday. She would like to have gone but there was a TV programme she wanted to watch so she declined the offer.

The situation went on week after week like a merry-go-round. Her intention to go out was always stated but her practical application was in a different direction. I tried numerous other manoeuvres and suggestions, all accepted with hope and anticipation, all negated by her actions. My belief is she will continue in this circular motion until it becomes *so* bad to stay at home she will find the effort required to make contact with other people.

When there is circular motion the underlying factor is that the person really does *not* intend to change however much she states that she does. Any progress will be diverted, as the person is not ready to accept the inevitable change that will occur with progress; she will also resist being pushed into change by well-intentioned 'do gooders' like myself.

It would be preferable to re-assess the aim or goal stated and either alter or reduce it, until the person feels confident to make a commitment to achieve minimal change in the right direction. Often too great a change is requested and this creates the merry-go-round movement.

This continued 'non-direction' is infuriating and frustrating for anyone who is sucked in to help. They jump in willingly with what appears to be reasonable and helpful advice only to see it 'fail' time after time, accompanied by plaintive cries for more help by the person using the merry-go-round as a safe retreat.

One way of helping is by not helping. Often they will seek help elsewhere and continue the same routine with different people, but sometimes leaving them without help enables them to begin the changes required.

5. THE TO AND FRO OR WAVE MOTION

This situation occurs when forward progress is being made and everyone is exclaiming how wonderful things are, then – 'whoops' – they slip back to the original position or even further back (like the tide coming in). This often happens when progress is too fast for either the person concerned or the surrounding family.

As the person improves he takes down his defences, so when a minor setback occurs fear and uncertainty in the new role provoke a retreat back to old patterns. At other times, friends and family, having become accustomed to the original situation, will direct him back there one way or another.

This often happens in therapy when the therapist shows his pleasure at the progress being made. At some level the patient is caught in a 'desire to perform for the therapist' situation and this extra pressure can be his undoing. It is as if he is in the limelight to succeed and gains relief in failing and going back to his anonymity.

In many situations when someone appears to be doing well they slip back and come into the surgery saying, 'It's all gone wrong, I'm back to square one.' There is a note of pride and even success at this statement of failure. The pressure to perform too quickly was uncomfortable. Often the superstition that once you say it is going well it will fail, also plays a part.

In order to avoid this to and fro movement, take it slowly, learn from any progress as well as learning from any setback. What occurred that made things go wrong? How did it happen, who said or did what? Did it really go that badly? Are you really back where you started or is it just a temporary setback you can learn from and use for progress?

A woman came to see me with insomnia (lack of sleep) which had persisted on and off for twenty years. She had seen many therapists and had taken numerous sleeping tablets but none had helped her problem. She related to me the eminent men she had seen – physicians, neurologists, reflexologists, herbalists, acupuncturists, homeopaths. All seemed to help her a little but her lack of sleep still troubled her.

She had two married daughters and she had lost her husband ten years previously. All her relatives were concerned about her lack of sleep and were constantly advising her of any new remedy that came on the market.

Her pattern with the various therapists appeared to be improvement and reasonable sleep for a couple of weeks then a return to insomnia and, I suppose, a bewildered therapist, who, when on the verge of success, was faced with failure.

I should have been forewarned as I wrote down her long history, but my belief that I would succeed where others had failed led me into the trap.

I spent an hour explaining the problems and difficulties she had previously experienced and how hypnosis and relaxation would 'cure her'. She left this first visit suitably impressed by my confidence and hopeful of overcoming this chronic problem once and for all.

On the next visit I made a relaxation tape and explained a routine for her if she did not sleep. She came back two weeks later saying everything was going very well, she had slept well for six nights and reasonably well for the rest. Full of self congratulations I gave her another session of hypnosis and relaxation and arranged to see her for a final check-up two weeks later.

You can imagine my dismay when she returned with a gloomy face saying it had all gone wrong. 'Just when I thought I was cured I was awake for three nights in a row.'

I launched into the fray with renewed vigour saying that the initially improved sleep pattern would be restored. I made longer tapes, and the wave motion got into full swing. Some nights she slept, others she didn't, and over the next three sessions we both seemed to have lost enthusiasm for each other.

When she left to find another therapist I spent some time analysing my notes and realised I had played a great role in allowing her to continue with her to and fro motion. It seemed to me she had a multitude of reasons for maintaining her sleep problem and was loathe to let go of it. It may well be sour grapes on my part but I believe she must still be seeking some therapist who will cure her of her chronic problem.

Often progress is halted and temporary setbacks occur on the way to recovery. Anticipation of these prevents regressions being a problem. It is sometimes beneficial to halt progress, to allow time for confidence and comfort to catch up with the changes occurring. Time is an essential ingredient and must be taken into consideration when any alteration in behaviour is contemplated, before assessing the results.

6. BACKWARD MOVEMENT

Many times a patient attends with a problem, we agree on an intended outcome and he leaves to put into practice what seems a reasonable way of dealing with it.

He returns crestfallen with the statement 'things are worse than when I started.' This is backward motion and there are a lot of things to learn from it.

Many times patients with chronic pain trying new tasks or attitudes cause the pain to increase. A worthwhile lesson can be learnt from most backward motions. It may well be that the intended changes were in the right direction but the protective mechanism of the unconscious mind caused the reverse result.

If you can drive a car in reverse gear, at least we know the car is working, and the possibility of finding a forward gear is greater than if it is stationary.

Learning about all the circumstances, people, feelings, efforts involved which caused this backward movement can be very helpful in overcoming the obstacles. Often one has to reverse to get out of a traffic jam and forward movement would be inappropriate.

The backward motion tells us a lot about the fears and insecurity the person has in making a change, the effects of relatives or others involved who are unable to accept any alteration of behaviour. Discussing and understanding this is often very helpful in allowing forward movement to proceed.

Tracey is a twenty-five year old housewife with three-year-old twin boys. She has had headaches for one year and in spite of many tablets etc. has not been able to find suitable relief. She is constantly on the go with the boys and looks after her husband when he gets home tired from work.

I talked to her about her lifestyle and the fact that she doesn't have much time to herself. 'How could I with three babies to look after?' she said, referring to her husband as one of the babies.

We discussed her lack of time to herself and she agreed it might be playing a part in her headaches. I showed her a relaxation exercise and asked her to practise it for twenty minutes when the twins were in bed and before her husband came home. She agreed to do this but she didn't want her husband to know she was seeing me. At her next visit two weeks later she was most upset and said the headaches were much worse. She wasn't very impressed when I commented that this was a good result, which I really believed because it helped me to understand what was happening.

She had started her relaxation after the boys were in bed but had enjoyed it so much that she was still sitting in a relaxed state when her husband came home demanding his dinner. A row ensued and her head-aches became worse, she was more upset and tension in the home was running high.

We spent some time discussing what had happened and I suggested to Tracey that perhaps she could have a long talk to her husband, explaining her problems and needs and also telling him about her visit to me and the relaxation exercise. She thought he wouldn't understand and would be annoyed but agreed it would be reasonable to try, as she didn't like hiding anything from him.

When I saw her a month later things had settled down, her husband had been more understanding than she expected and alterations were made to the timetable to allow her time to herself. As the routine changed the headaches got less and eventually she didn't require any medication.

The learning experience from the backward motion had been very helpful in solving some of the difficulties which had been present for a long time.

It seems to me that one's aims and forward movements are initiated by the conscious mind eager to change and tired of the old behaviour. The unconscious, cautious part of the mind instigates the halts and set-backs due to lack of confidence in the ability to maintain progress.

Analysing and questioning what is happening leads to an understanding of the roles both parts of the mind are playing. Self-hypnosis is very helpful if a halt to progress or a negative direction is occurring. Asking the unconscious about the benefits of these setbacks allows an understanding to occur and an incorporation of those cautions into the overall aim.

In any assessment as to how you are dealing with a difficulty, whatever movement you feel is occurring, if you can *learn* from the situations and behaviour, then this learning will be useful and if put into practice will help you to move in the intended forward direction.

PART FOUR

Hypnosis

13 Words

Words are loaded pistols.
JEAN-PAUL SARTRE

People who have had problems for months or years and have sought help from tablets, injections and tests without success may well ask 'How can words help me when all that powerful machinery has failed?'

It's a good question and the answer is difficult to explain. It reminds me of a man who owned a large factory. Something went wrong with the machinery and he had experts in who tested and adjusted it but to no avail. He was told about a specialist in these matters who might be of help but who was very expensive.

As the factory was losing money daily the man rang the specialist who came and strolled through the factory looking here, listening there. Finally, he went to one piece of machinery and taking out a little hammer tapped it firmly three times. The machines all started to work and production was resumed.

When the bill arrived the factory owner was amazed that it came to £500. He rang the expert to ask why it was so much for just tapping something three times. The answer came back, 'It was £10 for the tapping and £490 for knowing where to tap.'

Perhaps it is the same with hypnosis and words. With modern medical technology and machines like computerised axial tomography (CAT) scanners which cost a million pounds, it seems absurd that words can be more beneficial. Especially words that are simpler than the words 'computerised axial tomography scanner'. One would think them ineffectual against a problem or illness that had been going for a long time.

My own experience is that words are remarkably powerful and amazing changes will occur with the use of the correct words in a suitable situation. By words I mean either internal dialogue – talking to yourself in your mind (self talk), or external words spoken by someone else. I could reel off case after case where 'just words' have made the difference between illness and health, but I don't feel that just case histories would explain it all. So I'll try and analyse how words used in hypnosis can be such a useful method in helping change to occur.

Let us consider the mind to be a receiver and converter. Just as a TV set or radio receives waves through the air and converts them to pictures and sounds, the mind receives sounds, pictures, smells, feelings and converts them to thoughts, feelings and actions.

When people are being hypnotised, or doing self-hypnosis, it is the influence of the words, converted to thoughts or feelings, which have such a marked effect. The mind, like a computer, accepts the words in a way that is special for that person. Based on experience, memory and a thousand other factors, the mind will produce a result in the form of a thought, picture or feeling. It could be said that 'word energy' has changed into another form of energy.

The power of this recycled word energy can be seen in many examples. Hitler's oratory had an amazing power over thousands. The words and the way they were spoken caused people to behave in a way one wouldn't have thought possible.

Go to a religious crusade such as Billy Graham's and note the effect the words have on the listeners. If someone is dozing in front of the TV and you shout 'fire' in his ear, note how your word energy is changed into anxiety, action and perhaps 'punch on the nose' energy when he realises there is no fire. The word 'fire' has triggered, from previous experience, an alarm reaction. It has mobilised some latent energy into activity.

This is an absurd example, but it illustrates the power of the word. If we mobilise part of that energy to build self confidence, or to view things from a different angle, then we get a glimpse of the power that words can have on our behaviour.

One perspective of our continuing difficulties is that we use words or thoughts, which may be based on false or outdated assumptions, to cause or maintain our problems. In other words, we hypnotise ourselves *into* problems with self-talk, so why not use a similar method to hypnotise ourselves *out of* them.

Think of the effect words have in the self limitations we put on ourselves (see previous chapter). The tape recording in the back of the mind is repeating 'I can't, it's too difficult, I'll feel guilty, etc.' By changing the tape we can make alterations from within. I believe using the powerful internal resources of the mind, instead of the powerful external forces of drugs or operations, is a more natural way to deal with life. To realise the power of words, approach a friend who is looking really well and say, with a sombre look and downcast eyes, 'What's the matter, you look really ill?' He will protest and shrug it off, but a fragment of doubt will remain and if reinforced a number of times he *really will* feel ill. The words, few and simple, may change someone feeling well into someone feeling not so well, and the reverse is true.

The use of suggestions (groups of words) can facilitate enormous changes in illness. Not just people who are 'nutty' or 'imagining' their illness. It works with 'real' illness just the same. All illness has a psychological component which varies from being a minor factor to one of major importance.

Imagine the body and mind are like a radio. The radio normally broadcasts music and programmes which can be heard satisfactorily and provide entertainment. One day the radio sounds terrible, the voices are blurred, the sound is poor and the music is grating. Perhaps the set needs a new valve or spare part, perhaps a technician is required to find the fault or perhaps just a slight adjustment of the tuning and volume may rectify the problem. If the radio is not properly tuned we don't take the radio to the shop for an expensive overhaul, we only do that if all the minor adjustments fail to produce the desired effect.

So it is in hypnosis, where the words spoken by the therapist or by yourself may provide the 'fine tuning' necessary to overcome the difficulty. The words used by great orators and preachers rely on the powerful blasting of speeches heavily laden with emotion and guilt to create their effect. This is not necessary in hypnosis where the quietly spoken word (like the man tapping in the right place), the relaxing story or peaceful sounds may provide the basis for the mind to work out an alternative view of the situation.

How is it done? It is no trick. The elements are simple but it is not a simple process. The question of how hypnosis works has been discussed for centuries and no real agreement has been reached. Many theories shed some light on the problem and each has a grain of truth, but none explain it satisfactorily. I will try and explain a few aspects involved in the mechanism of hypnosis, to show how benefits may be obtained.

Let's look at an arbitrary situation and study the components, to note where and how hypnosis may be of use.

John and Sue have been going steady for six months. He is pretty nervous and shy but the relationship is going well and he is very happy to have someone like Sue to be his constant companion. One night he drinks too much and fails at making love. He starts to worry, he's 28 – perhaps he's too old, perhaps it will happen again. What will she think? She may leave me – and so on. Next time he tries, the worry and negative self-talk assures that it does fail and so his internal self-fulfilling prophecy goes into action.

He cautiously talks to a few of his friends who try to reassure him, but he doesn't believe their comments and things go from bad to worse. The worry spreads through the relationship affecting many other aspects of it.

Problem: John's 'self-talk' is convincing him he is impotent and is maintaining that conviction.

The 'self-talk' is on an unconscious level so reassurance by his friends will not reach it. Hypnosis allows a message to sink to a lower level in the mind, like the advertisement that claims the beer 'gets to the parts other beers can't reach'. The fact that the *positive* self-talk in a hypnotic trance reaches the unconscious, means it can over-ride the negative tape repeating 'I'm no good, I'll fail again'.

The words used in hypnosis by-pass conscious resistance, so the negative attitude John has need not be dealt with on a conscious level. Talking to him while he is relaxed means that the general anxiety and tension surrounding this very sensitive subject will be less. Explaining to his unconscious mind that he performed well previously and will be able to do so again, is very reassuring and builds confidence.

Encouraging him not to *try* to perform will allow him to act more naturally. Often the more you try, the less success you have. Allowing the problem to assume a suitable perspective in his life, allowing him to regain his confidence, will all help him to overcome his difficulty.

This situation occurs in a multitude of the adversities we encounter. The 'commonsense' attitude delivered on a conscious level – 'pull your socks up and get on with it' – generally has either a minimal or a negative effect by adding guilt to an already fragile situation.

One view as to how hypnosis can be effective may be its use in overcoming conscious resistance. As we grow, through years of painstaking trial and error to achieve the position we are now in, (often more error than trial), we don't take kindly to advice from outsiders who tell us to behave differently. For a multitude of reasons – fear, lack of confidence, disbelief or plain stubbornness, we cling to our position as a mountaineer clings to the rockface if he is unsure of his footing.

This resistance to change is something we may not be aware of. We will have sound logical reasons (according to our belief system) for refuting any advice offered. So, even with the best will in the world, it is often difficult to help someone who needs advice.

Imagine someone clinging to a half submerged boat (see diagram 7). She is not happy in her situation; it is wet and uncomfortable but at least she's afloat and alive. She knows this position as she's been there a long time.

Not far away is a ship floating normally and in good condition. In between there are fins; she believes they are sharks' fins. She stays where she is even though it's not too good, for fear of the danger between her and the safety of the ship. Therapists know (as they have looked under the water with their Scuba gear) that the fins belong to harmless dolphins. Her anxiety is such that she won't follow any coaxing or directing for fear she will lose her life if she swims towards the ship.

So it is with patients and their predicaments. They cling to their situation, resisting advice either from themselves or from others. In the altered

Diagram 7   Clinging to the comfort of discomfort

state of hypnosis, this judgement may be suspended and the courage to venture to the ship may grow. In small stages, allowing confidence to increase along the way, the journey is made.

Suzie, aged twenty-five, has had asthma since the age of four. She also has eczema and uses creams and inhalers to minimise the problem. She knows it gets worse when she is tense or upset, and has been told by a multitude of people to relax. She has tried many methods of relaxation from time to time, but she gets frightened of being on her own, so avoids having time to herself and is constantly on the go.

The advice seems sound enough, but something in Suzie prevents her following it. This could be termed a 'resistance' to trying something beneficial due to an unknown fear.

When I saw her, I achieved an agreement from her that she would spend ten minutes a day doing self-hypnosis for two weeks, then we would review the situation. During her self-hypnosis she discovered a number of things about herself when she was young. Two important things were,

a) that something unpleasant happened to her when she was on her own at about the time the eczema started at four,
b) on another occasion she became very angry and lost control with someone.

Discussing these two events and trying to fit them into the picture, Suzie believed her fear of being alone related to the early incident. When she was ten she had made a commitment to herself never to be angry or lose her temper again because she had lost control then.

After some discussion she agreed to spend time on herself either doing self-hypnosis or relaxing and also to gradually explore how she could express her feelings. So her resistance to change was due to two internal directions:

1. Don't be on your own or something terrible may happen as it did when you were four.
2. Don't express your anger or you may lose control as you did when you were ten.

Anyone directing Suzie to act differently would meet with this conscious protective resistance. In self-hypnosis she could circumvent this resistance and, using positive 'self-talk', direct herself that

1. Now she is twenty-five it is OK to be alone from time to time,
2. Expressing feelings, such as anger, is allowable at twenty-five, as she could make sure she doesn't lose control.

The eczema and asthma were results of her inability to have an outlet for normal feelings and experiences which were blocked by the resistance to change. As she learnt to explore these two areas, the eczema and asthma steadily improved. The new positive words she fed into her internal dialogue over the next few weeks allowed her skin to gradually clear and the spasms in her chest to subside.

This 'resistance' may be viewed as a protective role related to prior unpleasant experiences. Sometimes these situations still exist, so the resistance to change is preferable to the possibilities which may arise with change. The resistance could be seen as 'self-talk' from the past still in operation, where the internal dialogue is directing the person to be very wary of certain situations (similar to those which were previously painful).

Suzie is now using words herself that she had been hearing from others for years, but the conscious resistance is now understood to be out-dated.

It's as if we surround ourselves with a resistant wall to prevent change, because change represents the unknown (or the previously painful known); better the devil we know than the one we don't.

Imagine setting out on a long boat journey across unknown seas. As navigator, captain and bottlewasher you are in complete control of all aspects of the boat and journey. You study the map and work out the most suitable navigation course, keeping in mind previous sailing experience, and any other information you have at that time.

You plot the course for safety and speed, and feed the information into the computer which then locks the steering and engine into the set course chosen. The trip starts well and your expertise protects you from the minor winds and waves near the coast and you proceed through the first stage without any problems.

As the journey continues the weather changes, storms push the boat off course. Alterations need to be made to compensate for the wind conditions, but the computer is set and any attempts at change are 'resisted' by the locked in system set at the start of your travels.

You can see the treacherous rocks you are headed for and you know you are too shallow by the bumps heard from under the keel, but the computer guides you on into troubled waters and you are helpless to influence it with your up-to-date knowledge.

In life this 'locking device' is instituted in childhood as a protection against pain, sadness, guilt, etc. It comes about in our early life from experiences we have had, but as we grow up it may no longer be useful, as the computer program above.

Hypnosis is one way of unlocking the set pattern instituted years ago. It allows new facts and figures to be fed into the computer and this up-to-date software allows the competent and intricate mechanism of the machine to gently steer the boat away from the rocks and into calmer waters.

This new information may or may not be directed to the past. Self-hypnosis may be used to try and alter misconceptions about the past, or just inform the computer of the mind about present 'weather conditions and engine capacity'.

If we are locked into a course set in the past, then brute force and 'pull your socks up' advice has little effect. Telling yourself 'not to be foolish' and 'to act your age' or hearing this from others doesn't seem to have the desired effect.

I'd like to illustrate this 'set course' idea with another story. I'm sure you are having doubts about all these 'success' stories I'm relating. I can assure you they are true, they have occurred recently and are still happening. There are many which are not success stories, either due to my inability as a therapist or to the patient's inability to accept even *the possibility* that change may be useful. You don't need to read a book to learn about the cases that fail – they are all around you. The success stories here have been shortened and often many ups and downs occur along the way before solutions – either partial or complete – are reached.

Julia is a forty-year-old housewife with four children ranging from six to sixteen. Her life has the usual ups and downs and she deals with these very well. She is bright and cheerful and appears thoughtful and concerned, but she has been troubled for years with migraine headaches every one or two weeks. These are so severe that she needs to lie down in a darkened room for most of the day. Over the years she has had tests and treatment. She was taking tablets which did ease the pain but had side effects that she didn't like. She was also becoming more and more frustrated by her dependence on drugs.

There did not seem anything obvious in her present situation which was causing the headaches. Her relationship with her husband and children was good and she didn't seem to be using 'self-talk' in the present to cause the headaches.

She was a good and willing subject for hypnosis and agreed to learn self-hypnosis to see if she could help her headaches in any way. When she described the headaches to me initially she called them '*punishing headaches*, which keep me in bed for the day'. The word 'punishing' seemed to have some significance, so I wasn't surprised when she returned after two weeks practising the self-hypnosis to tell me that she believed the headaches were due to something she had done when she was young.

In a trance, in my surgery, she went back to when she was eight years old. She remembered playing in a park, being swung around by the park attendant. He had his hand under her dress but this was only to hold her properly whilst swinging her around.

When she told her mother about it, her mother reacted with anger and went to the police to complain. The man was brought to court and little Julia had to identify him and say what happened. Even though she wailed through her tears that he'd done nothing wrong, he was sacked from his job. She remembered the very sad look he gave her as he was led from the courtroom, and the extreme guilt she felt at having caused so much trouble was still with her. Her face filled with grief as she told her story in a trance and tears ran down her face. She still felt that terrible guilt after thirty years, from the words that she was repeating in the back of her mind and the associated pictures and feelings.

I let her cry for a few minutes and then gently suggested that perhaps it was not all her fault, perhaps she behaved as a normal child would have behaved, but her parents' fears took things out of her hands. Even if she was guilty, did she need to be punished with the migraines after all these years?

She spent some time altering the message on her internal tape recorder and helping the young Julia in her mind understand that there was no need to be punished any more for the upset to the kind park attendant.

Julia had set a computerised course at eight years of age; 'I've done a very bad thing, I must be punished.' She left that message locked into the computer out of reach of conscious interference or logic.

Why it took so long for the punishment to occur I don't know. Perhaps it was a particularly happy time in her life and hence the 'computer judge' decided to carry out the sentence passed years before. Learning about this was of great benefit to Julia who gradually, over some months, let go of her unnecessary guilt from the past.

The words which are the vehicle of these situations are often evolved from simple situations. At other times more complex scenes have occurred for the literature of the mind to be set in concrete. One example of the power of words is a situation called *imprinting*. This is related to the imprinting that occurs in birds and animals which has been brilliantly studied by Konrad Lorenz and others.

Imprinting is a term used to describe the powerful way words are planted in the back of the mind and their effect remains there for years, sometimes even for a lifetime.

An imprint is a (1) command made by (2) someone in authority to (3) someone under stress or very frightened. Such a command or imprint may go deep into the mind and leave its mark there long after the initial situation has been forgotten. The command continues to exert its authority for years as a form of compulsion, being followed without question.

Here is an example of the effect words can have in the form of an imprint on someone very nervous by someone in authority.

Mrs Jacobs was in hospital having a baby. I was looking after her and delivered a normal baby girl. The baby developed a problem with her chest and was put in an isolette (a humicrib or plastic box with humidified air and raised temperature) to help her breathing.

Mrs Jacobs was understandably anxious about her baby and developed nervous diarrhoea, going to the toilet many times during the night. There was a very officious sister on duty who aggressively blamed her for disturbing the other patients.

Mrs Jacobs became more nervous and the diarrhoea persisted. After a few days I decided to let her go home to see if she would settle down. By this time the baby was well.

The night before she was due to go home the aggressive sister came to her and said, 'If you go home tomorrow you'll be sick for a very long time.'

She was! For months and months she had abdominal pains that defied any positive finding, in spite of all the investigations performed. Specialists prodded and probed, looked into every orifice and X-rayed her from top to toe, and took pieces of her bowel to examine. No abnormality could be found.

The imprint of the sister was being carried out and there seemed nothing we could do about it. In hypnosis it was revealed that the sister's words were having a powerful effect and they seemed to be locked into her mind. I couldn't help her change them.

I last saw Mrs Jacobs a year after her baby was born. She was still having tests and treatment for her abdominal pains. I was still receiving letters from specialists trying to find the cause of this distressed woman's problems.

Often this imprinting occurs in childhood and is lost in the backwoods of the mind. It may be reinforced by other words or events and the time between the command and the carrying out of the command may be many years.

I saw an overweight woman of thirty who had struggled since she was very small to lose the fat which continued to be a burden to her. She had tried every diet, every club related to weight loss and consulted numerous helpers in the field of obesity (of which there are many).

During a session with self-hypnosis she went back to the time when she was four years old. She was fat at this time and her mother dragged her along to a doctor for help. The doctor was overpowering and very frightening to the little girl, who was terrified by all the sights and smells of his surgery.

The doctor, after examining the girl, said to her mother, 'She's just a fat girl and will be fat for the rest of her life.' This edict somehow registered with the little girl and it was like a prophecy which must come true. It had the three components of an imprint:

1. Figure of authority,
2. Frightened child,
3. A command.

The unconscious takes words very literally. The doctor said she would be fat for the rest of her life, that is, if she got thin she would die.

So she started on a see-saw battle, her conscious mind struggling to lose weight, her unconscious terrified of losing weight and dying. So the battle continued in a similar way on many fronts, keeping the imprinted command in mind at all times. A loss of weight would be rapidly followed by a binge.

There needs to be 'fallow ground' for these imprints to take hold. We have all been given commands by authoritarian figures whilst being nervous and they haven't controlled our lives. The fertile soil of low self-esteem, guilt and perhaps a basic inherent belief in the edict even before it is spoken, may be necessary.

Often these imprints may be altered by repeated self-hypnosis and by 'updating' the unconscious mind, reassuring it about the fears it has harboured for years. At other times the imprint seems to persist in spite of the various manoeuvres available to patient and therapist. The fear of changing may be too great to allow any light to be shed on the old command from the past.

14 *What is Hypnosis All About?*

It is difficult to say what is impossible, for the dream
of yesterday is the hope of today and the reality of
tomorrow.

The word hypnosis is associated with a long history of mystique, fear
and the supernatural. It is false to continue to think along those lines
so I propose to analyse some components of hypnosis in order to describe
how it may be more easily understood.

There are various components of a hypnotic state which you in your
daily life have already experienced but haven't labelled as hypnosis.

A A DAYDREAM COMPONENT

We have all stared into space for seconds or minutes at one time or
other. We may be looking at something – out of the window, the TV
or the traffic in front of us – and our mind 'turns off' from what we
are watching. Part of the mind is aware of what we are looking at, another
part is 'away with the fairies', thinking about a holiday or what the boss
said. I call this a daydream and this is a major component of a hypnotic
state or trance.

B A RELAXATION COMPONENT

Nearly everyone who does self-hypnosis maintains how relaxing it is.
'I've never felt so relaxed in my life,' 'I wish I could have stayed there,'
'I nearly dozed off,' are all common remarks from people coming out
of a trance. The mind and the body are relaxed as the stress and tensions
associated with modern life are moved to a distance, resulting in a peaceful, calm or tranquil feeling.

C   A PASSIVE COMPONENT

Going into a trance is a passive process like going to sleep. You cannot *try* to go to sleep, *effort* is in the opposite direction and will keep you awake. So it is with going into a hypnotic state, it is a feeling of 'letting go' rather than 'doing' something.

D   AN EXPLORATORY COMPONENT

Hypnosis may be used to explore and discover aspects of life that are unavailable to the conscious mind on its own. Things long forgotten come to mind. Aspects of behaviour are looked at from different angles, new light thrown on old problems.

E   BUILDING OF CONFIDENCE

During hypnosis one comes more to terms with oneself. The ability to understand and say 'I'm all right' is a great confidence builder, diminishing the eroding qualities of guilt and self-doubt which limit enthusiasm about life.

F   A REMEMBERING ASPECT

During hypnosis things may come to mind which have been completely forgotten for years. Age regression may occur where the person in a trance goes back to an early period in life and actually 'is there'. The speech, actions and abilities are those of that age.

Memories that have been repressed but are still affecting the person may be looked at and reassessed, hence removing the 'shadow' being cast over their lives. This may occur with or without their conscious understanding of what happened and they may not remember these incidents when they come out of the trance.

G   BEING RECEPTIVE TO SUGGESTIONS

Directions received in a trance may be carried out without interference by the conscious mind. This post hypnotic suggestibility is very useful in hypnosis and self-hypnosis to circumvent conscious resistance to change. Abilities possessed by the unconscious may be brought into play by this unquestioned reaction to suggestions and hence increases the choices available for future use.

H   POST HYPNOTIC SUGGESTION

Suggestions received in a trance state may be carried out at a future date with little or no interference from the conscious mind. Therapeutic suggestions to feel better, overcome difficulties or deal with problems have a much greater effect than if given in the conscious state. Change can therefore take place following hypnosis in spite of the conscious doubts. This effect is commonly seen in stage hypnosis when people return to their seats then do something humorous.

I   PARALLEL AWARENESS

This is a term used to describe the feeling of being in a trance. 'I'm here but I'm also somewhere else' is a common description. The trance state allows the mind to accept the fact that the person is sitting in a doctor's surgery but is also lying relaxing on a beach in the sun. In the conscious state these two situations could not be logically accounted for but in hypnosis they are not questioned.

J   A FORGETTING ASPECT

Many memories or thoughts occurring during hypnosis, if not needed to be remembered, may be forgotten. This ability is a defence mechanism as if the unconscious mind is saying 'There is no need to think of that any more, it is being dealt with satisfactorily, get on with other things.' So it is with things being remembered at an unconscious level which drag on for years after the event. Hypnosis may help us to forget what we don't need to remember.

K   A SURPRISE ELEMENT

People are often pleasantly surprised on coming out of a trance. Emotions like 'I feel strange, unusual, different' are often commented on. This feeling is in contrast to the down to earth, matter-of-fact feelings we all have most of the time and which may last for minutes or hours in a most pleasant way. To use these elements in your own personal way is the aim of learning about hypnosis and putting that learning into practice. An overall view may be to *expand your capabilities in dealing with life*.

A working concept that has proved useful is to regard the mind as a vast warehouse. This warehouse contains all the components necessary to deal with the situations confronting you. These may be calmness, willpower, confidence, assertiveness, whatever is required is there, has been experienced previously and forgotten – the door to the warehouse is closed.

Hypnosis is one way of opening the door to abilities *you already possess*. There is no new learning required, it's all been done before. Certainly it's a different situation, but the abilities required to deal with the present problem are in store, tried and tested, in the unconscious warehouse.

This warehouse is not a Pandora's box. The fear that peeping into the back of the mind will unleash evil spirits is unfounded. The unconscious will only release thoughts which can be handled by the conscious mind.

Many times whilst doing hypnosis the patient and I have a vague feeling that something that happened years ago is affecting the present day situation. But no matter how hard we try to find out what it actually was, the message from the unconscious is 'you are not ready to know yet' and the protective role of the warehouse will not let it out.

The word 'trance' frightens a lot of people. I use it to mean an altered state, the daydream-like feeling I've previously discussed. It is not frightening or awesome, it is just a word and correctly translated contains no fearful elements.

As you read the following paragraphs allow the words to form pictures in your mind. Your own pictures from actual experiences, films, stories. Don't rush the reading, let it flow – like watching a film in slow motion. See if feelings can be associated with the pictures – perhaps like a passenger in a car looking out of the window at the scenery passing by, allowing the pictures to drift in and out of his mind.

Imagine being in a large green valley. You have been there a long time. The sides reach up to block the sunlight and cast a shadow on the valley floor. You are alone. You feel restricted and uncomfortable being down in the valley blocked off by the mountains.

You sit down in the grass and look along the valley floor as far as you can see. It stretches out for miles, green, smooth with irregular shapes forming in the mountain sides. A little claustrophobic and you feel very small, enclosed and uncomfortable.

As you sit and the minutes pass by, you come to a conclusion. To stay there doesn't hold much future for you. To climb the mountain side will take a lot of effort and discomfort but you make the decision to do just that.

You get up and walk towards the mountain with a mixture of feelings – apprehension, hope, sadness.

The walking goes on and on at a steady pace until you reach the mountain base. Looking up it is just possible to see the top and blue sky beyond. You decide to take it step by step. Looking at the top makes it more difficult and you question your decision, falter, then move on.

Soon you are climbing, slowly, methodically, grasping a rock, pulling yourself up, getting a foothold and then on again. You feel yourself getting tired, starting to ache. You sit on a rock and look down.

A good feeling begins to creep in as you see the valley floor below you. A sense of achievement, of leaving something behind, of moving in the right direction. A few minutes rest then on again.

Monotonous, slow methodical actions of hands and feet crawl up the side of the valley. The sun is getting closer to the horizon. The valley is in shadow. You are halfway there and the air seems clearer, fresher, you begin to feel the joy of progress, the aches of solid hard work.

The disturbing feelings of the valley floor drift further away as if your steps up the mountain-side push them into the background and reinforce your own ability, your own confidence, not only of making the decision but carrying it out.

You stop from time to time to admire the view. You can see further to other valleys, plains and mountains. The light is improving the higher you climb, as if coming from night to day. You remember seeing a sunrise long ago. It's a similar feeling.

You realise the valley you were in was a small, inconsequential part of the landscape. You remember how cramped and restricted you felt there and for how long you put up with that feeling, telling yourself there was no alternative, that it would be too difficult to do anything about it. You feel free and full of energy as you continue the climb and start to notice a different perspective becoming apparent without even trying.

Thoughts drift through your mind about other times when you said 'It's too difficult.'

Eventually you get to the top of the mountain. It is bright sunlight, fresh, clear and invigorating.

You sit in the grass on the top and look out, allowing all your senses to take in the beauty. The sights, the smells, the breeze, the feelings and thoughts and you realise that although you are the same person who was in the valley a while ago you feel completely different.

In all directions are valleys, plains, mountains, rivers and you notice a feeling of confidence and optimism for whatever journey lies ahead. You have an appreciation that there will certainly be problems and difficulties ahead but you feel more capable of dealing with them. It's as if the journey up provided a basis for learning about your own potential and you have a sense of anticipation in applying that confidence.

You rest and store up energy before moving on.

So it is with the journey to the warehouse of the mind in self-hypnosis. A journey at your own pace, gathering what you need and being involved in the process of integrating it with all the other aspects of your life.

The experience will certainly be relaxing, most likely refreshing and invigorating, and will provide a basis for confidence, learning and altered attitudes. The body's appreciation will be noticed by a feeling of comfort and energy; the mind with calmness and clarity.

Perhaps this sounds like all the other 'how to achieve inner peace in five easy lessons' books. I don't suggest for one moment that going into a trance and learning self-hypnosis will be the answer to everything.

It is a learning experience. It will help provide a basis for you to make the necessary adjustments you require. Building a swimming pool in your home doesn't make you a good swimmer. But if you wish to be one, and are motivated to work at it, the pool would be a great help and make it easier than going to the local swimming pool every time you wanted to train.

What I am writing are only words. If you allow them to remain as words and not attempt to change them into practice they are valueless, just as that pool can only be of use by being the vehicle for practice and time spent training.

If your fear of drowning is so great you will not venture into the water, then the best pool in the world is of no use to help you become a strong swimmer. Hypnosis, relaxation, self-hypnosis etc. are things to be tried, at your own pace, experienced and improved or discarded. By not trying them you are making a choice to stay on the valley floor with all its associated difficulties.

It is important to proceed at your own pace, in your own comfort, so any progress will be made without concern and fear. Don't start learning to swim at the deep end. There is nothing worse than learning something at someone else's pace. Much better to go slower with the feeling of being safe and in control than follow directions which cause uneasiness and concern.

If you decide you would like to learn more about hypnosis, read the relaxation section on stress, perhaps buy the tape and only allow yourself to proceed at a rate that feels safe and comfortable for you.

I can assure you of the following:

1. At any time if you need to come out of self-hypnosis you will. If you feel uncomfortable, the doorbell rings etc., you will automatically come out of the trance.
2. The majority of feelings you experience will be comfortable ones. Any discomfort from previous memories will be remembered in a way you can deal with.
3. Any feelings of lightness, heaviness, tingling, will go away within seconds or minutes of coming out of the trance state.
4. You will not disclose anything to yourself or anyone else that you will not be able to integrate into your normal way of life. Any emotional reaction which may occur will be a learning experience that you will benefit from.

15 *The Mind as a Computer and its Protective Role*

We are generally the better persuaded by the reasons we
discover ourselves than by those given to us by others.
PASCAL

An endless tapestry the past has woven drapes the halls
of my life, compelling my soul to conform.
D.H. LAWRENCE

If we regard the mind as a computer it helps us to understand some
of our actions, and also some of the difficulties in achieving our aims.
A child growing up feeds experiences into the mind computer. All this
information is used as the software for future experiences.

To the baby and young child the most powerful force is that of *survival*.
This is an internal force inherited from the cave man, and prehistoric
animals before him. Without survival, all the other emotions and actions
are useless.

Survival comes first. So the computer acknowledges, and underlines
in red, any experiences which may put survival in jeopardy. Those situations are stored in a special compartment. They are magnified to ensure
that protection is at a maximum.

It's as if a wealthy man has had his house broken into and something
of importance stolen. He fits a burglar alarm, which helps for a while,
but when he is again burgled, he installs a more sensitive, protective
alarm. This alarm is so sensitive that even the slightest movement triggers
it off, even the movement of a cat or a curtain. All goes well, but one
day he forgets to switch it on and he is nearly burgled again.

He then leaves the alarm on all the time, as his fear of being burgled
is now all-consuming. His thoughts, actions and dreams are all concerned
with protecting his safety. The alarm is successful in guarding him from
burglary, but it is so sensitive, so protective, that he can't move freely
without setting it off. He can't have any pets, his windows are sealed

so the breeze won't move the curtains, and he remains in one room so as not to disturb the alarm. An extreme and absurd story but it illustrates the protective role our computer minds play in limiting us in adult life.

The baby learns how important it is not to upset his mother. She is his lifeline – if she is upset she may cut him off. He may need to limit thoughts, feelings and actions in order to safeguard himself from parental disapproval.

The guarding function of the mind says, 'Don't do that, don't think this, don't feel that,' in order to screen the child from rejection, desertion. In childhood when parents are in control these devices may be life-saving and very successful. The child restricts his thoughts, feelings, actions in a similar way to an animal which remains motionless when caught in a snare, realising every movement may bring great pain.

The program of the computer is made up of experience upon experience, fear upon fear and these become magnified as time goes by. The guardian role of the mind uses these enlarged fears to protect the person from present situations. Often these protective devices are not required and are in fact limiting and disturbing in themselves.

Imagine a young child wandering off at a picnic and becoming temporarily lost in the woods. He is frightened and cold and misses his mum. Let us assume there are two alternative mothers who find him.

Mother A shows her relief and love by cuddling him, reassuring him everything will be all right, that it wasn't his fault but he must be wary of wandering off in the future. His fears are minimised (although still part of his memory), he feels minimal guilt and rejection.

Mother B finds him, and her anxiety and concern are shown in anger and disapproval. She cries and screams at him – how stupid he is to wander off and cause so much trouble. 'You could have died of cold and think how Mummy would feel then.' She is not only criticising his action but also criticising the child himself. That child will have fear, guilt and pain built into his computer and underlined with the big red pencil so that any future experience, with any similarity, will bring the guardian angel in to restrict him and so prevent the pain occurring again. Any experiences in the future involving independence or exploring may be severely curtailed.

The mind acts as radar does, screening each second we live and comparing it with the past, noting any similarity to previous danger areas and bringing in protective devices if needed.

The problem with the protective devices in the mind is that they can still operate to protect a child long after childhood has passed.

This blocking of abilities in the adult, when implemented by fear or guilt, is a very powerful force. A child in whom fear and guilt played a great role in his learning experiences will find it difficult to overcome these feelings when tackling life's normal problems in adulthood.

Even though he may have had many positive experiences to boost his self confidence, the protective radar picks up the fears and guilt much more easily, than the pride and confidence from successful actions.

Toby is forty, a businessman, married, successful. He has trouble talking to people, relating, expressing himself. When he meets strangers, he knows what he wants to say but he seems to freeze and smile in an embarrassed way. He feels foolish and thinks people regard him as dumb. He avoids these situations because they are too painful. He laughed when he told me a quotation which appealed to him, 'The human brain starts working the moment you are born, and never stops until you stand up to speak in public.' He said, 'That's me to a tee.'

After a few sessions using hypnosis and teaching Toby self-hypnosis, he recognised two parts in his mind advising him how to behave. One part, the adventurous one, said 'Go ahead, say what you think, it will be received well.' The other part, the protective one, then said to him, 'Don't say that, they will all laugh at you.'

The protective part had been implanted when, as a child, he had a number of experiences where people ridiculed things he said. So the radar came into action every time he spoke to people he didn't know well.

He seemed to be a pawn in the game played between his adventurous and protective parts, playing no role himself except that of puppet with two string pullers.

He learned to join with the two parts into a three way discussion as to how he should act – he had a say in things. Gradually he allowed the guardian protector, which was still treating him as a child, to go off duty. With time and experience he became more comfortable in company and chose not to avoid it as he previously had.

Studying Toby's reaction to an intended cocktail party we can represent it as in the figure overleaf. The situation (cocktail party, talking to strangers) is fed into the computer. Instant protective scanning by the radar picks up threatening painful situations in the past. *It is interesting and important to note that any successful situations which may be similar, are overlooked and don't register on the radar screen.* This device provides *instant* reaction to danger, without presenting positive and negative options to the conscious mind and so delay things.

If there is some similarity between the present situation and any fearful situation in the past, then a protective mechanism comes into play in order to avoid the present challenge.

This explains Toby's frightened reaction to the cocktail party, which is out of his conscious control. The conscious mind will endeavour to produce logic to explain the feelings, but the real reason is hidden in the unconscious mind.

The flaw in the unconscious mind's argument for protection is that

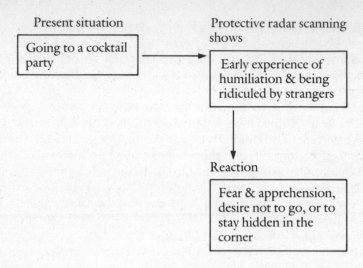

Present situation

Going to a cocktail party

Protective radar scanning shows

Early experience of humiliation & being ridiculed by strangers

Reaction

Fear & apprehension, desire not to go, or to stay hidden in the corner

it has not been updated by the abilities which Toby has gained since his early fearful reactions. Toby may have had many experiences where he has felt comfortable talking with people, but these are not taken into account when the defence strategy is implemented.

Hypnosis is a useful mechanism to re-program the computer and look at early experiences from the distance of the present time. It is also helpful to feed in positive experiences and abilities, to help the unconscious realise that the protective mechanism is no longer needed in such strength. Hypnosis can remove the unnecessary blocks placed on emotions and abilities many years previously. Removing these blocks allows freedom to 'be yourself', to be able to accept your feelings as your own, without associated guilt, to react to situations without fear and insecurity, but with the confidence to use the powers that are available.

Two of these blocks are guilt and fear.

Guilt is one of the least beneficial emotions; doing things or not doing things because of a guilty feeling is most restrictive. The majority of inter-reactions due to guilt do not provide growth for either the giver or receiver. It is an emotion brought about by parental displeasure, and continued in the mind as its most powerful negative force. Many people who have had 'guilt-making' parents go through life feeling guilty of saying, feeling, thinking even the most trivially assertive things, virtually guilty for being alive. They have lived with this guilty feeling for so long it has become part of them and they may feel guilty without it. Any attempt by them to gain access to their adult resources, used to wend their way through life, is stopped by the all-pervading guilt.

Fear of what may happen is an extremely limiting force, preventing people from exploring their abilities in present day situations. The feeling of fear will have been learnt at an early age, and it may be so sensitive that it immobilises the person and prevents any challenge being met. It can be completely illogical and so does not respond to any conscious discussion or encouragement.

We can compare it to someone who in early life swam out of their depth. The fear of drowning is heavily underlined in red in the mind's protective pattern. The child grows, has swimming lessons and is capable of looking after himself but this is overlooked by the radar when it searches in a similar situation in the future. So the person has an unnatural fear of going swimming; even though logically he knows he can cope, he may even have a fear of going into the pool up to his ankles. These fears may pervade other areas of life, relationships, his self-confidence. They are often illogical and always limiting.

I believe that we *all* have the abilities to deal with the problems that confront us each day. We have the strengths, the confidence, the power to deal with them and to feel comfortable within ourselves. If we are limited by fear or guilt, then hypnosis could be a useful way of overcoming those blocks, reaching the resources that have been dormant for so long, to lead a more fulfilling life.

Another way of understanding how the mind affects our appreciation of things is to regard it at birth as having a *basic attitude*, and experiences will act as magnifiers or diminishers of how we view things.

The 'real mind', that is the structure upon which experiences are added, can be theoretically believed to be untainted, unbiased. Foetal experiences, delivery and growing up all exert influences on the mind's ability to perceive reality. As everyone has different experiences, we all view reality in a slightly different way.

We can compare it to having your eyes tested at the optician. You sit in a chair facing an illuminated screen showing letters of different sizes. Special frames are put on, and different lenses added and subtracted, while the optician questions the clarity of the letters. Some make the letters blurred, others make them clearer, some are too strong, others too weak, until the right combination of positive and negative lenses is reached, so that the picture is really clear and precise. The letters are seen as they actually are.

So it is with the experiences affecting the ability of the mind to see the world as it really is. Assuming the original mind could see clearly, or that it required some experiences (magnifications) to enable it to do so – loving, caring, support, constancy, understanding, then the comparison begins to make sense.

Now we can begin to understand how people differ in their view of situations. They may be wearing blurring lenses due to inadequate experiences to help them use their original abilities. Many of our growing experiences alter our vision drastically. Our view may be severely limited, just as if dark glasses had been put on. It may be negatively altered, as if a lens is worn which magnifies only negative aspects of reality, thus diminishing the positive ones.

The hypnotherapist can be seen as the optician altering the lenses to suit the individual, to help the natural eye use the correct magnification in order to see the letters of experience more clearly. Previous colouring, blurring or magnifying lenses may be removed if not suitable for the requirements of the eyes. A more accurate representation of the *present* situation can then be seen.

I'm not suggesting that self-hypnosis will enable you to see the world through rose-coloured glasses. I am suggesting it may help to reduce the magnifying power you are (unconsciously) applying to negative situations, and so be more comfortable and realistic in your appreciation of events and relationships.

Once again I'll reiterate: the capacity *is* there to deal with things by alternative, more appropriate ways. It requires commitment to find those alternatives. Just as the optician will keep varying the lenses until the sight is clear, so hypnosis will try to gain the best from the mind. The optician doesn't change the letters or the patient and we don't need to change the situation or ourselves, we just need to vary the way we view things.

16 Our Early Learning and its Effects

The most important words you'll ever hear are those you
tell yourself.

Footsteps echo in the memory
Down the passage which we did not take
Towards the door we never opened
Into the rose garden.
T.S. ELIOT, *Burnt Norton*

Adult life is an extension of childhood learning. What and how we learn
as we grow provides the foundation for further learning during the rest
of our lives. The stages – sitting, crawling, walking, running, riding
a scooter, a tricycle, a bike – were probably gone through by most of
us. If we remain at the crawling stage, as some children with brain damage
do, the likelihood of riding a bike is remote. So any pause in our learning
process may have limitations later when more difficult tasks are encountered.

Our early learning comes from experiences. These are often directed
by our parents: 'Behaving in a certain way will be better for you.'

Even if our personal experience differs we need to satisfy 'the authori-
ties' *so we do it their way*. That is a most important phrase, because when
we are young and 'defenceless' we have to behave in the manner required,
to some extent, by our 'protectors' – our parents. As we grow older
'doing it their way' may not be appropriate, and as it is *their* way it
may not be suitable to incorporate it into our own growing pattern.

If a young tree is bent over and staked it will grow in the direction
of the stake and gradually bend back to grow towards the sun. But that
bend will be incorporated into its growth structure. If it continued to
grow just in the direction of the stake, all the *natural* tendencies of growth
would be hampered and its suppleness and flexibility lessened. It may
be brittle and not bend with the wind. So it is as we grow. If our own
special talents, feelings and strengths are guided, and allowed freedom

of expression, we are close to 'being ourselves' and much more strongly based, more able to bend to the vicissitudes which will put pressure on us through life.

If our parental direction, for whatever reason, is different from our natural tendencies, we don't develop a naturally strong base. It is an artificial base to perch on for the rest of our lives. It is not flexible or malleable and is unable to bend with pressures as they occur.

If we could imagine ourselves as a solid triangle (difficult though that may be – we certainly need a good imagination to carry us through a lot of situations) – some people have the base of the triangle on the solid ground. Hence any pressure will move the triangle over but its tendency will be to rock back to the original position (see diagram 8A).

Those with an 'artificial base' of parental influence in early learning have the apex of their triangle resting on the ground and any pressure will topple them to an uncomfortable position. A lot of work is required to restore them to the original position (see diagram 8B).

Self-hypnosis is useful in understanding the early learning principles by which we act in the present, not only in discovering what juvenile methods we are using to deal with things, but how to include the new learning that has been consciously acquired.

It's as if in our youth we built a ladder to get over the obstacles confronting us (see diagram 9 on page 120) and this was suitable at the time. As we go through life the obstacles grow and we may still be using the small ladder, hence we hit a brick wall. What we don't realise, and this is where self-hypnosis helps, is that the ladder is an *extension ladder*. We don't need to get a new one but to extend the one we possess – a much simpler process.

This early learning situation can be exemplified by Mary.

Mary is a thirty-year-old housewife, mother of three, always busy with the kids, their activities, luncheons, charities, etc. etc. Her week is full of engagements. She complained of tension headaches and when I heard of her activities I said to myself 'no wonder'. I talked to her about having time to herself, relaxing, and she said she'd have a try.

Two weeks later there was no change. I asked her how her ten minutes a day relaxing was going. 'I can't get ten minutes to myself,' she complained.

'What? Out of sixteen hours a day you can't make ten minutes?' 'No,' she replied, tears starting to fall. 'I can't get ten minutes a day alone.'

I saw how upset she was, so I didn't persist. I asked if we could use hypnosis to look at her early learning which might explain this difficulty. She agreed and over the next ten minutes she drifted into a trance and gradually in her own time she went back into childhood. I asked her how she was. She beamed and said 'I'm a good girl and I'm busy.' This seemed a reasonably strange remark so I questioned her further. 'I was always good and busy and everyone liked me because of that.'

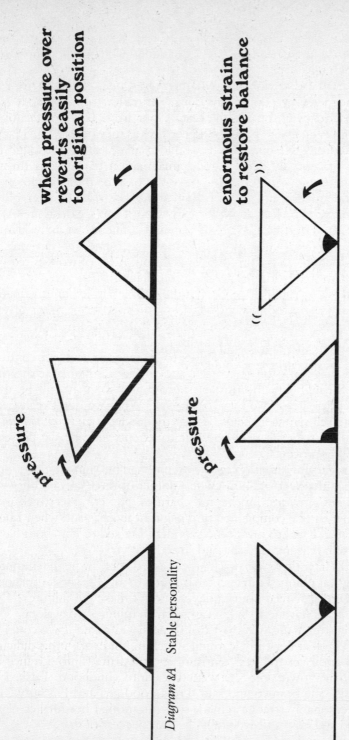

when pressure over reverts easily to original position

pressure

Diagram 8A Stable personality

enormous strain to restore balance

pressure

Diagram 8B Precarious balance

Diagram 9 Making use of natural resources

'How would you have been accepted if you were naughty and lazy?' I queried. 'I don't know, I never was. I was always well-behaved and liked.'

So Mary had built a rigid ladder to climb to the top of her childhood wall with rungs of being busy and being good. These rungs were very satisfactory to her parents because they obviously helped her achieve the reward she required: love and acceptance.

Now as a grown up these rungs are meeting a brick wall. She is not happy. She uses adult logic to be more good and more busy to gain the acceptance she desperately needs, and spending ten minutes a day relaxing is 'selfish and lazy', so it doesn't fit in with her childhood ladder. Hence the tear stained face at the impossibility of making a change from the short ladder she had built.

The first step to using the extension ladder was somehow, somewhere, to find ten minutes a day for Mary. It might be lazy and selfish but what she was doing was not working. She, luckily, trusted me enough to accept my offer to help her use her own extension ladder – not her parents', not mine or her husband's, but *hers* which she didn't know existed.

It was necessary to go at her pace – to tread the additional rungs very carefully, so as not to upset the balance in her mind and in her home situation. Gradually over weeks and months she found the ability to discard the early rungs of 'good and busy' and built some more flexible ones for her extension. She now does have times when she is good and busy. Times when she is liked and disliked. Times when she spends energy on herself. The tension and tears are much less and I believe her ladder will scale much greater heights now she's learnt of its real potential.

17 *Understanding a Trance*

All our interior world is reality – and that perhaps more
so than our apparent world.
MARC CHAGALL

When we have understood we hear in retrospect.
PROUST

Self-hypnosis, or going into a trance, is a basic ability we all possess
to a greater or lesser degree. It is an instinct which, due to lack of training
and neglect, has become inaccessible to many people.

I think most people's attitude to self-hypnosis is similar to that of
a man who walks around with his eyes closed, because he is unaware
of how to use the muscles of his eyelids. When shown how easy it is
to open his eyes, he then sees things and exclaims how simple it was
to make the change, questioning why he didn't do it before.

The ability to use our senses can be increased by training so they
provide us with more information, more pleasure. We all possess the
ability to taste, but a wine taster or a tea taster has, with practice and
experience, increased that ability to a remarkable degree.

Self-hypnosis, communicating with our unconscious mind, is an ability
we possess already. It is not something 'someone else with unique powers
does to us.' Society and progress direct us to act outwards not inwards,
to *try and achieve* from the moment we are born. We are directed to
try and walk, *try* not to cry, etc. As adults this same direction continues
at home, work, etc.

This may be why the art of *being* has become obsolete. If one is constantly reminded to look forward, then looking backward becomes much
more difficult. Think of the times during the day when you sit and 'contemplate your navel', look inwards or daydream. 'A waste of time,' you
may say, 'We were always told as children not to daydream but to get
on with things.' I'll relate a story to explain why this may not be such
a useful approach.

A sixty-year-old businessman sought some help from a friend. He felt at sixty that he did not want to work every day from nine to five, although he didn't want to retire. The business was running well and he enjoyed it, but he needed some new ideas to keep up with his competitors and the more time he spent at his desk thinking about this, the more frustrated he became. He didn't want to put in the longer hours necessary to upgrade his business. His hobby was collecting and reading western magazines. He never seemed to have the time to do this, or when he did have the time he was too tired.

His friend advised him to work at his business from nine to one, then to have lunch. After lunch he was to go back to his office and sit in a comfortable chair on the other side of the room from his desk. On a table next to the chair he was to put a pile of westerns and a pencil and paper.

During the afternoon he was to read the westerns, and to jot down on the piece of paper any innovative thoughts about his business that came to his mind. He wasn't to stop and think about them or try to understand what he'd written, but he was to keep reading until four o'clock. At four o'clock he was to look at what he had written and to see if the notes were of any use.

The businessman found that he was doing much more for his business in the afternoon while he was reading, than he was doing in the morning when he was *trying* to think of things that would help. By not consciously *trying*, he was allowing some of the creative knowledge in his unconscious mind to filter through in a most pleasant way.

Learning self-hypnosis is re-learning a forgotten art. By communicating with a large part of our mind we can find peace of mind which provides us with a firm basis with which to deal with problems. By gaining access to part of our vast learning experience the many supportive feelings we discover, help to increase our self-confidence.

Hypnosis is a word, an unfortunate word, which describes one method of achieving this communication. I say unfortunate as it has connotations of mystery, fear, of being controlled, all of which are untrue because it describes a process which is inherently natural. Would someone be frightened to learn the art of wine-tasting, would he believe he was under the control of his teacher? No, indeed, most of us would be pleased to have our senses heightened and be able to discover things previously unknown.

As children grow up they are often told not to daydream. 'It is a useless waste of time, get on with your work,' is the common admonition. 'It is wrong to daydream, selfish to spend time on yourself.' And so the instinct diminishes and in time may be temporarily lost. We may compare our ability to use self-hypnosis to a child who inherits a vast wealth at birth. Any enquiries he makes about his future are met with negative responses, perhaps anger. In time he may feel it is wrong to make use of what is his, and forgets about his great inheritance.

Hypnosis is a word used to describe how we may *regain* this inheritance; it is *our* birthright and not dependent upon any outside influence. All we need to learn is the pathway to it. Just as money can be put to a multitude of uses, so can the ability of the unconscious mind. At different times it serves different requirements.

Imagine driving two horses – the conscious and the unconscious. Hypnosis helps you gather the reins of both so that one is not out of control. Hence the powers and abilities you consciously possess are greatly enhanced (see diagram 10 overleaf).

Imagine you have difficulty facing up to a problem; perhaps a neighbour is continually noisy at night and you would like to let him know, but fear the consequences. The more you think about it the more angry you get and the more frustrated at not disposing of your anger. In your 'inheritance' there will be part of you that is courageous and able to deal with the situation. You are unaware of this because all your thinking leads you in a negative direction, so you bypass any positive thoughts. In hypnosis you may gain access to this positive part and you can be more optimistic about quietly and easily knocking on your neighbour's door and explaining the difficulty with the noise. It may or may not have the desired result but the benefit of expressing your feelings is worthwhile in itself.

Ignoring these resources means you are only using a proportion of your strengths and abilities. This proportion may be suitable for the majority of your life but may not be sufficient for some of the challenges that come your way. The fear that many people have of 'looking into the mind' may be based on superstitious beliefs suggesting it was dangerous to 'meddle with the mind'. I maintain it may be dangerous *not* to meddle with the mind if you are having difficulties in coping with your problems. To repeatedly ignore the possibility of learning to do something better and to understand more about yourself seems to me to be an ostrich-type attitude.

Chugging along in a car with only three out of six cylinders working may be suitable for flat roads and short distances, when no speed is required. But repeatedly having difficulty going up hills or constantly being late for important meetings may not bring you the satisfaction you desire. Refusing the suggestion to change the spark plugs, on the grounds that the engine may blow up if the bonnet is opened, is another ostrich-type attitude.

People who have used hypnosis are often amazed at the simplicity of it. They expect difficulties or tricks and in reality are often persuaded *not to try*. Once people learn to sit quietly with their eyes closed and allow thoughts to drift through their minds without trying to stop them, they acquire the peace of mind I've described. This peace of mind,

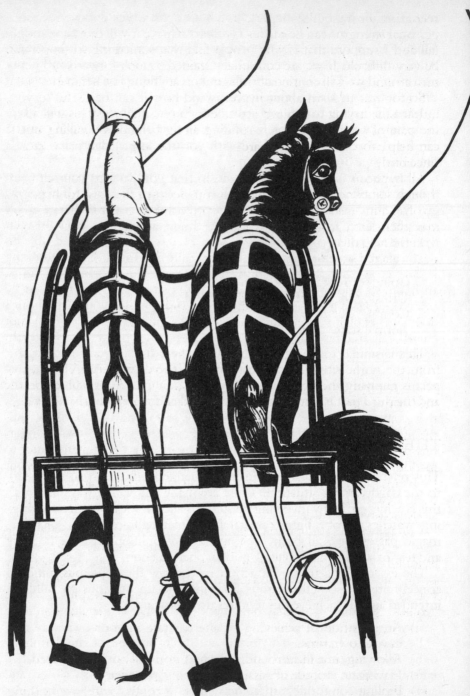

Diagram 10   Loss of unconscious power

relaxation, or tranquillity represents a basis upon which discoveries about personal strengths can be made. *Trying* to achieve it will most commonly fail and I suppose that is why people find that something so simple can be very difficult. If we are continually trained to look forward and never turn around we will continually miss out on anything just behind us.

So for you to learn about hypnosis and how it can be useful to you, unlearn the 'trying to achieve' attitude for a few minutes. This will allow the part of your mind that is running along behind you calling out 'I can help', to catch up and share with you the knowledge it has stored since birth.

All hypnosis is really self-hypnosis, in that you do it to yourself even though someone else may be helping you. Seeing a therapist for hypnosis involves him instructing you on how to achieve an altered state. You may then learn from this and achieve a similar state on your own or with the help of an audio cassette.

The altered state or trance may be artificially divided into three parts:

1. Going into a trance – induction.
2. Utilising the trance – using the altered state to achieve an aim.
3. Coming out of a trance – returning from the altered state to a normal state.

This is similar to going on a holiday, where the first part is changing from the home situation and travelling to the destination. The second part is enjoying the holiday and hopefully gaining the benefit expected, and the third part is returning home, relaxed and with a sun tan.

THE INDUCTION

This refers to the means by which we change from a normal alert state to the daydreaming situation. There are many and varied ways in which this is achieved, many involving mysterious and mystical practices. Swinging watches, strobe lights, crystal balls, metronomes, scenic pictures, magic passes have all been used and in my opinion create a mystery and fear of what is an absolutely normal phenomenon.

The essence of a trance induction is to allow the conscious mind to concentrate on something thus allowing the unconscious to fulfil an intended aim. To achieve this requires the following:

i) An intention of achieving an altered state in your own way and in your own time.
ii) Allowing time in surroundings where you will not be disturbed.
iii) Having an attitude of passivity, of 'being' not trying.
iv) Feeling comfortable that you will be in control and have nothing to fear.

The first time you try self-hypnosis and are in a suitably peaceful situation for about twenty minutes, try and make *relaxation* the intended aim.

There are many ways, as I've said, of inducing a trance. I will describe a simple one for you to follow. If you have contact lenses it is preferable to remove them. Make sure you do not need to go to the toilet.

1. Sit in a comfortable chair or lie down.
2. Look up with your eyes as if you are staring at your eyebrows.
3. Take a deep breath in and hold it a few seconds.
4. As you breathe out, slowly allow your eyelids to close.
5. Concentrate on your breathing and at every breath *out* imagine *letting go* a little bit of tension from your body.
6. Allow your breathing to become slow, calm and regular, and gradually check different parts of your body – starting at your head and working down to your toes – to ensure the relaxation continues.
7. Allow any thoughts or feelings that occur to drift past; don't *try* and stop them and don't try and hold on to them, any effort of *trying* will slow the process down.
8. When, in your own time, you feel really relaxed, notice how nice it feels to *not do anything* for a few minutes. Perhaps 'talk' to parts of your body – your arms or legs, commenting on how peaceful they feel.
9. Store that calm feeling in a manner you can remember, as it will be useful as a basis for most of the hypnotic utilisation.
10. Allow any peaceful, calm, confident scenes from the past, present or future to drift into your mind to be associated with the relaxed feeling, a feeling of acceptance. Use your imagination to *be* there. If they are beach scenes feel the sand and the warmth, notice the sounds of the sea or seagulls, look at the colour of the sea and the sky. Be a *receiver* of the pleasant experiences you have stored.

Remain in that state for five to ten minutes being aware of the lack of tension or stress, as if it is an oasis in the desert of life. Perhaps you may like to view some present day situations from that vantage point of tranquillity.

Perhaps you may have been enlarging on difficulties as if looking at them through a telescope. Reverse the telescope so that they appear much smaller, much less of a problem, much easier to deal with. See if you can feel the relaxed response, as if your body is thanking you for 'turning off' for a few minutes. Maybe some thoughts will drift into your mind which don't have a chance during the normal busy day. It's nice to think of things that haven't occurred to you for a long time, maybe put a new slant on some situations.

After five to ten minutes, gradually, concentrating on each breath *in*, count slowly from 10 to 1 and feel yourself coming out of that relaxed state. If it takes a little longer it may be because part of you enjoyed the experience and doesn't want to rush back to the 'conscious' world.

When your eyes open sit for a minute or two contemplating the ten minutes relaxation. Ask yourself if it was worth repeating on a daily basis. As it is so simple you may wonder if it has any effect at all.

Watching Grand Prix car racing, it is interesting to note the need for cars to go into the pits for tyre changes, etc. It only takes a few minutes (while the other cars are whizzing by) but without these pit stops the cars would not make the distance. Spending a few minutes a day doing self-hypnosis is a pit stop you may not be able to afford to miss, if you want to make the distance in the best possible condition.

18 Self-hypnosis: The First Step – Time for Yourself

The value of hypnosis is that it makes your mind optimally
receptive to your own thoughts.
DR H. SPIEGEL, AMERICAN PSYCHIATRIST

It is said that we can only learn what something feels like by experience.
Someone else's description cannot convey the feeling we will experience
in that situation. How often does someone say 'You must go and see
that film, it was the funniest thing I've seen. Laughed so much I almost
cried'? As you sit stony-faced through the worst film you've been to,
you wonder why something so funny to your friend is so boring to
you. You may try and look for what they found so funny and perhaps
end up with the conclusion that your sense of humour is so different
you won't follow any suggestions in the future. You had to experience
it yourself to learn to fit that experience into your own framework.

A child learns about the danger of fire by being burnt or feeling the
heat, not by the warnings of parents. After the experience, then modifica-
tion by description may occur, but the original learning needs to come
from experience.

So how can I explain how hypnosis will be for you? I can use words
and descriptions from my own and other's experiences but until you
yourself experience a trance these words will be no more than words,
and you will understand them as little as the child understands pain
before ever feeling it.

Perhaps it may be of help to use words other than hypnosis which
may touch on some experiences you've had which you can relate to.

I'd like you to think about the phrase *constructive daydreaming* or *creative
daydreaming*. What do these words convey to you?

Do they bring a picture, feeling or experience to mind? They appear
to be contradictory and opposite. How can one create or construct if
one is daydreaming? Surely daydreaming means drifting, vacant, of no
use?

128

The first step to learning self-hypnosis is to allocate ten to fifteen minutes a day. Make a commitment to have this time for yourself, your thoughts, your feelings. Remember a daydream experience or, better still, create one. Stare at the wall and allow your mind to drift anywhere, any thoughts that occur are allowed, be passive in receiving them. Stay staring at the wall for a couple of minutes, achieving the feeling that there is nothing else to do for now except this apparently silly experiment. Allow any feelings from your body to be experienced: even the feeling that this is ridiculous, nothing will happen, how could this be of use?

Allow specific feelings from any part of the body to come to mind, (as if starting a communication between your mind and body). How does your right hand feel, your left leg?

If you feel more comfortable allow your eyes to close and let the regularity of your breathing come into your mind. Allow yourself to focus on the breathing and, as you breathe out, feel yourself letting go a little. Let go of your concentration, control, allow a drifting, floating feeling to be related to your breathing.

You will need to read and re-read this a couple of times then put the book down and experiment in your own way. Learn what it means to *you*. This is the beginning of learning what hypnosis feels like.

I'm not saying that the experience will be a hypnotic experience – there are many varied properties of being in a trance. Like experiencing motion, you can move by walking, running, driving, going in a speed-boat or a 'plane. Each experience is different and has its own individuality. So it is with a trance experience, but like learning to crawl, it is a precursor of walking, running, etc. Sitting for a few minutes *passively* experiencing thoughts and feelings will be a precursor of using self-hypnosis. And just as crawling really gives no semblance of the feeling in Concorde, so the possibilities of experience in hypnosis cannot be gauged by experiences of relaxation.

It may help by describing some of the ingredients of self-hypnosis or the trance state. Hypnosis is described as 'an altered state'. This means it is different from the everyday conscious state we live in most of our lives.

It has been compared to the brief time between being awake and going to sleep at night or from being asleep to being awake in the morning. A twilight-type feeling where the concrete realities of the conscious may not be so concrete. A dream state where the mind has wandered, under no influence or direction. 'I knew I was in this room but I was also lying on a beach,' one patient indicates the split feeling often experienced. 'I could hear your voice but I didn't take much notice of it, as I was so relaxed, strolling through the woods listening to the birds.' Many years ago I saw a man who requested hypnosis for stress and tension.

I asked him what was a most relaxing situation for him. He said he loved fly fishing in mountain streams. I began by telling him he was walking along a most beautiful mountain stream casting his line out into the rippling water. The sun was sparkling on the water, the sounds of the birds and the breeze in the trees, and the river splashing on the rocks could be heard. I repeated this a few times, then suggested he had come to a grassy bank which was so inviting that he lay down on the grass in the sun and went into a really relaxed state.

I noticed some frowns crossing his face as I said this but I continued to talk to him about his difficulties and how to deal with stress. Later on when he came out of the trance I asked him how he enjoyed it.

'It was fantastic. I was near this beautiful mountain stream casting my line out and I hooked a large trout. I was pulling him in but some idiot kept telling me to lie down in the grass. I kept resisting him until I'd landed the 3 lb trout, then I lay down and relaxed as the fool had directed me.' This gives an indication of the split in appreciating what is happening. Part of him was near the mountain stream, another part was listening to me, and the illogicality of it didn't bother him nearly as much as 'that idiot telling me to lie down in the grass.'

19 *Self-hypnosis : Understanding the Possibilities*

> The mind is a gold mine of inexhaustible abilities.
> The fortune of the fortunate is knowing how to find them.
>
> Would you go through life hopping on one leg, if you
> could walk or run on the two good legs you possess?

All hypnosis is self-hypnosis. You go into a trance by being both the subject and the hypnotist, and in the altered state make use of the extra abilities present in the unconscious to deal with whatever problem is troubling you.

To practise self-hypnosis on a regular basis may, like brushing your teeth, become a useful daily habit. The requirements are the (1) intention and (2) making time. The following steps may be of use.

1. Ascertain what you wish to achieve in the allotted time. It may be to relax, remove tension or for a more specific complaint such as to relieve a headache. Be concise, realistic and specific in your aims. Approaching self-hypnosis as a cure all or a happiness-maker will be met with failure.

2. Choose an appropriate time and place. It may be helpful to set a routine of the same time and place each day. It should be somewhere where you feel secure and will not be disturbed. It may be your bedroom, the train, the toilet at work, the bath, the car in the car park.

   Make sure those around you will not interfere with your session. Don't approach it with the attitude, 'I've got to spend this ten minutes relaxing but I'll be late for work and I've got so many other things to do.'

   Ten to twenty minutes a day is an average time spent on self-hypnosis and many people set their alarms to 'reclaim' twenty minutes of sleep for this activity.

   Don't do it when you are exhausted and nearly asleep as the

relaxing aspect will send you to sleep. *Sleep and self-hypnosis are not the same thing.*

3. Choose a position that is comfortable, such as an armchair, resting your head on the back of the chair. If you find you are going off to sleep each time, make it less comfortable.

   Go through the stages in Chapter 17 or the section on Stress, pages 175–91.

   To start with you may find it easier to use the tape as a guide (see page 252).

   Have in mind your problem or what you wish to achieve by the self-hypnosis session. Talk to yourself about this before you go into a trance, then let it float around undirected. Do not try and achieve any result consciously; *trying is the opposite of self-hypnosis.*

4. As you drift into the altered state be a passive observer of any thoughts or feelings you have. They may not be related to the problem you are having: don't worry – the picture may become clearer in time, piece by piece, just as a jigsaw puzzle does. Direct your mind inward rather than outward.

5. Enjoy the relaxing feeling that goes with self-hypnosis and appreciate the benefit of the 'oasis in the desert of stress' for a few minutes. Perhaps you may recognise some components of your problem in the dream language of the unconscious, but these may come to you later on during the day or night. Don't try and logically investigate or make sense of any of the hazy thoughts as they will disappear as shadows in the light.

6. Remain in that state for ten to twenty minutes (or however long is suitable) as a receiver of messages or no message at all. Allow a feeling of parallel awareness to be present. Don't expect too much – many things may be occurring beyond your conscious recognition.

   You may talk to yourself in a positive way, praising, promoting, reassuring, as if talking to a shy child, in order to remove guilt, fear or negative attitudes. Look at things from different angles and find an avenue to establish confidence and possibilities of success.

   Don't hope for great changes in each session. A small change in attitude each day will bring about suitable improvement in time. Constant dripping wears away the stone. Continually assessing and worrying that there is no progress will ensure that there will not be.

7. When you are ready, come out of the trance in any way suitable. By counting slowly from ten back to one is a good starting way; in time you will find this may be unnecessary.

   Don't allow your conscious mind to dissect and analyse different aspects of the trance. This is very important. Enjoy whatever feeling you have for a minute or two before getting on with your daily routine.

If you are a deep subject and feel disorientated when coming out of the trance, spend a few minutes allowing yourself to return to normal before getting up and getting on with things.

8. In time you may find yourself drifting in and out of a trance for a few seconds during the day when appropriate. Your experiences and abilities to use self-hypnosis will vary from time to time, depending on the situations occurring in your life.

   As it becomes part of your routine you may not use it on a daily basis but wait for a specific problem to occur before using the combined conscious-unconscious approach of a trance to deal with it.

9. Some specific ways in which self-hypnosis may be useful:
   A To sleep better use self-hypnosis once you are in bed or play a sleep tape as you turn out the light. Use positive suggestions of relaxing, not waking until the morning, being refreshed and in a positive frame of mind on waking.
   B Using time which is normally wasted in travel to and from work as a passenger in a train or bus (not as driver of a car). Sitting in a trance during a train journey is a great way of reclaiming wasted time. Program yourself for the day ahead, looking at specific problems you may encounter.
   C Before a normally tense-making experience which may range from after dinner speaking to meeting new acquaintances, is a good time to use self-hypnosis. Many professional sportsmen and performers use this technique to create positive attitudes before an event. A dress rehearsal in the mind often boosts confidence.
   D In the bath at night to review the day's activities, observe the positive aspects of the day and put into perspective any negative occurrences – as if you are writing a confidence-building mental diary.
   E To look at future experiences in a positive, relaxing way. During pregnancy to anticipate an easy, relaxing delivery of a healthy baby. Before exams or driving tests to imagine a calm, successful performance.

To hypnotise oneself to go into a trance is an individual experience. I cannot describe how you will feel, except that you have most likely been there before many times. It is like the feeling you have just before going to sleep or just as you wake – a twilight zone.

There is a feeling of 'parallel awareness', that is, you know you are in a room but part of you is somewhere else, half dreaming. This is different to a dream while asleep, as then the sleeper is totally in the dream and only occasionally will be able to say 'this is a dream'.

The use of self-hypnosis may be compared to a surfer going out to catch a wave. This is a very popular sport in Australia and the surf beaches are filled with people enjoying the thrill of being carried into shore by a large rolling wave.

The novice surfer wades into the sea, swimming out to where the 'big ones' are. He swims out ten yards and is buffeted back by an incoming wave. He tries again and struggles out a few more yards before being washed shorewards by the next wave. This process continues as he slowly makes his way out, becoming more and more exhausted with each stroke.

When he eventually reaches a place where he can catch a wave in, he is so tired he hasn't the energy to enjoy it.

As he learns, he realises that swimming out to catch a wave may be easier. Every time a wave comes towards him he takes in a deep breath and dives below the surface; it is calm there and the powerful force of the wave passes harmlessly over him. He bobs up again two seconds later to continue his journey out.

Time and time again he allows the incoming breaker to flow over him as he gradually makes his way out to where 'the big ones' are. Arriving there he floats on the swell waiting for the right wave to take him in. As it arrives he turns shorewards, swims powerfully for a few strokes, so his momentum is the same as the wave's, then relaxes and enjoys the exhilarating ride to the shore, using the energy of the wave to effortlessly carry him there.

Self-hypnosis is like the surfer ducking under the wave. It allows us to conserve energy and the 'dumpers' of life to pass by. By going into a trance state regularly we can avoid much of the tension continually swirling around us. We can allow it to pass by while we catch our breath for the next 'wave' of the day.

In a trance a common feeling is described as being here and being somewhere else at the same time. This is called 'parallel awareness' or 'dissociation'. 'I knew I was here in this room and I was also lying on a beach in Spain.'

This ability to dissociate is an important factor of self-hypnosis and varies from person to person. To let go, suspend critical judgement, to use imagination and allow the benefits of self-hypnosis to be explored, these all play a part in the hypnotic trance.

Parallel awareness occurs when someone with a broken leg in severe pain can allow part of his mind to accept the possibility that an imaginary block of ice is making it numb. Part of his mind accepts he is without pain, another part knows he has a painful broken leg.

Stage hypnotists make use of this phenomenon when subjects act in a humorous way contrary to their beliefs. People who are normally shy and reticent suspend that aspect and behave like Hitler and order people around. In medical hypnosis the ability can be put to use to overcome hurdles that are difficult to surmount otherwise.

One way of using this dissociation is, in a trance, to imagine that someone else 'over there' is going through the difficulty while you are watching from 'here'. All the emotional conflicts occur to 'him over there' and you can be an observer of the procedure without suffering the painful feelings involved. I used that technique with a very nervous man who had been trying for months to pluck up courage to ask his boss for a rise. He was a reasonable subject and I taught him self-hypnosis. He practised daily imagining he was watching 'the other him' going through the motions (and emotions) of asking his boss for a rise. This 'other him' felt all the nervous tension involved while my patient sat and watched as an unemotional observer.

On the big day when he had an appointment to see his boss he remained in a trance throughout the whole procedure. He got his rise and when he saw me later on he said his only problem was not smiling during the interview.

'For some reason,' he said, 'It reminded me of a Laurel and Hardy-type film, where the nervous employee asks the stern boss for a rise. All the time I was in his office I couldn't stop imagining him as the character in the film and me as the "fall guy", all of which I found very funny. At one stage I had to cough to avoid laughing.'

He had used the dissociation technique not only in the practice sessions but in the actual event itself. I received a note from him some months later saying he had found many opportunities for using this technique of 'distancing' himself from his problems.

Another person who used this technique to her advantage was a girl of sixteen who had a problem visiting an uncle of hers. The family visited this uncle every two or three weeks but some years previously he had shown her excessive emotional attention and she was angry and frightened of him. Her parents were unaware of what had happened and she did not want to tell them.

Every time they went to visit she felt all her hostilities come to the surface and sat in the corner the whole day in a sullen mood. Her parents chided her for her behaviour and complained she was upsetting her 'lovely uncle'. She dreaded the visits and the situation was getting worse. All her attempts to avoid these meetings failed.

I explained to her the dissociation ability of self-hypnosis and asked her if she would like to be at her uncle's but not be there at the same time. This idea appealed to her and as she was capable of going into a trance easily I explained some alternative ways of using her ability. She could 'go off into a daydream' by staring into the distance and concentrating on her breathing. She didn't even need to close her eyes and remained relaxed and calm in my surgery, ignoring the 'phone ringing and other disturbances.

She agreed to practise this 'day dreaming' and allow her mind to wander to other, more pleasant, situations whilst at her uncle's place.

It worked very well. She sat in the corner as usual and began daydreaming using the same method as she did at my surgery. She saw her uncle as a wild beast or Dracula; when he was drinking his tea she imagined it was poisoned; she saw herself lying on a beach in the sun, all on her own, really relaxed.

In fact she actually began to look forward to the visits to her uncle as she could express in a trance all the pent up emotions that had previously no outlet. She called them her 'theatrical afternoons' and as her creative ability increased her anxieties diminished.

Imagine that when you were born a small candle was placed in your vital centre (which is wherever you imagine that place would be). This is a special candle, a little like the Olympic eternal flame. It can't be extinguished until you die.

However, its brightness, radiant light and warmth are dependent upon being tended properly. It needs care, attention and respect in order to grow as you grow. If it remains as that tiny initial candle its effect will be lost as the body grows. What would be sufficient for a baby is inadequate for an adult.

As you grow many things happen which dampen the flame, reduce its intensity and threaten to blow it out. Just like a candle in the breeze, it flickers and wavers constantly.

If as you grow it receives inadequate attention in the form of time, praise, acceptance, respect, it will become stunted and drop behind the growth rate of other parts. Less candle power may be a way of describing our lack of self-confidence.

Self-hypnosis could be regarded as directly tending that candle in an appropriate way. Giving it the time, respect, oxygen and protection that will allow it to stabilize, grow and become powerful enough to resist the winds of fate which continually blow.

During self-hypnosis one may concentrate on that 'essential candle' allowing the feeling of warmth and exuberance to grow and last long after the trance. This candle power will not only be felt by you but others will notice the change, the 'radiance' coming from that internal source of energy, the different attitude not only of you to others but of them to you.

This may sound too much like propaganda from a faith-healer promoting his wares. I do not intend it to be so and I make no promises. I write this way to encourage an attitude of respect and acceptance of yourself, as you are, 'warts and all'. This acceptance will, I assure you, have a marked effect on many aspects of your life. Self-hypnosis is one way of providing this acceptance and in my experience has increased the 'candle power' of many people who have used it.

PART FIVE

Hypnosis and You

20 *Symptoms as Messages*

The body never lies.
MARTHA GRAHAM, AMERICAN DANCER

The medical profession (of which I am one) often regard a symptom – that is a complaint the patient makes to the doctor – as a problem that needs to be dealt with by removal. Removal of the symptom I mean, and the approach is generally to discover the cause by history, physical examination and tests and to give appropriate treatment in the form of tablets, or perhaps surgery, to *remove* the problem. This is very satisfactory for a proportion of symptoms and the medical profession is very successful in curing a vast number of illnesses.

I maintain that there are a proportion of symptoms which may be viewed as *messages* to be understood, rather than problems to be removed. The most obvious of these conditions are the chronic illnesses which do not respond to the 'removal of the problem' technique. These 'message' illnesses are many and varied and may be seen as a message from the body to the mind, about a situation which occurred in the past.

Kate is 18 years old. She has had psoriasis for two years. She has tried many creams and tablets but the psoriasis remains as red, blotchy, scaly areas almost covering both arms to the wrists. She is embarrassed by her skin and wears long sleeved clothes even in the summer. She is very shy of boys and doesn't go out much.

At night, while she is asleep, she scratches, and the condition remains in its red angry state most of the time. She has no idea what caused it or what maintains it, nothing makes it better or worse and the doctors just say it will settle eventually. In the meantime, life isn't much fun.

Using the theory that her condition is a message and that she had no conscious idea what that message may be, we decided to use hypnosis to decipher it.

Kate went into a trance quite easily and I directed her back to when the psoriasis started two years ago. In the trance she talked about her parents separating and how upset she was at her mother leaving. The psoriasis first occurred at about the time they were violently arguing before they separated.

I directed her to go back further in time, as Kate had also told me that she had psoriasis for a year when she was six. In the trance she talked about a bitter argument her parents were having at that time and her skin became blotchy and the psoriasis developed.

It appeared as if young Kate believed that her parents stayed together when she was six, after a terrible argument, because of her skin condition. This of course was not so, but the logic of the unconscious may well have believed it.

So as her parents started to split up when she was sixteen the same reaction occurred. As they stayed split up this time the psoriasis remained in a desperate bid to bring them together. The rash was a message for Mum and Dad to reunite. This was impossible since they had both remarried so the message was in vain.

I directed Kate to do some self-hypnosis daily to educate the unconscious mind that there was no need to reunite her parents. She knew they were both happy and she saw a lot of each of them so there was no reason for the psoriasis to continue.

She was very dubious about the possibility of being able to help her skin condition this way, but did as she was told. Over the next month, in time for summer, the condition settled down and new healthy skin took the place of the scaly red blotches.

There are a multitude of conditions that may be regarded as *message diseases*, some of which one could call psychological and others physical. How do we recognise these as different from symptoms to be dealt with by removal?

This is not an easy question to answer. If the medical profession have nothing more to offer than stronger tablets and no real diagnosis or treatment, then using hypnosis to seek a message, even if it does not find the answer, can do no harm.

Conditions that go on and on, bringing with them associated fears, anger and frustration may well be helped by looking for a message. Even conditions which show positive X-ray results, such as peptic ulcers, may well be part of a complaint from the body about the patient's attitude to himself.

Peter is thirty-five and works in an office. He had two problems – he was very overweight (18 stone) and since the age of ten has had boils every two or three weeks. His weight problem had been part of his life as far back as he can remember. Photos of him as a four year-old show him as very tubby. His boils occurred one or two at a time in the groin, armpits and bottom.

He had many treatments for his boils and repeated dieting for his weight, which fluctuated between 16 and 18 stone. Nothing he did seemed to help these two conditions.

I talked to him about his weight and boils possibly being messages which originated when he was young and may no longer be of any use. He told me his early life was very unhappy as his Dad was very strict and he was constantly teased at school and home about his weight.

He agreed to see if we could find any bodily message which would explain his weight and boils. And so I used hypnosis to go back to when the 'message' first occurred. I directed him under hypnosis to go back to the first time the boils appeared.

In a trance he talked about being at home aged about ten. He wanted to go out and play in the street, but was frightened of the boys calling him Billy Bunter and making fun of him. His father was picking on him and he complained about pain in his armpits. His father and mother examined them and found he had two large boils there. They gave him a lot of attention and made a fuss of him. It felt nice and was a good excuse not to go outside.

So the message seemed to be that the boils provided attention from Mum and Dad and a reason to avoid being teased by his mates.

After this the boils occurred regularly every two to three weeks for the next twenty years. No treatment in the form of pills or injections helped, so Peter just allowed them to occur and dressed them when necessary. There were times he couldn't sit down and needed time off work and at other times they were just a 'damn nuisance'.

I asked Peter to do self-hypnosis and explain that the boils may have been useful once but now served no purpose at all. He was now married with children and didn't need to receive extra attention with the boils. There were no kids outside waiting to tease him.

The boils didn't recur after that session and what was also interesting was that a boil that was becoming larger actually went away, the first time he can ever remember that happening.

The message from his weight was really that of comfort to a young un-happy boy, and he spent time in a trance dealing with that message also. He has managed to maintain his weight at about thirteen stone since, and has become a keen follower of 'the symptom as message' philosophy.

To deal with the symptoms such as pain, sleeplessness, skin conditions, abdominal upsets, headaches, etc. instead of 'running away' from them by trying to get rid of the problem, confronting them by thinking about them may prove more successful.

If you have a condition that has been present for a long time and the doctors don't seem to be able to offer much help, then may I suggest you approach it as a message?

Let us take an arbitrary problem such as persistent diarrhoea. All the tests show no positive cause – perhaps some spasm in the bowel shows on X-ray – and you are taking regular medication to minimise the discom-fort.

Approaching it as a message, think about the following questions.

1. When did it first start? As accurately as possible.
2. What was happening at that time or before that time, which may have been relevant? Some stress-provoking situation, perhaps.
3. Are there any situations since it started which make it worse or better?
4. Can you offer any thoughts about how the problem could have been of benefit to you at any time?
5. Did the symptom help in a conflict that was occurring or a release of emotion, such as anger or fear?
6. Do you feel the problem acts as a punishment for any guilt you may have felt?
7. Can you get any response if you spend some time 'communicating' with the part of the body where you feel the discomfort?

If the answers to all the questions are negative it may be that it is not a message or it may be that something like hypnosis could help to find some answers.

In my experience many problems can be dealt with in this way. And the learning process that occurs whilst dealing with the 'message' is very beneficial in helping confidence to grow. An appreciation of the mind-body communication as an important structure results in its use in many other ways and the changes that occur may be far and wide.

Spending time 'talking to your body' is one way of improving the two-way communication between body and mind. If you are feeling pain – that is, the body is sending a message to the mind – then returning the message by talking internally to that part may be of use.

Many of the patients I see have learnt to spend ten minutes a day relaxing and communicating with parts of their body which were causing problems. I know you will think this is stupid and I don't offer any logical explanation other than we too often take our bodies for granted. We assume it is there and doesn't need any recognition; if something is not working properly the doctor will fix it with a tablet.

If this philosophy is not working for you why not try spending more time understanding your body's needs. Perhaps devoting time to it may be very rewarding. Sitting in a relaxed posture and 'going' to the site of the problem, 'being there' and observing how it feels, what associated thoughts or emotions are involved, what past experiences come to mind, may all be very helpful.

Assuming a co-operative attitude with it rather than a blaming one may also be useful. Offering the possibility of an open mind is the first step in the right direction.

As you need to live with your body, any knowledge about it and the way it is attempting to help you can only be of benefit. To realise that the discomfort and suffering you have had for years may really be your body trying to guide you, will surely be a relief. The responsibility to understand the intended message and to deal with it is up to you. If you allow your scepticism or limited thinking to prevent you exploring this possibility, you may continue to seek answers outside when they are really coming from within.

21 Being Yourself

No bird soars too high if he soars with his own wings.
BLAKE

If a man carries his own lantern, he need not fear
darkness.
HASIDIC SAYING

We are all, to some degree, twisted and bent away from our 'real self'
by circumstances which occur to us during our life. Parental guidance,
social and financial pressures, the pace of society and directions from
others all affect us. Let us assume that the *natural* person is one who
grows under ideal conditions, loving parents, good schooling, enough
money, a suitable marriage and a secure job. No such person exists but
it is valuable to consider this 'ideal person' inside you as a guide to understand difficulties you may be having.

Diagrammatically this can be represented as a tree (see diagram 11).
The 'natural' tree grows in nourishing soil with ideal weather conditions.
It grows straight upwards towards the sun. The reality is that it may
be forced to bend and bow to the elements, disease may affect its boughs
and drought may wither it. This tree will be deformed and gnarled to
a degree, depending on the situations through which it has grown.

We, like the bent tree, are guided from the moment of birth in different
directions by our parents and environment. So our growth is forced,
to some extent, away from the ideal, our strengths are thus reduced
and our abilities 'to be ourselves' limited.

Another comparison may be made with horses pulling heavy loads.
At one period it was thought fashionable for the horses to hold their
heads up at all times, in order to look proud and to please their owners.
A special harness was devised to prevent the horses from lowering their
heads and they trotted around looking pretty to suit the fashion. The
problem was that the muscles of the horse are developed in such a way
that the pulling power is greatly increased by putting the head down
and using the shoulder muscles to take the strain. The structure of the

Diagram 11   Being yourself

bones, muscles and tendons in the 'real' horse are arranged to function best if it is allowed to assume its 'own' position for pulling.

These poor animals were forced to struggle and exhaust themselves trying to drag heavy loads uphill with their heads held high to suit the fashion, only having access to a small proportion of their strength. So it is with humans who are directed to behave according to someone else's beliefs. They only have access to a proportion of their resources and so struggle uphill unable to act 'naturally'.

You may be able to think of some aspects of life which appear to be a struggle for you, but which others find easy. Maybe there is some behaviour you are following which is not 'yours' but has been grafted on by someone in the past or present. This is where hypnosis may be useful in pruning the 'dead wood' and helping you to realise that you can do things you are unsure of. Hypnosis can help in understanding the artificial restraints placed upon you or which you are placing on yourself.

These restraints may be understood without hypnosis as in the case of Mrs Sewell, a sixty-year-old woman who had seen me two years ago with some problems. She rang me two weeks prior to the interview stating that she had put on six stone in weight during the last year and needed some help. I would like to analyse the interview and notice the *false logic* (see page 72), *lack of responsibility* and *loss of control* involved in not being herself. The following is a summary of the visit:

MRS SEWELL: Hello, doctor, you can see my problem without even asking.

DOCTOR: You certainly look as if you've put on weight, is it really 6 stone? How did that happen?

MRS SEWELL: My father died.

DOCTOR: Does that cause so much weight gain?

MRS SEWELL: Well, I was very upset because we were very close.

DOCTOR: Yes?

MRS SEWELL: And I wanted to cry a lot, but my husband wouldn't let me.

DOCTOR: Why not?

MRS SEWELL: It would only make things worse. He said I shouldn't cry but get on with living.

DOCTOR: And did you try it his way?

MRS SEWELL: Yes, but I felt worse, so I ate to comfort myself.

DOCTOR: Did that help? Did eating comfort you?

MRS SEWELL: No, it didn't. I think it made me more uncomfortable, in fact I'm sure it did.

DOCTOR: So you are now carrying six stone of uncomfortable non-comfort around with you.

MRS SEWELL: Yes, I suppose you could put it that way.

DOCTOR: Mainly because your husband said you shouldn't cry?

MRS SEWELL: That's right, he wouldn't let me.

DOCTOR: How could he stop you?

MRS SEWELL: Every time he noticed I was starting to cry he told me to pull myself together. He said nothing would bring my father back.

DOCTOR: Does he love you?

MRS SEWELL: Yes he does, and he felt he was trying to help me.

DOCTOR: But he didn't really help you.

MRS SEWELL: No, I think he made me worse.

DOCTOR: Why, after you had put on three stone didn't you decide you might know what was best for you and cut down on your eating?

MRS SEWELL: I don't know. I just kept feeling low and stuffing food down; I got into a habit. The food, instead of helping, made me more depressed because of my weight.

DOCTOR: Did your husband have any 'shoulds' about your eating?

MRS SEWELL: Yes. He kept telling me to stop, but I didn't. When he wasn't looking I'd binge and say to myself 'I'll show him', 'I'll get back at him for stopping me crying'.

DOCTOR: And did you get back at him?

MRS SEWELL: Not really. All it did was upset *me*; after a while it didn't seem to worry him at all.

DOCTOR: Sounds like cutting off *your* nose to spite *his* face or punishing *him* by making *yourself* uncomfortable. That's strange logic isn't it? Why are you coming to see me now?

MRS SEWELL: Because I'm sixty-one next week and I'm deciding to do things *my* way from now on; I think I'm old enough to make up my own mind don't you?

DOCTOR: Yes I do, and you look as if you have *really* made up your mind.

MRS SEWELL: I'm determined to follow it through, until this prison (*indicating obese abdomen*) has gone. Perhaps life can begin at sixty-one.

This interviw occurred with Mrs Sewell after she went from eight and a half stone to fourteen and a half stone over the previous year. It illustrates a number of features I would like to discuss.

Perhaps you may be able to recognise the illogical thinking which directed this lady off the rails. You may be able to understand some of the ways you are behaving in a similar manner.

Firstly, Mrs Sewell stated, 'I put on six stone because my father died.' In other words she was blaming her father's death for her excess weight. By doing so she didn't take the responsibility herself and made it much more difficult to be in control.

On further questioning she blamed *her husband* for her problem: 'he would not let me cry.' In fact it would be very difficult to stop someone's tears from rolling down their cheeks. She was saying, 'I wanted to be myself, mourn my father my own way, but I let my husband direct me as he saw fit.'

Her husband probably acted in good faith, believing that if *he* was in that situation he wouldn't cry, therefore it must be the best thing for *her*. He may have thought she would become more depressed so he applied the 'pull your socks up' attitude, even though it did not seem to be working as time passed.

After some time of putting on weight and feeling lousy she still didn't take control of her actions, but began to blame her eating on 'feeling low'. She realised that eating was not helping her low feeling, but developed a habit of following this policy anyway. She added fuel to the fire by telling herself *her* over-eating would annoy *him*. This may have worked for a short while but when she noticed him wandering off to read the paper while she gorged herself in the kitchen, she may have recognised it was time to stop that tactic. I suppose she could have had in mind humiliating him by being in the Guinness Book of Records as the fattest woman on earth, but somehow I think this was too big a task for her to contemplate.

In any event the approaching birthday seemed to be the vital factor causing Mrs Sewell to make a decision for herself. The realisation that time was running out and it was *her* life that was wasting away (even though *she* surely wasn't) helped her to come to her senses. At sixty-one she said to herself, perhaps it's time for me to do what *I* want and not get caught up in this tangle of interpersonal conflict where I lose part of myself. Her attitude and tone of voice implied she was determined to make the necessary changes.

Her visit to me was really for support, her decision was made and she needed someone who agreed with her to share the difficulties she might encounter. She continued to 'be herself' over the next six months, she lost the weight, felt happier, got on better with her husband and indeed life for her did begin at sixty-one.

One way of 'being yourself' is to be aware of the stresses and strains you are putting on your mind or body in behaving the way you are. Asking yourself, 'Is this *really* what *I* want to do, say, how I want to behave? If it's not, then what would I do or say if left to my own devices?' Talk to yourself to find out how 'the real you' would act.

If you have difficulty knowing what you really are and where you are being directed, hypnosis could be very helpful. In hypnosis you could go 'inside' and using the trance state observe your thoughts, actions, feelings as if from a distance. It may help you to remember words or situations in the past which have influenced you to behave 'out of character' and whether you have continued that behaviour after those influences have terminated.

The reason hypnosis is useful in helping you see the wood in spite of the trees, is that it allows contact with an 'inner self' by reducing the multitude of additional thoughts and misbeliefs you have acquired. It's like listening to a radio station with a lot of interference from static and other stations, and then moving the dial slightly and just hearing one commentator coming through loud and clear.

To give you a framework to begin understanding what I mean when I talk about the 'real you' and how it may be useful to have a working knowledge of this concept, I would like you to ask yourself the following questions. It may be necessary to adapt them to suit your particular situation.

1. Is there any part of your life in which you act contrary to your beliefs or desires? Do you think this is part of any problems you are having?

2. *What* are you doing or not doing and *why* are you unable to do what you believe is best for you?

3. Are the reasons preventing you from 'being yourself' unchangeable, or are they mainly in your mind?

4. Is your opinion about what may happen to you if you 'do your own thing' the limiting factor? Is this a factual and realistic opinion?

5. Is someone else – either past or present – preventing you from 'being yourself'?

6. Do you think by acting according to your feelings you will hurt someone? Is this your interpretation or do you actually *know* it will hurt them? If so, is that their problem and are you taking it from them?

7. Can you notice any 'false logic' similar to Mrs Sewell's which you are following?

8. Is there an appropriate time in the near future which may be suitable for you to 'temporarily be yourself?' Are you prepared to put this

into practice for a brief period of time in order to discover how the actual event differs from your anticipated belief?

I would like to relate how a patient responded to these questions and used hypnosis to overcome a difficulty she was having.

Suzanne is a thirty-year-old bank clerk. She lacked confidence and felt uncomfortable expressing her needs or wishes. She found many reasons why she should not speak her mind and the word 'selfish' seemed to be a basic part of her vocabulary preventing her from being herself.

She had been in the same job for some years and many months prior to her visit to me she had been promised a promotion but nothing had happened. She came to see me with symptoms of depression, lethargy, constant crying and generally feeling lousy. 'I'm not my usual self,' was how she described her plight. She had seen me previously and had learned self-hypnosis but had not been using it recently.

I asked her to answer the questions I've enumerated above.

1. DOCTOR: Is there any part of your life in which you act contrary to your beliefs or desires? Do you think this is part of your problem?
   SUZANNE: Yes to both those questions. I would like to know about my job change but I'm too nervous to ask the Manager.
2. DOCTOR: What are you doing or not doing and why are you unable to do what you believe is best for you?
   SUZANNE: I'm not enquiring about the promised promotion because I feel the Manager may be annoyed by my asking. I think they just want me to wait until they are ready.
3. DOCTOR: Are the reasons preventing you from 'being yourself' unchangeable or are they more in your mind?
   SUZANNE: They are in my mind. I've always been nervous about things like that and when I think of asking the Manager I get so frightened I can't find the courage.
4. DOCTOR: Is your opinion of what may happen to you the limiting factor? Is this a factual and realistic opinion?
   SUZANNE: Yes it is the limiting factor. I don't think it is factual but it is real to me.
5. DOCTOR: Is someone past or present preventing you from being yourself?
   SUZANNE: Well I'm not sure. My father was very strict and I know I was often upset and weepy when he kept telling me to do things that I found very difficult. He never used to praise me, he just criticised me and my sister all the time. I don't know if that's what you mean when you ask if I was prevented from being myself.
6. DOCTOR: Are you concerned that if you act according to your feelings someone will be hurt?

SUZANNE: No, only me. I may be upset by the Manager's reaction but I don't think he would be hurt.

7. DOCTOR: Can you notice any false logic in your actions?

SUZANNE: I suppose so. In fact it really doesn't matter if he gets angry as I'll be leaving the job anyway. I am annoyed at all the delay so perhaps the logical thing is to ask. If only I wasn't so nervous.

8. DOCTOR: Is there a time in the near future suitable for you to 'be yourself' and ask the Manager?

SUZANNE: Well, next week is the last week the Manager is there before he goes on holiday. If I don't ask him then it will be another month before I can see him.

It seemed from the answers Suzanne gave that she really wanted to ask about her job, but part of her feared the Manager's response. I believe this 'part' was not the real Suzanne but perhaps the part grafted on by her father's criticism – the frightened part. It really doesn't matter if this is actually true or not, the aim here is to help her do what *she* believes is best for her.

It is interesting that when I discussed her feeling of nervousness about speaking to the Manager, she said it was an identical feeling she had as a child when her father criticised her. So it is likely that this grafted part, the 'frightened Suzanne', who had repeatedly been upset by her father, was frightened of the same thing happening with the Manager. I maintain this is not the *real* Suzanne but an added part that may be no longer useful in helping her deal with present day problems.

I asked her to go into a trance and imagine *all* the alternatives which might occur over the next month, at the same time getting the feeling as to what the 'real Suzanne' would want to occur. She was to pay particular attention to the way she, the Manager and staff reacted in her imagination and the various outcomes resulting from the different alternatives.

She sat quite still with her eyes closed for ten minutes and was obviously involved in what was happening in her mind. Then she slowly opened her eyes as if coming out of a dream. After a little while she told me the different experiences she had imagined in the trance.

'Firstly I imagined doing nothing, the Manager went on holiday unaware of my distress, I became more and more upset as the days went by. I definitely didn't feel right with this choice.

'Next I saw myself going to the Manager's office. I felt pretty nervous but I was determined. I asked him politely about the promised job promotion. He was very pleasant, apologised and made a phone call there and then. He told me something would be done in the next few days. Both he and I felt the meeting was satisfactory. I felt good after this choice.

'Then I imagined asking him and he got annoyed and told me to wait. I felt frightened but put my case politely and firmly and explained I had been waiting some months. He remained annoyed and when I left

I cried, but after a while I felt glad I'd seen him. I felt pleased that I'd spoken my mind, I felt much better, even though I cried, than the first choice of doing nothing.'

Suzanne seemed quite pleased with what she had discovered about acting as herself even though it may not have gone smoothly. The thing that seemed most striking to her was the lousy way she felt when she did nothing.

In fact she did go and see the Manager, not once but three times, over the next month and eventually, after a lot of excuses and procrastination, she got her promotion. She wrote to me some months later saying how glad she was that she'd persisted, as she was really enjoying the change and felt so much better in herself.

Her words about the self-hypnosis session were, 'I didn't know I could do it. In the trance I saw all the possibilities and realised they weren't as bad as I'd imagined. I really felt unhappy when I let the Manager go on holiday without asking him.'

In my experience one of the requirements of 'being yourself' is to spend time on yourself. Time relaxing, thinking about yourself, understanding your difficulties, talking to yourself. In this way you will begin to feel more confident, more able to deal with situations and you will feel happy about your behaviour. You may learn to like yourself or feel proud of the way you are acting. This may sound like boasting, being egotistical and selfish. I maintain it is none of those things – it is just an important basis from which to deal with the knocks that inevitably seem to come our way.

Learning to do this is not difficult. It is not time-consuming: it is just different from the attitude of people today and so we may not feel comfortable about spending time on ourselves. As *we* are all we have and, to the best of my knowledge, we only have one life on this earth, if ten to fifteen minutes a day will make life easier, more comfortable and more rewarding, it doesn't seem too big a price to pay.

It takes courage for a man to listen to his own goodness and act on it. Do we dare to be ourselves? This is the question that counts.
PABLO CASALS

22 Body and Mind

Disease tends to leave me rather rapidly because it finds
so little hospitality inside my body.
ALBERT SCHWEITZER

The mental attitudes of patients have a lot to do with
the course of their disease.
NORMAN COUSINS, *Anatomy of an Illness*

Humans may be placed into many categories, men/women, adult/child,
rich/poor, black/white etc. Also each human may be divided into body
and mind.

It is my belief that there is some benefit in looking at ourselves as
made up of the two distinct parts: *the body* – with its own needs, desires,
capacities and capabilities; *the mind* – separate and often with different
desires and capabilities.

These two are like Siamese twins joined at the neck, pulling and pushing
to 'do their own thing' the one not being able to escape from the other;
a love-hate relationship with a long memory to bring about pain, suffering
and sometimes destruction, one to the other and hence to itself.

Imagine a pair of Siamese twins with circulations joined – one wanting
to eat all the time, the other not; one wanting to work all the time,
the other needing rest; one aggressive, the other shy.

But because they are joined they must both participate in what the
dominant one wants, which may be to the detriment of the other and
hence both suffer.

The mind is the dominant twin. It has its own set of likes, dislikes,
needs, desires, etc. The body is the partner without much say. It goes
along with and suffers at the excesses of the mind.

The mind is the controller. It runs the show and directs the body.
The mind orders the body to put hand to mouth to eat, even though
the gigantic distortion of the body is imploring otherwise. The body
must obey even against its own interests. Like a sergeant major telling
a private what to do, the body has no alternative but to follow the mind.

Obvious examples of abuse of the power of the mind are seen every-where – smoking, drinking, over-work, no exercise: stresses and strains the mind places on the body. Ask yourself how often do you think about your body and its needs during the day? How many activities are to satisfy the mind, irrespective of the resulting problem for the body?

An interesting example is the disease *anorexia nervosa*. In this illness, mainly in young girls, the mind has a mistaken belief that the body is too fat – a false body image – and endeavours to correct this by minimal eating and excessive exercise. There are a multitude of psychological reasons why this has come about. The girl looking like a skeleton will see herself in the mirror and exclaim how fat she is.

In this extreme case the mind's distorted desire not to be fat punishes the body to the extent that there is a high mortality rate with *anorexia nervosa*. Thank goodness the body has methods of 'fighting back' in many situations to prevent the continuation of 'mind dominance'. These ways start off simply but may build up in intensity if the message is not recog-nised.

Many of our medical and surgical conditions may be viewed as the body's attempt to alter the mind's self-destructive pathway.

A man working too hard, worrying too much, not relaxing or getting enough exercise may develop 'bodily messages' of indigestion. He may complain it's the stress of the job, take some tablets and continue punish-ing his body. After a period of time the indigestion becomes more severe. Worry about the pain makes things worse and tests show a peptic ulcer. The body is fighting back, trying to get 'the host' to slow down.

As is often the case the mind takes no notice, the ulcer becomes more severe and surgery may be undertaken. Isn't it a shame that the part that is trying to help us needs to go to such lengths to get recognition?

Wouldn't it be silly to hear of someone sailing along in a small boat, when he decides he feels like hammering nails into wood to deal with his aggression. He gets out a hammer and starts to hammer nails into the bottom of the boat. He ignores the water seeping in and continues making holes in the boat. As the boat sinks, he exclaims in amazement and annoyance at his discomfort.

Stupid isn't it? Yet this is what we do to ourselves every day in stressing, straining and abusing the body which has to carry us through life's jour-ney.

Obesity is a classic example of a breakdown in mind-body communica-tions. The mind says 'I want to eat' for reasons associated with habit or emotions. As the mind is in control the body cannot refuse the com-mand and excess food is pushed through the opening in the face.

In spite of the obvious lack of need for food this mechanism continues. The body may try and give a message to slow down by shortness of breath, depression, and lack of confidence.

Unfortunately these messages are misinterpreted and the mind says 'I want to eat more because I feel lousy', so the poor body groans under the excess weight forced upon it.

Many of the 'symptoms' which we feel may be messages (See chapter 20) from the body to the mind to try and make changes. Pains, bowel problems, skin rashes, tension in muscles, tiredness, indigestion and many others could be viewed as messages to be interpreted, not problems to be removed. The body may be 'demanding respect', like a car whose noises or slow starting indicate the need for a service or lubrication. If the car doesn't start properly, we can ignore it and continue to overwork the starter motor, or we can take notice and have it checked and corrected. Often a minor alteration can save a lot of future problems from occurring.

John was a bright twenty-two-year-old working in a garage. He was carefree, he played football and squash and enjoyed life to the utmost.

He had a pain in his left leg but thought it was nothing. Perhaps it was due to a knock at football or a fall from his bike.

The pain persisted. He put a bandage round it, took a few aspirins and ignored it, in spite of his parents' suggestion that he should see a doctor. 'It'll be OK, it'll go away soon,' he thought.

This state of affairs went on for two long years. Eventually the pain became so bad he went to see a doctor. The doctor arranged an X-ray and later solemnly told John the bad news. He had cancer of the bone.

John treated it all as a joke. It's no big problem he told Mum, Dad and himself. They'll fix it and I'll be 100 per cent. He went to hospital and had radiotherapy on the leg and gradually the cancer diminished and X-rays showed it was gone. He was 'cured', for the time being anyway.

But the pain didn't go away. In fact it was more severe. The doctors thought perhaps it was due to the radiotherapy and prescribed pain killers.

John took the pain killers three times a day and still the pain persisted. He doubled the dose to six a day – but there was still no significant relief.

The pain killers were increased in strength and prescribed at the highest dosage. He was woozy from the side effects, but the pain was still there.

He had days off work, days in bed and days he just can't remember except for the interminable pain through the haze.

How could it be? The cancer was cured. Why did the pain persist?

The hairs on his leg had gone due to the radiotherapy so when he went in the sun the leg blistered. He was angry with the leg. It was letting him down. He was ashamed of the way it looked. He hid it behind the other leg when sitting, wore long trousers most times, even on the beach, to hide it.

One day, in a daze of pain killers, he took too many tablets. Not on purpose. It wasn't a suicide attempt, but he was very depressed by the pain.

He went to hospital for three months for depression and when he came out was referred to me for hypnosis as the doctors were wary of prescribing more drugs.

John went into a trance easily and I began to show him how to reduce the pain by imagining his leg in ice cold water. Suddenly his face became contorted and he started to cry. I had no idea what was happening and asked him to explain his feelings. He said 'It's my leg, it's talking to me.' 'What's it saying?' I asked. 'It says it's dying inside, hollow, dead. It says it's bloody angry at me for letting it down. It's annoyed that I continually blame it, hide it.'

I asked him to continue this communication with his leg in a trance and for the next hour he sat there intently muttering to himself. Then I asked him to come out of the trance and we discussed what went on.

In a theoretical way part of his body, his leg, was angry with him for ignoring the original pain for two years; it was annoyed with him for not taking the problem seriously and was punishing him for lack of respect.

I realise this doesn't make conscious logical sense but I'm reporting how it happened. It was a starting point from which to work with John to help deal with the chronic pain he'd been having.

I saw him a week later and we went through a similar performance, this time with John agreeing to respect the needs of his leg and to spend ten minutes daily doing self-hypnosis to communicate with the leg.

After these two sessions John's pain became minimal. He still had some discomfort but it didn't bother him. He worked well, felt better and I noticed his leg was crossed *in front* of the other one. He had been out in the sun and his leg hadn't blistered – a strange and unexplained happening.

It's six months since I saw him and he hasn't taken any tablets since. The discomfort is well under control through his daily self-hypnosis.

PART SIX

Specific Uses of Hypnosis

23 *Pain*

The strain in pain lies mainly in the brain.
DR DAVID SPIEGEL, AMERICAN PSYCHIATRIST

Those who do not feel pain seldom think that it is felt.
DR JOHNSON

There are two types of pain – acute (for a short time) and chronic (for a long time). They are completely different conditions and I would like to describe the latter, its effects and how hypnosis is used to alleviate it.

Firstly I would like to describe the Pain Clinic in a London teaching hospital where patients with chronic pain attend for relief. The clinic is similar to other outpatient clinics – crowded with patients, sparse with furniture and time. Waiting time varies but is often up to two hours, time with the doctor varies from ten to thirty minutes.

The patients are a cross-section of the community in age, race and occupation. Pain is no discriminator and is the common link of all those gathered seeking help. Chronic pain – although just two brief words – spells a history of suffering, depression, frustration, anger and fear.

The patients walk, hobble, limp, are wheeled into the clinic or brought in on mobile beds. They gather in the corridors and settle in for the morning. Philosophers all, wise in the knowledge of their experience. Discussing with intense looks and shaking heads the history of their tragedy. Fragments of medical jargon, picked up on the long journey, are heard wafting to and fro.

There is a constant attempt to understand 'why?' There seems no answer as to why the pain started or is continuing year after year. Every avenue is followed to explain the curse that is ruining their life.

The doctors are concerned at their limitations in stemming the flow of woeful tales that continue to pour out at each session. Frustrated by the lack of knowledge or ability to deal with this soul-destroying problem, they are eager to find an answer, a solution to lessen the pain.

The stories continue – out of work five years with a bad back, marital discord due to chronic headaches, inability to walk due to painful hips, difficulty in driving a car due to a stiff neck, etc. etc.

The treatments are many and varied. Some patients have had operations to help the pain and are referred on when the pain persists. All have been through a myriad of attempts to remove the pain by their local doctors, osteopaths, chiropractors, herbalists, faithhealers, etc., before they arrive at the Pain Clinic.

In the clinic therapy commences after a diagnosis is made. Many of the patients have hospital notes so large that they give you a backache when lifted! Tests are performed – X-rays, blood tests, diagnostic injections to ascertain where the site of the pain is and what may be causing it.

Many times it is more difficult to arrive at a precise answer than in other areas of medicine. The diagnostic tools are limited because the problem is subjective – that is, the pain is only measurable by asking the patients how they feel, rather than using a scientific instrument. Chronic pain is a leveller. From the judge to the prisoner all are reduced in stature by the eroding capacity of their tormentor.

How can we tackle this immense problem? There are so many attempted solutions that there must be more than one answer. Each form of therapy has a place which is helpful in some way, some more than others.

When the diagnosis is made and a treatable underlying condition ruled out, the battle begins. Tablets and pills of all shapes, sizes and strengths are used to deaden the pain, provide relief, help blissful sleep wash away the day's memories. Many chronic pains are greatly helped by analgesics and the aim is to provide maximum relief with minimum side effects.

After many trials of different tablets with no success, alternative therapies are used. Injections of local anaesthetic to block the pain pathway or cortisone to alter the tissue response. Success may be short-lived, long-lasting or non-existent, only time and trial can tell.

Acupuncture is beneficial in many cases. This time-honoured oriental therapy is increasing in popularity and success. Many people who doubted its effect are pleasantly surprised at the relief obtained after a few visits. Side effects are minimal and the acupuncture needles are so fine that the discomfort is generally of no consequence.

Nerve stimulating machines (TENS) are small boxes strapped to an appropriate part of the body and worn under the clothes. Many people find these are very beneficial in reducing the pain to a tolerable level and find them a great strength in the fight against pain.

But for those who leave the Pain Clinic smiling, there are many who return time after time, the pain still not under control, act after act of their life story repeating itself like a never-ending tragedy. The persistence of chronic pain affects the sufferer in a multitude of ways. It is a constant shadow throwing its gloom over every aspect of life, reducing enjoyment and happiness.

The total range of emotions may be released by this tormentor, anger, frustration, guilt, sadness, self-doubt and desperation. The fact that no logical reason can be given for its existence adds fuel to the emotional fire.

If you are a sufferer of chronic pain you may recognise some of these feelings. My aim will be to help you to understand the pain and perhaps to approach it in a slightly different way using hypnotic techniques so that you can be involved with reducing or removing it.

Firstly I'd like to discuss attitudes towards pain and then interweave hypnosis to change negative feelings to positive ones of gaining control. I do not wish to promote hypnosis as the answer to chronic pain. I believe it plays a major role, in conjunction with other forms of therapy, or on its own.

I. *Take responsibility* for your pain. You may well ask 'How do I do that? I don't know what caused it, I'm not to blame for it.' I agree with you and I am not entering a moral discussion. I am saying, it is *your* pain. Other people may try and help, but in the long run it is *your* problem and any way you can become involved with treating it will be to your advantage. Setting your mind to take responsibility and being prepared to spend your own time doing something for it means you are heading in the right direction.

The most common attitude is 'Doctor, here is my pain, I don't want anything to do with it, you fix it.' In other areas of medicine this may be appropriate; for a high proportion of people with chronic pain, it is not. Learning what part you can play in understanding and reducing the pain is a difficult concept to grasp but I will point out methods of doing this using hypnosis.

The aim is to use the powers of the conscious and unconscious mind to rid the body of this unrelenting distress. If you consider pain is a parasite draining you of energy, the more you can learn about its habits and lifestyle, the easier it will be to find a way of getting rid of it.

Firstly, I do not believe there is any benefit in dividing chronic pain into *organic* (where pathology can be demonstrated by tests and X-rays) and *psychosomatic* or *functional* pain (where no pathology of the tissues can be shown) which implies that the mind is involved in the cause or continuation of the discomfort.

My understanding is that *pain is pain* and the sufferer of chronic pain feels the same intensity of discomfort whether it is caused by the body or the mind. The treatment using hypnotic techniques may well be the same in each case. Unfortunately a stigma has become attached to psychosomatic pain as if the sufferer was to blame, had intentionally caused it and should feel guilty. As if it is *his fault* in some way and no-one can help him.

Nothing could be further from the truth. Unfortunately due to lack of training, many in the medical profession, unable to treat non-organic pain, label it as due to 'neurotic malingering' and increase the aura of guilt and blame. Many patients have described the 'pull your socks up' attitude of doctors frustrated and annoyed by their failure to take away the pain.

The inference often is that if it is organic and tests show pathology, it is acceptable. If no abnormality can be found, nothing much can be done so don't waste the doctor's time.

II. *The mind plays a major role in chronic pain.* All pain is felt in the mind. Whatever part of the body is affected the pain centre is in the brain and learning to use the mind to reduce pain is often very helpful.

Hypnosis, learning to control some aspects of the mind, acts in many different ways to reduce pain.

A DISTRACTION

We all can forget things for a brief period of time when distracted by something exciting or enjoyable. The mind cannot concentrate on everything at once so if pain being top priority is pushed down the scale by something else it will diminish accordingly. Using self-hypnosis we can learn to use the 'forgetting part' of our mind to reduce the pain. Learning to concentrate on the comfortable parts of our body may seem difficult but it's not impossible. Going into a dream-like state and recalling happy memories will automatically provide relief from the pain. This relief may last long after the trance has finished.

Helmut is a German Office Manager with a very busy and hectic job. He is constantly under pressure. He had a kidney stone removed three years prior to seeing me and had constant, intense pain in a nerve involved in the operation scar. He had been in hospital on and off for the pain and the nerve had been cut, frozen, lasered and burnt, all with no relief.

The man was distraught from the continued saga of doctor versus nerve in which he was the continual loser. When I saw him I asked how I could help. He said 'If only I could have a little relief each day I could cope.' He wasn't asking for a cure just a little daily relief from the agony.

I hypnotised him and asked him to imagine a scene he'd enjoyed previously. He imagined he was alone on a lovely beach in France, the sun was hot, the water blue and the sand fine and warm under his feet.

He stayed on that beach in his mind for half an hour and his face showed the appreciation of that relief as he opened his eyes.

He learnt to do self-hypnosis for ten minutes twice a day during his hectic work. He went to his French beach twice a day and although he didn't develop a suntan he gained all the benefit of a brief holiday.

After a few weeks he noticed the pain had diminished during the rest of the day so he decided to reduce his workload and relax more. After three months the pain was negligible and he was able to enjoy life again as he had done three years previously. Helping him to use his mind to distract his attention away briefly, allowed him to gain control of the pain.

B   REMOVING NEGATIVE EMOTIONS

Often due to the disturbing nature of the pain or because of emotional situations involved in its causation, many negative feelings become intertwined in the pain itself. If these can be disentangled the suffering is often remarkably relieved.

I call negative emotions those which direct their sufferer to feel worse, add a burden to the problem. Such emotions as anxiety, fear, guilt, self-punishment, conflict, all may play a role in causing or maintaining the pain.

Hypnosis is an ideal way of understanding these components and putting them into a realistic perspective. By reassessing the value of the negative component and analysing it 'in the light of day', it often disappears.

Some examples of what I mean :

i) Guilt

If the pain is caused in an accident and someone else is hurt or killed, the pain may be maintained by the guilty feeling. Guilt requires punishment; what better punishment than long term pain.

In hypnosis, reassessing the guilt, adding logic and understanding, having an imagined trial and alteration of sentence, often reduces the guilt and allows the 'punishing pain' to diminish.

Mrs Johnson, a thirty year old housewife, is very nervous and tense. She always has been. She was driving home one night two years previously and failed to see a child on a zebra crossing. She braked hard but knocked the child over. She thought she had killed him. In fact he was only shaken and, after a short while, he walked home.

The instant flash in her mind that she had killed him remained with her. For two years she had an unusual pain in her joints, investigated and treated with a multitude of tablets without success.

She agreed to try hypnosis only after she believed it was her last chance. She was very dubious and fearful of 'meddling with her mind' and required her husband to sit with her at all times.

She relaxed gradually and after a few sessions was able to do self-hypnosis at home with a tape I made. During these trances she reassured her unconscious mind she did *not* kill the boy and did not need the punishment she was receiving. She also learnt to relax more.

After five sessions her pain was much less; it was still present but not nearly so limiting or destructive to her life. She continued to reassure her unconscious mind and gradually she no longer needed to see me or to continue punishing herself for a crime she did not commit.

ii) Fear

Many patients whose pain continues, unexplained, untreatable, develop a fear that there is an underlying condition, such as cancer, which is being missed. This fear is reinforced by the repeated attempts to prove there is no cancer. Every negative test seems to point to the fact that cancer must be present but the test is not strong enough or suitable enough. Each failed attempt to identify and remove the pain is proof that 'something' is causing it. 'The pain is real, doctor, I know you don't believe me, but it is destroying my life.' Any discussion seems to make matters worse and further tests seem to deepen the quicksand.

The continued cycle of hopes being raised and dashed, by therapy continuously being altered, adds to the problem.

The problem becomes illogical – that is, out of control of the logical, conscious mind. This is where hypnosis is useful; it avoids logic and deals with the emotional aspects of the unconscious mind. The calming effect, the altered attitude, the reassuring evidence, is put to the unconscious mind to lessen the fear. Optimistic thoughts are included in the self-hypnotic routine.

Often in such cases, seeking the *cause* of the pain takes priority over the pain itself. Talking to patients, they continually ask 'Why?' and when I say 'Would it be all right to lose the pain and never know why it existed?' the answer is often a shake of the head. Because no-one can give an answer as to *why* a pain persists, some these sufferers continue on their endless quest, adding all sorts of emotional problems along the way.

A comparison between pain and a burglar alarm seems relevant. The alarm notifies us something is wrong in the house, we investigate and take appropriate action, turning off the alarm when we are reassured all is well.

If there is a fault in the system or if we are not satisfied that nothing is wrong and we leave the alarm on for days, weeks or months, it serves no purpose. It will upset the household and disturb the neighbours and certainly have no effect on an intruder.

The alarm can be safely turned off or down with no detrimental effects. So it is with chronic pain, the message is no longer useful, it no longer warns us or causes us to take appropriate action. The pain can be diminished with safety even if we do not know the cause, so long as suitable medical tests have shown no underlying treatable disease exists.

iii) Anxiety

Generalised anxiety from a chronic stressful condition such as pain may reinforce the situation. The hopelessness of it all, the lack of direction or understanding, all drain the energy and resources of the sufferer.

Going from place to place, having test after test, treatment after treatment, causes a downward spiral of feeling. Loss of a job, the humility of being on the dole, being dependent rather than a bread winner, being treated as an invalid, all cause massive disruptions to the functioning of the personality and lower self-esteem.

Hypnosis, by its very nature, lessens anxiety, produces a calming or tranquil effect and so may stem the flow of strength and determination 'down the drain'.

Intertwined with this is the realisation that 'someone understands', 'someone is prepared to spend time with me, to listen to me and realise I am not putting it all on'. The hypnotherapist often takes an understanding, supportive role and this plays a major part in guiding people through their difficulties.

One of the difficulties is the *non-acceptance* of hypnosis as a form of therapy. 'If hypnosis can help it must be in my mind, I must be mad' and this is unacceptable. Many patients refuse to contemplate hypnosis as a choice on these grounds; they prefer to continue the never-ending search for a physical treatment that will take the pain away.

In a pain clinic I asked one hundred consecutive patients with chronic pain the following three questions:

1. If you trusted your doctor and he recommended tablets for your pain, would you take them?
2. If you trusted your doctor and he recommended an operation, would you have it?
3. If you trusted your doctor and he recommended hypnosis, would you let yourself be hypnotised?

I was amazed at the replies I received.

1. 100% said they would take tablets.
2. 65% said they would have an operation.
   15% said they would think about it.
   20% said they wouldn't.

3. 40% said they would allow themselves to be hypnotised.
   20% said they would think about it.
   40% said they wouldn't.

What amazed me was that more people would accept an operation with all the pain, side effects and dangers, than hypnosis with none of those problems. The fear of having 'their minds meddled with' was so great that even the remote possibility that their pain may be diminished was not enough stimulus to 'have a go'.

The attitude that 'it's not in the mind, doctor' also added to their negative response and this attitude is a very real, limiting factor in the general acceptance of hypnosis as a useful tool for pain relief.

iv) Anger

Many patients are understandably angry and this may be known or not known, expressed or not. The cause of the anger varies considerably and may be caused by an initial incident where the anger is directed at someone else, or at oneself. As the pain continues there are multiple opportunities for creating anger but not many targets to vent this anger on.

Repeated mishaps which tend to occur, doctors who fail in some way, misunderstandings, the pain or painful part of the body itself, the hospital, operation, etc., all may be the source of the anger but the poor patient is in no position to express anger in the direction where he feels his saviour may be.

A young boy was knocked off his bike by a drunken driver. He received severe injuries to his leg and developed a permanent limp. Some years later he still had a lot of pain in spite of repeated attempts to control it.

On the surface he appeared calm and resigned to his fate and he had accepted all the pushing around and delays which occur in chronic cases. He was also involved in legal action where the delays were interminable and he received no suitable response to his questions.

After seeing him a few times it became apparent to both of us that he was understandably very angry. He was angry at the drunk who knocked him off his bike, angry at the medical profession for not curing his condition, angry at the legal profession for their delays, angry at his leg for ruining his life, angry at the pain for the discomfort it caused. I taught him ways in hypnosis and out of hypnosis to express his righteous anger and 'get it out' of his system. He recognised that it was acceptable to feel angry and there were some avenues where he could show this without destroying his hope of help. He wrote letters to all the people he was angry with and stated in no uncertain terms how he felt. He didn't post the letters. He made tapes about his thoughts and feelings and described in detail what he thought of the people and situations he had become ensnared in. He didn't listen to the tapes.

After a few weeks he felt much better, he was reducing the pent-up anger caught in his chronic pain system, and by reducing this energy he reduced the pain. He also used the relaxation and analgesia of self-hypnosis to help the overall situation.

v) Attitude to the painful area

After part of the body, say a limb, has been causing pain for some time, it is understandable that you would get annoyed and aggravated with it. 'If only the pain would go. Cut off my leg, and I'd be happier than with this blasted pain', are words I've often heard.

It's as if the person looks upon the painful part as an enemy that he wants to be rid of. Hour after hour, day after day, year after year, a constant reminder and cause of his distress.

I believe this attitude to the painful limb may play a part in the pain continuing. It's as if the affected limb says, 'Damn you, it wasn't my fault that you had the accident. You did it and now you're blaming me for the consequences. I'll show you, I'll pay you back.'

Now I'm not suggesting there is any logic in this. I have found in many cases that altering this attitude to one of understanding, apology, may completely relieve the pain.

John is a delightful sixty-year-old who came to see me in a wheel-chair. His right leg had been amputated above the knee three years earlier. He had suffered constant intolerable 'phantom limb' pain since. Phantom limb pain means pain in the limb that is no longer there. It is real, painful and causes much distress because you cannot touch the painful area – it doesn't exist in the flesh, only in the mind.

John had been subjected to every form of treatment to remove the anguish of constant pain day and night. He had received analgesic tablets to the limit, sedatives, sleeping tablets, injections into the stump, operations on the nerves, injections into the nervous system, all to no avail. The pain persisted unchanged. He came to me in desperation with tears in his eyes saying 'You are my last hope, I don't know what to do if you fail too.'

I had mixed feelings of being put on a pedestal in this way and also feared I may not be able to help this gentle, tormented man. I discussed the various aspects of hypnosis and spent some sessions just chatting with him, understanding his fears and strengths.

He had been a successful businessman and had had disease of his arteries limiting his circulation. He had been advised to rest, but concerned about financial security for his family, continued working very hard. As time went on he developed gangrene in his foot and eventually it required amputation. He was most distressed after the operation and lost his confidence; the pain and the fact that he was a one-legged man got him down. He tried to use an artificial limb but it hurt. His stump constantly jerked with the nervous tension he was under, he felt very annoyed with the leg that had literally let him down.

After a number of sessions I taught him relaxation and the twitching in the stump was gradually brought under control. But the pain persisted. I made hypnosis tapes for him to play, still the pain persisted. I helped him produce analgesia in the stump but it only lasted a short while.

In a word I was 'stumped'. After three months I wasn't getting anywhere and I felt I was going to have to say to him that I couldn't help his pain. Then one session, for some reason, I asked him about his attitude to the stump. He described his anger, frustration and annoyance at this 'non-limb' which was causing him so much trouble.

I asked him to go into a trance and remember the times he neglected his leg. He recalled many occasions since childhood when he had injured the limb in accidents, horse-riding incidents, falls, bruises, etc. I then asked him about times he didn't treat or rest the leg when it was required. In particular he hadn't rested when advised three years ago and gangrene had set in.

I suggested that perhaps his leg was angry with him for all the problems he had caused it. Perhaps he should assume an apologetic attitude towards it now.

He agreed to spend time daily talking and apologising to his leg. And wonder of wonders the pain started to recede. It wasn't all plain sailing, but from that point on we began winning the battle with the painful phantom limb. Over the next three months the pain completely disappeared. He still required to take a mild sleeping tablet for some time to ensure a good night's sleep, but after three years of hell he is now able to enjoy life with his wife, children and grandchildren. He also says with a smile 'I still pay my daily dues of respect to my old friend the "little leg".'

Pain often produces muscle spasm in the area surrounding it. A headache may be caused or maintained by tension in the neck or scalp muscles. As relaxation is part of the hypnotic experience, this may be put to great use to reduce the spasm and hence break the pain-spasm cycle as in the figure opposite.

To demonstrate the effect of tissue tension on pain, with the left hand open pinch some loose skin on the back of the hand, register how painful it is. Then holding on to the skin slowly clench the hand and notice how the pain increases as the skin tightens. So it is with muscle spasm and by doing self-hypnosis and relaxation this muscle tension can be greatly reduced.

Pain

Muscle spasm

Hypnosis can produce analgesia: using the trance state, patients can imagine part of their body as going numb. This imagined numbness can produce real diminution in sensation. In the daydream-like state of a trance patients are asked to imagine one hand is immersed in ice cold water. As the coldness continues numbness develops; this numbness may be transferred to the painful area.

Using thermometers measuring skin temperature it can be shown that a very marked reduction in temperature actually occurs using this method. A patient of mine had chronic backache. He had been off work for two years and was becoming depressed at being on the dole. At home he was unable to lift his young baby because of the back pain.

He was suitable for hypnosis and developed a reasonable ability to make his back numb by imagining ice on it. When he came out of the trance and moved around the pain returned. After many visits with no lasting improvement I asked him to go into a trance, make his back numb and come out of the trance from the neck upwards. In other words, leave his back in the trance but bring his head out.

He looked perplexed at my request but did so and was surprised that he no longer had the pain when he walked around. I asked him to go outside and walk down the street. When he returned he had the same bemused look on his face so I knew his back was 'still asleep'. He touched his toes and did many things he had not done for months.

PAIN AS A MESSAGE

As with other illnesses, I believe, in many cases, chronic pain may be a message of some sort. If we can learn to understand the message the pain improves. Hypnosis is an ideal state in which to decode these messages and tackling the problem this way rather than 'taking away' the pain is often successful. I would like to relate an unusual case of this kind.

Philip is a forty-year-old jeweller who had experienced joint pains for as long as he could remember. He had missed many weeks from school due to these pains and he had seen numerous doctors, but no real diagnosis or cure had been obtained. He had taken 'almost every pill in the book' to see if the pain could be removed.

Most days the pains occurred in one or more joints and he came home to rest at lunch time to relieve the discomfort. His family life was very happy and there was no obvious stress or emotional upset apart from the nuisance value of his continuing pain.

He agreed to use hypnosis to find out more about the pains and was a co-operative subject who easily went into a trance. I asked him to indicate when the pain had occurred for the first time, as I counted back from his present age of forty.

He indicated something of importance happened at the age of three. I asked him what this was. He related that his mother had died then. His father, a poor Australian graduate doctor, couldn't afford to keep him and he was adopted by another couple who moved to England.

On further questioning, when he came out of the trance he explained that he knew all this and he also knew his father was still a doctor in Australia. He had never contacted his father as he did not want to cause him any problems.

I tried to figure out how the pain could be a message for such a long time since his mother died and he was adopted. Then I had a brainwave. Could it be possible that the pain was trying to help the little boy find his real father by constantly directing him to visit doctors? Illogical, but the unconscious mind often works on childish logic.

I explained my thoughts to him, how the pain was an outdated message to find his father. He went away thinking about that and practising a relaxation technique. He was pleasantly surprised over the next two months as the pain gradually disappeared. The suffering he had experienced for forty years was no longer necessary when he realised how out of date the message was.

Pain can be used to transmit messages which are not as dramatic as Philip's. The pain can represent self-punishment, attention gaining, conflict, a need to spend more time on yourself, to relax more, to stand up for yourself, and many more. It is only by questioning under hypnosis that some of these messages can be deciphered and a course of action decided upon.

Hypnosis can be useful in going into the pain in order to understand it. I know this sounds crazy but I have found that by directing patients *into* the pain – that is, in the opposite direction to the one they usually choose – many aspects of the pain can be analysed.

In a trance 'going into the pain and being there' helps us learn about various components of the pain. I divide them artificially into descriptions which may be applied to the feeling. Again, this is not logical just helpful.

I ask patients to concentrate their mind on the pain and to describe:

1. The colour of it.
2. The temperature of it.
3. Whether the muscles are tense or relaxed.
4. Whether there are associated memories there.
5. Whether there are associated emotions there.
6. Their attitude towards the pain.
7. The physical limits (outline or shape).
8. How it sounds.
9. Any message the pain may be giving.
10. How it feels.

So you can see that instead of running away from the pain I direct them towards it in order to really dissect and understand it.

For example, a man with chronic headaches whom I asked to describe the pain in the above categories, answered:

1. Red.
2. Hot.
3. Tense.
4. Missing out on many outings.
5. Anger at doctors for not curing the headaches.
6. Angry at it, blame it for a lot of problems with work and home life.
7. Like a plate pressing on my head.
8. No sound.
9. No message.
10. Like pressure.

I next asked him to make some alterations to these components using his imagination in the trance.

1. Imagine the red changing to a relaxing blue.
2. Imagine a block of ice on his head to reduce the temperature.
3. Relax the muscles.
4. Realize the memories are from the past and let them go.
5. Deal with the anger he had felt for the doctors.
6. Alter his blaming attitude to one of understanding and tolerance.
7. Imagine the plate to be smaller.
8. —
9. See if any message comes to mind as you think about the pain.
10. Imagine the pressure to be lifted, lighter.

I asked him to practise this daily for ten minutes and, with much guidance, after a period of weeks he gradually learnt more about his headaches, what they meant to him and how to control them. After a few months the headaches became much less frequent and less severe. One of the messages the headaches were giving him was to relax more and when he did this the message was no longer needed.

SLEEP

Often people with constant pain sleep poorly. This sleep loss adds to the problem and lowers their tolerance for the pain. The night is very long if you are in pain, you can't sleep and your partner is snoring away blissfully. Hypnosis and sleep tapes are often very helpful in improving this situation.

All in all, chronic pain still has the upper hand. I have illustrated different ways hypnosis may be useful. I do not suggest that it is useful in every case or that it can 'cure' chronic pain. I do maintain that it is a very helpful tool amongst all the others we have to offer and may be used in conjunction with any other therapy to reduce pain.

It is important that you don't get the idea that all these patients lost their pain easily in a short time. There are often many hurdles to overcome in order to achieve comfort. It often needs an astute therapist and a co-operative patient who has rapport with the therapist, to get the best results.

I have only mentioned 'success' stories here. If I were to mention the failures I would need a much larger book. Hopefully as we learn more about hypnosis the ratio of successes to failures will increase.

If you have pain I suggest you try and develop the ability to use self-hypnosis and with some of the above suggestions learn more about *your* particular pain. In that way you may be able to wrest control from the unrelenting intruder.

24 *Stress*

More than any other time in history, mankind faces a
crossroads. One path leads to despair and utter
hopelessness. The other to total extinction. Let us pray
we have the wisdom to choose correctly.
WOODY ALLEN

Stress is a word becoming more and more popular in the press, in books
and medical circles. It has been quoted as the 'modern day killer', 'the
underlying cause of most diseases', 'the high cost of progress', and so
on. Many volumes have been written about stress, its cause and effects.
What I have to say here will be a summary of a number of thoughts
and ideas to help you understand how stress may be affecting your life,
and how to deal with it.

WHAT IS STRESS?

The dictionary definition in relation to physical stress can also be applied
to the emotions – 'a force or system of forces producing deformation
or strain'. We are all under some form of strain; the only person with
no stress is a dead one. A gradation occurs between creative or *constructive*
stress and *destructive* or immobilising stress.

I go to bed at night and realise I haven't put out the milk bottles.
I feel a minimal irritation over this and get up and put them outside
the door. This is *constructive stress*.

I go to bed at night, realise I haven't put out the milk bottles. I develop
severe anxiety at the thought of going outside, perhaps I'll be mugged,
I toss and turn not deciding what to do, the tension mounts, I dwell
on the problem for hours, I can't sleep. This is *destructive* immobilising
stress as it taxes the mind and body with no resolution.

Variations on this theme occur in a multitude of ways in most people's
lives. The physical reaction to stress is called a 'flight or fight' reaction.
This means that chemicals and hormones are produced in the body to

either fight or run away from the stressful situation. These reactions began with prehistoric creatures millions of years ago as a means of survival, thus they were extremely important. Those animals without this system, calmly grazing while a predator approached, understandably didn't live long enough to worry about putting the milk bottles out.

As man evolved, he too developed this fight or flight response to stress. He developed a constructive reaction to deal with a hungry dinosaur (see diagram 12A) and either used his club or his feet to advantage. Due to the demise of the dinosaur our modern day stressful situations are not solved by the feet or club method. The stress of every day life requires vastly different and more subtle ways to subdue it.

Wouldn't it be nice if the boss asked you to work late one night when you had tickets to the opera and you pulled out your club and boffed him on the head? Unfortunately this may well increase the stress in your life if you returned home from the opera to find some men in blue waiting with handcuffs at the ready.

So the internal reactions which help fight or flight, that is, increased blood pressure, pulse rate, breathing, sweating and muscular tension, have no outlet in modern society. But this process places an immense long-term strain on the body and the mind (see diagram 12B).

In fact this stress syndrome, as it is called, feeds upon itself. The more stressed we become the more tense, anxious and worried we are, which in itself produces stress. So a vicious (and that is a very appropriate word) cycle is set up, leading, in many cases, to physical or emotional symptoms. A few definitions may help our understanding of this very complex subject.

Anxiety is defined as 'a state of uneasiness or tension caused by apprehension of possible misfortune, danger' and is intimately tied in with stressful situations. It may be divided into two groups:

i) Anxiety learnt from the past, from others, usually parents, and incorporated into the system. This is medically called *'free floating anxiety'*.
ii) *Specific anxiety* related to present day situations such as mortgages or traffic jams.

A *stressor* is something that *produces* stress and ranges from a stubbed toe to a bank manager. In the times of the cave man the stressor was a predator and the normal resting state was maintained after the predator was disposed of. In today's society the predator (the bank manager or tax man) is constantly with us, so no return to the resting state occurs.

Our bodies have not changed with the times and our protective stress reaction gets ready to deal with the stressor using out of date weapons.

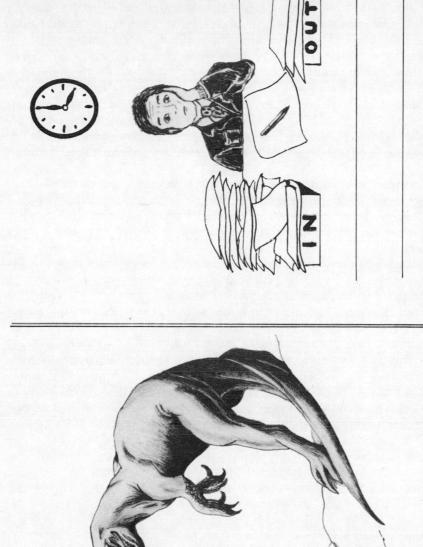

Diagram 12A   Constructive stress reaction – 165 million BC

Diagram 12B   Destructive stress reaction – twentieth century

In fact it's as if the guns are so rusty they explode in our hands when fired at the enemy.

When we are caught in a traffic jam and feel the adrenalin flow in readiness, it is of no use to fight or fly, we are hemmed in and the taxi driver in front is six foot six and eighteen stone. So we, understandably, sit fuming in the car thinking of all the problems which will occur, while the stress reaction causes all sorts of havoc with our 'vitals'.

The adrenalin increases, the sympathetic nervous system comes into action, we feel tense, the heart races, blood pressure rises, hands sweat, increased acid pours into the stomach and a feeling of 'eating up your insides' literally occurs. Energy is drained, and completely wasted. Woe betide the first person you meet when you eventually reach your destination.

Another way of looking at it is to imagine an Olympic sprinter training for years for his big race at the games. He is in peak condition on the day, his mind and body finely honed by all he has gone through in preparation for the ten seconds when he will give his all. All systems are on alert.

He walks to the starting blocks, adjusts them, looks at his competitors and the massive crowd filling the stadium. Everything inside him is racing as he gets on his mark, he leans forward, his eyes staring ahead, his muscles straining. The starter calls 'get set', he takes a big breath, raises his body slightly in anticipation, takes his weight on his fingers, he has an explosive feeling inside, a ton of energy waiting to be released.

Nothing happens. No pistol shot. He waits. Internal systems on the alert draining precious energy, still full of anticipation he waits. Minutes pass by, he has to keep at the ready for that starter's gun, all those years of work flash by as time progresses. Hours pass, he is still there waiting, his rocket fuel is burning out and he is going nowhere.

This imaginary situation illustrates in an exaggerated way how our bodies' reaction is constantly being unfulfilled. The chronic results are a breakdown in many different aspects of the internal systems.

Emotional stress reactions cover the spectrum of mental and physical disorders. Headaches, hypertension, ulcers, heart attacks, bowel disorders, pain, skin conditions, irritability, premenstrual tension, asthma, insomnia, 'nervous breakdown' to name a few.

Many doctors believe our immune system efficiency is reduced by stress. This may be the underlying cause of infections and even cancer, as the body's defence mechanisms are depleted by the constant fight against the dinosaurs of the past.

So it would be hard for me to overestimate the problems stress may cause. As hypnosis and relaxation are one way of dealing with stress, it is important for you to realise first if you are under undue stress, then I will explain ways to reduce this to a safer level.

HOW DO YOU KNOW IF YOU ARE UNDER STRESS?

There are a multitude of signs, some of which are obvious, others require a trained eye to detect.

Let us take an imaginary morning in the life of John Smith, insurance salesman, average man with a wife, two kids, house mortgaged, car on hire purchase.

At 7 a.m. the alarm bell rings, starting him off in an irritated mood. It is raining. His wife gives him a peck on the cheek and gets to the bathroom first. He looks at the clock and thinks, 'I'm going to be late' and lights up the first fag of the day. Coughing violently at the first drawback (in more ways than one), bracing his nerves for the busy day ahead, he gives a big sigh.

His wife takes longer in the bathroom than he expects, he goes downstairs and picks up the mail. All the letters have windows – bills for the car and house: electricity, 'phone, gas, plumber, etc.

When he gets to the bathroom the kids are screaming, they can't find their socks, the dog is jumping all over the bed with muddy paws. He looks in the mirror through the smoke haze and doesn't like (or even recognise) what he sees. He lathers his face for a shave, turns on the tap. The water is cold. His wife has used all the hot water with her shower.

And so it goes on. Is it not understandable that our body equipped to deal with brontosauruses has trouble with cold shaving water? Stressors are everywhere. Hidden in the cupboard is a shoelace about to break, keys hide themselves under cushions, shirts develop a stain in the wrong place at the wrong time, and so on.

In those situations we do not need a portable adrenalin meter to tell us we are under stress, the glance in the mirror told us that. But there are many long term events which cause us stress which we do not recognise. These events may be in the past, but the memory in the back of our minds still causes the stress reaction of panic, nervous tension, irritability, etc.

In order to detect if you are under stress from whatever cause, let's look at the various systems of the body and mind and do a check. What we are looking for are signs of stress that are not being dealt with satisfactorily.

1. The skin
Excess sweating, skin rashes, itching, blushing, psoriasis, eczema, boils, dermatitis, hair falling out (not hereditary baldness), worry wrinkles from constant frowning, nail biting, recurrent skin infections.

2. *The muscles*

Increased muscle tightness or tension. This is commonly found in the neck or scalp, jaws, shoulders, abdomen, clenched fists, tremors, tension in back muscles. Often this constant tension causes pain in the area such as back pain or headaches, painful neck or abdominal pains.

3. *The heart and blood vessels*

Palpitations, angina, history of heart attacks, high blood pressure, chest pains.

4. *Gastrointestinal system*

Recurrent diarrhoea or constipation, bowel cramps, indigestion or peptic ulcers, abdominal pains, increased wind.

5. *The nervous system*

Nerves 'on edge', headaches, insomnia, depression, anxiety, uncontrolled temper, wide mood swings, memory loss, nervous habits, chronic tiredness, 'uptight', 'not able to cope', etc.

6. *Weight*

Our weight may be a useful indication of how we cope with stressful situations. Being either overweight or underweight may be a sign that stressors are being dealt with by our eating pattern. Eating, like smoking, is one not so successful way of dealing with stress.

7. *Reproductive systems*

Pregnancy and delivery are often very stressful situations. Pre-menstrual tension, difficulty with intercourse either from the male or female situation. Painful intercourse, premature ejaculation, failure of erection, are some of the psychosexual disorders, as well as reduced libido (sexual desire) that result from strain.

You may feel I have gone 'overboard' in my list, but I can assure you I have not. I am not saying every condition mentioned is always due to stress, but stress plays a major role in many such cases.

WHAT CAN WE DO TO DIMINISH THE STRESS RESPONSE?

Now that you have some idea what stress is and how it may be caused, let us move to the important part of the chapter. How you can reduce the punishment your body is receiving.

There are four levels at which you can reinforce your weapons in the battle. You may choose to use one or all of these tactics.

1. Deal with the stressor in a more appropriate way.
2. Alter the internal 'self-talk'.
3. Relax the body.
4. Relax the mind with self-hypnosis.

1. Dealing with the stressor

If John's stress level rises to a fever pitch when his wife stays too long in the bathroom he could

a) talk to his wife about it then or later,
b) make sure he gets to the bathroom first,
c) occupy his mind with something else such as reading the paper.

With many stressful situations there are practical alternatives to the way we are handling them. I won't enumerate them but I'm sure you can think of alternative ways of behaviour (especially when not actually involved in the situation) which would be more suitable next time.

2. Altering the internal 'self-talk'

We constantly talk to ourselves in our minds. This 'self-talk' may be negative and so magnify the problems we face and its associated tension. It may be painting a disastrous picture which is far from the truth.

'If she stays there much longer my breakfast will be cold, I'll miss the train and I'll have to wait twenty minutes, the next train will probably be crowded, I won't get a seat, the driver may go to sleep, the train will be derailed, we'll all be killed. All because she stays in the bloody shower all morning.'

This sort of self-talk is not very helpful. Perhaps an alternative, more appropriate, internal dialogue may be suitable.

'She's got a long day ahead with the kids and her job, and her mother's ill, I'll let her enjoy the hot water a little longer, in fact I'll slip down and get her some tea and toast when she eventually decides to come out of the bloody shower.'

Sarcastic and facetious I may be, but I'm sure you get the point. I don't say it is easy, but I maintain it is possible.

3. Relaxing the body

This is a very important and practical way you can reduce the stress level in your system. I will take you through a ten minute relaxation exercise which I feel is 'life-saving' in many situations. Doing this exercise daily or twice daily may seem a real chore, but being off work for three months following a heart attack isn't much fun either.

Allocate a time and place to do this exercise on a *daily* basis. Don't *find* the time, *make* it. You should not be disturbed by 'phone, wife, kids, dogs, etc. If necessary hang a sign on the door 'Survival time, interruption may cause death.' Make sure you have no need to go to the toilet.

Sit in a comfortable chair or lie down on the bed, couch or floor. Ensure the temperature is suitable (one patient complained he couldn't relax; I understood when he told me he had chosen to lie on a stone floor during a winter when snow had stopped the city).

When you feel comfortable concentrate on your breathing, close your eyes if it makes you feel more relaxed. Allow your breathing to become slow, not forced, more in your abdomen than your chest. At each breath *out* imagine you are breathing some tightness or tension out of your body.

Concentrate on a part of your body and breathe the tension out of it. Notice the muscles becoming more relaxed as you do so. If you feel more comfortable you can have appropriately calming music playing softly in the background.

After a few minutes, starting at your toes and working your way up, *slowly contract* then *relax* each part of the body. I will name them in order:

Toes:	Screw up your toes, feel the tightness, then let them go, notice the difference.
Ankles:	Pull your feet towards your head so you feel tightness in the ankles. Let go.
Calf muscles:	Tighten then relax.
Thigh muscles:	Tighten then relax.
Abdominal muscles:	Tighten then relax.
Clench fists:	Then relax them – imagine squeezing any irritating thoughts or feelings out of your body.
Bend elbows up:	Then relax them.
Shrug shoulders:	Then relax them.
Clench teeth:	Then relax and let the jaw drop open a little.
Screw up eyelids:	Then relax.
Raise eyebrows:	Then relax.
Tense neck muscles:	Then relax.

Take a deep breath in, then slowly let it out and feel the relaxation all over your body.

Remain in that state for a few minutes. Check that all your body is relaxed. If there is some part still tense concentrate on reducing that tension.

When ten minutes is up gradually open your eyes and slowly get up and get on with your daily life.

In this way you can reduce the tension and stressful effects incorporated in your body.

During the day your body may be giving you signs that stress is building up and you can help that situation by altering the body's response.

If you notice your breathing is more rapid, slow it down. If your muscles are tense – jaw tight, hands clenched – loosen them. If you are assuming a tense position with neck stiff, shoulders hunched – relax them. If you notice your voice is louder, higher pitched and more rapid – slow it down (see diagram 13 on page 184).

Hyperventilation is a term used to describe overbreathing. Many people breathe too rapidly or too deeply for their body's requirements. This produces a decrease in carbon dioxide in the blood and *many many* symptoms may result from this.

Learning to breathe correctly, that is at a suitable rate using the diaphragm rather than the chest, can make dramatic changes to how you feel. This requires some instruction from a qualified physiotherapist as hyperventilation is often a long-standing habit. Doctors are finding this to be related to a multitude of illnesses which were previously thought to be due to other causes.

Anxiety is greatly increased if the breathing pattern is incorrect and just altering this pattern may change someone from a 'nervous wreck' to a competent relaxed person. In order to tell if you are a hyperventilator, stand up, place one hand on your chest and the other on your abdomen. Breathe normally and notice if the upper or lower hand is moving. If it is the upper hand you are breathing incorrectly and this may be an underlying cause of unexplained symptoms.

If your lower hand is moving and your upper (chest) hand is still, then you are using your diaphragm, which is the correct organ for breathing at rest. The chest is used for extra oxygen as in the fight or flight response.

4. Relaxing the mind

I regard the mind as a container. It has a certain capacity to hold stressful situations but when it overflows all sorts of problems occur as listed in the illnesses previously. There will always be a certain base level of stress but we can minimise the overflow by:

1. reducing this base level,
2. dealing with ingoing stress so as not to raise the level (see diagram 14A on page 185).

Relaxing the mind is incorporated in self-hypnosis and is a very useful way of dealing with the stress level to prevent it overflowing. Energy requirements are improved by blocking the drainage of energy caused by not coping with stress properly (see diagram 14B on page 185).

I will now describe one way of relaxing the mind which is called a *visualisation method*. It would be suitable to follow after the body relaxation previously described.

Let us assume you have achieved relaxation in your muscles and are sitting or lying comfortably. Think of a scene you find most relaxing.

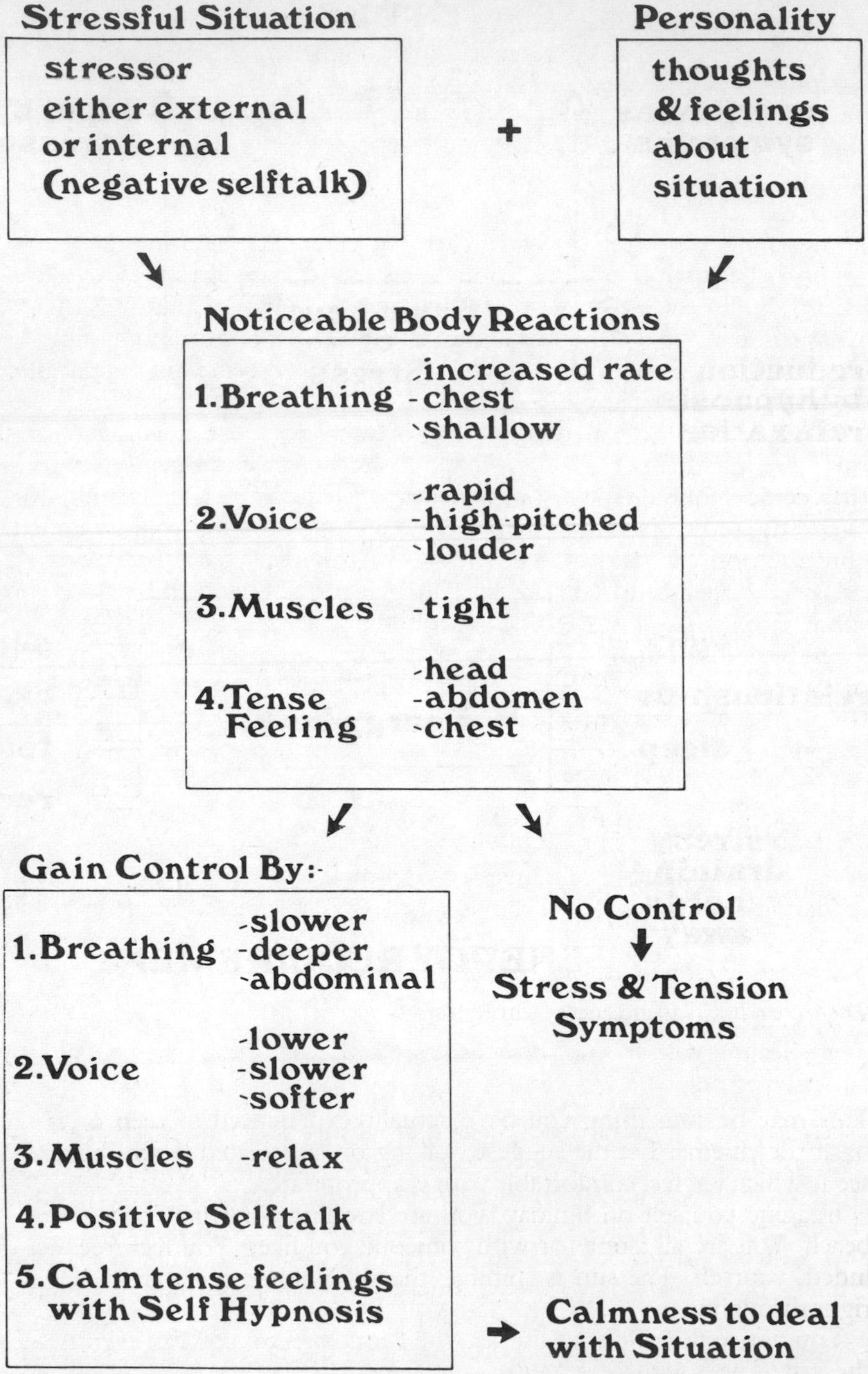

Stressful Situation

stressor
either external
or internal
(negative selftalk)

+

Personality

thoughts
& feelings
about
situation

Noticeable Body Reactions

1. Breathing
- increased rate
- chest
- shallow

2. Voice
- rapid
- high-pitched
- louder

3. Muscles
- tight

4. Tense Feeling
- head
- abdomen
- chest

Gain Control By:-

1. Breathing
- slower
- deeper
- abdominal

2. Voice
- lower
- slower
- softer

3. Muscles - relax

4. Positive Selftalk

5. Calm tense feelings with Self Hypnosis

No Control

↓

Stress & Tension Symptoms

→ **Calmness to deal with Situation**

Diagram 13   Stress awareness and control

STRESS

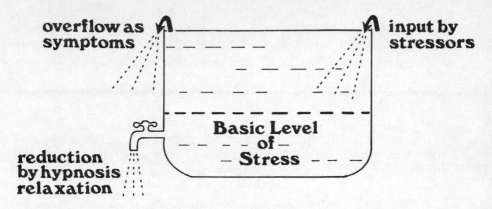

overflow as symptoms ╱╲ _____ ╱╲ **input by stressors**

Basic Level of Stress

reduction by hypnosis relaxation

Diagram 14A   The mind as a stress container

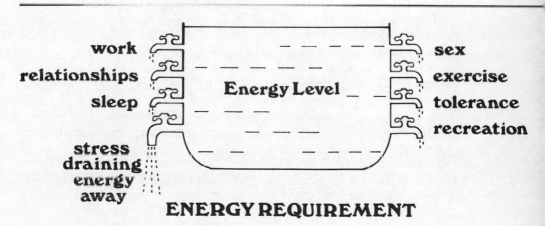

work **sex**
relationships **exercise**
sleep **Energy Level** **tolerance**
recreation

stress draining energy away

ENERGY REQUIREMENT

Diagram 14B   Wasting energy through stress

This may be something you have actually experienced or seen on TV or at the cinema. Let me suggest walking on an isolated beach, but *any* scene which *you* feel comfortable with is appropriate.

Imagine yourself on holiday, you are strolling (or lying) on a lovely beach. You are all alone (or with someone you like). You feel free, secluded, yourself. The sun is shining, the sky is blue, the warmth filters right through you.

You notice the colour of the sea, the gentle breeze; you can even smell the salt. The sound of seagulls can be heard and time is non-existent.

The soft sand feels so good under your bare feet, the gentle lap of the waves on the shore makes you feel sleepy.

You decide to lie in the warm sand, perhaps let it run through your fingers. You feel dreamy and dozy and a wonderful appreciation of having nothing to do but just *be* there. Allow your mind to wander in a really passive way. Allow any thoughts of 'the other world' to pass through, don't try and stop them. Don't try at all.

Allow yourself to be a 'receiver' of any messages from the mind or body. The comfort of it all right through you. As if energy is being restored, tension draining away into the sand.

Just *be* there. Nothing matters, nothing to do. Allow the sounds of the scene to be a part of the relaxation; perhaps view 'the other world' from the safe distance of the beach, allowing things to settle into perspective.

Perhaps allow some thoughts, some decisions, commitments for an altered attitude when you 'return' there.

Be aware of how calm, how serene, how tranquil you feel. Store that feeling for future use. Remain in that state as long as you wish.

When you are ready gradually allow yourself to 'come out' of that relaxed state. You may feel refreshed as if you have had a swim in that blue water, perhaps noticing you have more energy.

Get into a routine of doing this, not when you are tired at the end of the day and in bed about to go to sleep – although it would be helpful if you have sleep problems – but first thing in the morning or at lunch time to restore your mind's capacity for dealing with stress.

Here is another example of this form of visual imagery for self-hypnosis, using a different scene:

1. Stare at a point in front of you. Choose a specific point and continue to look at it as if your beam of vision is connecting your eyes to that point.
2. Keep your eyes open until the eyelids feel heavy and want to close. Allow your mind to wander, your breathing to become slow and calm, your muscles to relax.
3. When your eyelids become heavy and it is a strain to keep them open, allow them to slowly close, breathing out at the same time.
4. Just enjoy doing nothing for a minute or so, being aware of any of your thoughts, your body, your breathing. Don't try and do anything, whatever happens is all right.
5. Imagine you are at the top of some stairs. Ten stairs in all. Slowly, in your own time, count from 1 to 10 going down one step with each number; coincide your breathing out with each number, with each step down. Maybe you'll have a picture or a feeling of the stairs.

6. At the bottom of the stairs is a garden. A very special garden of your own choice. You go into the garden. You feel really good in this garden, nothing to worry you there. You stroll around the garden feeling more and more at peace, more and more tranquil, more and more your real self, all in your own time, little by little.

7. You allow the world at the top of the stairs to drift away. Passively strolling around the garden, time is irrelevant; you notice the flowers, shrubs, trees. Feel the cushion-like grass under your feet, the fresh air scented with flowers, the colours of leaves and the blue sky.

8. After a while you sit on a garden seat and let all the surroundings engulf you. *Be* there absorbing the sounds of the birds, the rustle of the leaves, the sound of silence. Notice the warmth of the filtered sun, the pattern of dappled light and feel the peace, serenity and calmness filtering through you.

9. You may talk to yourself, give yourself advice about activities in the life at the top of the stairs. Realise the benefit that this tranquillity will make to counteract the stress. Store the feeling somewhere for future use. Perhaps the picture of it all or the sounds or feeling of that place will come to mind at a future time.

10. Notice how your body feels. Perhaps it's warm and heavy, or peaceful and floating. Notice how you don't want to move, to think, to do anything.

11. Begin to learn from the plants, insects and trees around you. Notice how different they all are, yet they fit into a group, a society. The colour of each blade of grass is a slightly different shade of green, each is unique, yet fits into the overall pattern of the lawn.

12. Allow the conscious, critical, controlling part of your mind to drift away. It has no role in this garden. This is a passive garden to allow the back of the mind to drift into view.

13. Remain there for however long you feel comfortable, for your own time. When you are ready to come out of that scene, come slowly up the stairs counting from 10 to 1, one number for each stair on each inspiration.

14. Allow a little time to enjoy the experience, whatever it was.

Each time you do this you may find it becomes easier, deeper, less under conscious control. I doubt if you will feel any change the first few times, but gradually as you become familiar with the routine you will notice yourself 'letting go' a little more. It's as if you are exploring unknown territory: as you discover little things you will feel more secure and safer to progress, and you will proceed further and further into the trance state at your own pace. Your ability to relax will increase and the tension and anxiety will diminish.

You may feel it will help to read what I have written out loud and tape record it; listening to your voice or someone else's voice saying the words will allow you to let them passively float through your mind. I often use a tape of birdsong as soothing background noise.

Your personality plays a major role in how stress will affect you and how you can deal with it. As well as external stressors, the ruminations of the mind also produce stress. People who are perfectionists, rigid and inflexible, those who have a low self-esteem and continually run themselves down, shy people, pessimists, worriers, those who bottle up their feelings, who resort to alcohol or drugs to calm themselves down, those controlled by guilt or who brood over past events all have an increased tendency to become stressed. I suppose you could sum them up as being inflexible, unable to cope easily with life, not being themselves.

With such people there is voluminous negative self-talk, where they tell themselves 'I'm no good, it won't work, I can't do it, it will all go wrong, it's not fair, why does it always happen to me.' This negative attitude often plays a role in the tension felt by these people. Their 'failure' in society or with themselves brings about both internal and external strains and pressures on their lifestyle and those around them.

We all have a little of those characteristics in us and there are many books and charts to help you understand your 'stress rating' or ability to deal with the stressful situations of life.

PERFORMANCE STRESS

In some areas of life when we are called upon to perform, the nervous tension involved minimises our performance. After dinner speaking, exams, cocktail parties, driving tests, competitions, meeting strangers and many other situations, are so stressful to some people that they avoid them or 'make a mess of them'.

Using self-hypnosis to have a 'dress rehearsal' of the event and to be your own 'coach or director' will often provide a means of coping with the situation in a more relaxed way.

Imagine you have had some driving lessons. Your teacher thinks you are competent and ready to take the test. You have heard so many stories of failure that you dread the day of the test and you develop panic feelings just at the thought of it.

1. Allow yourself twenty minutes on your own each day.
2. Do the physical relaxation mentioned earlier.

3. When you are relaxed imagine setting out for the test. If you feel nervous thinking about it wait until you have calmed down before proceeding.
4. Get a picture in your mind of how it will be with the instructor driving you to the test site. Allow your breathing to relax you.
5. Imagine the examiner greeting you and asking you to lead him to your car. Remain calm and keep telling yourself you will be all right. Repeat your instructor's words of encouragement. Ignore the negative messages which may be spinning around in the back of your mind.
6. Go through the test route in your mind. Calm, comfortable and confident. It is only a test route not a war. It is not a life and death matter; at the worst you will repeat it and learn from the experience. Correct any negative tense-making thoughts or feelings. Go through the whole test course and then walk back with the examiner and receive his congratulations at having passed.
7. Stay with that feeling for a little while and give yourself a 'pep talk' about how nice it will be when it is all over.
8. Allow your eyes to open and keep any positive, confident feelings that remain.
9. Do this every day and again on the morning of the test.

Similarly with exam nerves: for some weeks before, have a 're-run' of the exam in a relaxed state, and perhaps spend five minutes at the start of the exam in a relaxed state after reading the paper. This will help the unconscious to allow its knowledge to filter through to the conscious mind. A recent Mastermind winner stated he used self-hypnosis before and during the competition.

Many great sportsmen have used hypnosis before and during their events. This allows the restrictive nervous tension to be diminished. Golfers, tennis players, snooker players, all play better if their muscles are allowed to move unhindered by spasms created by tension.

PANIC STATES

In these situations the person feels a panic coming on for no apparent reason. He feels well, then gets an ominous feeling that an attack is about to occur. His pulse races, his breathing increases, he goes pale and sweaty, has the 'indescribable feeling he is going to die'. This may last seconds or minutes and sometimes longer.

The cause is most likely an unconscious memory flooding the conscious mind, due to a thought or trivial incident that brings the recall. The fear of it recurring often plays a role (see page 73, self-fulfilling prophecies) and treatment may vary from a glass of brandy or a sedative to a long analytical process.

Hypnosis is very useful in this condition either to uncover the initial situation or to provide relaxation and calmness when a panic attack is imminent. Realising that these attacks can be controlled by progressive relaxation, slowing the breathing and preventing hyperventilation, often reduces the fear and allows self-confidence to return. By regularly practising self-hypnosis the attacks will be reduced.

In conclusion, I would like to describe a metaphor to illustrate how we can cope with our difficulties on a day to day basis.

Imagine life is like a road. You are on one side of the road and you have a daily quota of bricks to carry across. You then move up the road a little and carry the bricks back. So day after day you are transferring these bricks further along the road of life and zig-zagging across the road on your way.

The elements concerned with how your journey proceeds are:

1. The number of bricks you carry,
2. Your ability to carry bricks,
3. The traffic along the road,
4. The distance you move each day.

Let us consider the components.

1. The bricks

These are like our problems and difficulties. If we deal with the daily quota then we may be able to carry these quite easily. If we carry bricks from the past and also from the future (past and future worries) our job becomes much more difficult and tedious.

2. Our ability

Our ability to carry the bricks depends on our actual strength and our opinion of ourselves. If we feel we are competent and capable we *will* be. If we have self-doubt, low self-esteem and are critical of our ability, we will be able to use only part of our strength. So carrying the daily quota will be a strain.

3. The road traffic

These are events beyond our control, daily mishaps and stresses which interfere with our progress. The ability to deal with these stressors depends on our attitudes, how slow or incompetent at crossing the road we are, if we give up or hurry too much. This illustrates how we cope with the regular misfortunes that come our way.

4. The distance we move each day is of our own choice

Some people try and do too much and cross rapidly from side to side, running unnecessary risks. Others choose minimal progress and are slow to learn about life and its ups and downs.

If you are having trouble coping with the stresses of life as you progress, there may be some factors which you can alter to make your load easier. Providing an 'oasis' of relaxation and self-hypnosis on your travels in the hot sun may allow for a more enjoyable trip.

25 *Obesity*

We live on one-third of the food we eat. Doctors and
diet organisations live on the other two-thirds.

If life is a journey, obesity is the excess luggage which
spoils the trip.

If there is any part of our life for which we cannot delegate responsibility
to other people it is for our weight. It is your hand that puts the food
into your mouth. In life's other problems we can find reasons outside
ourselves which we can use as excuses.

With weight, unfortunately, it is up to you to be in control. Yet of
all the conditions we are affected by, there are more excuses for being
overweight than any other I know.

'I only drink twelve pints of beer a day – that won't put on weight, will
it?'
'It's my glands doctor.'
'It's not fair, my husband eats like a pig and is as thin as a rake.'
'I only eat a lettuce leaf every three weeks, I don't know why I'm 20 stone.'
'I only have to look at food and I put on weight.'
'It's all the hassle of work that makes me put on weight.'
'It's my husband's fault; whenever he nags I binge.'
'The problem is I'm retaining too much fluid.'

And so it goes on time after time; people allocate responsibility to
something or someone else other than the hand which feeds them.

Obesity is a very difficult condition to cure. The multitude of diets,
books, clubs, theories on the market demonstrate that we don't have
the answer. I don't have the answer either, but perhaps I can help you
understand the problem a little better which may be useful in teaching
you how to control your weight.

In order to understand the problem let's start at the beginning. A
baby is born with a need for milk to survive, a metabolism to digest
the milk and convert it into energy and protein for building tissues.

The amount required will vary for each individual – this is an important fact to grasp.

Mother and the doctors don't know *exactly* how much that baby requires but they have a good approximation from experience. The only way the baby can let anyone know it needs more milk is by crying. The problem is that it may cry for other reasons, but, as we don't know what they are, we generally give milk to deal with the crying.

In time the baby may enjoy the attention associated with feeding and therefore drink when it is not necessary. Let us assume that at birth a baby has a mechanism which could be represented as:

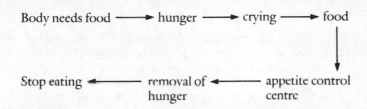

After being digested, the food goes via the bloodstream to the brain. In the brain there is a small area called the appetite control centre (or satiety centre) where what has been eaten is registered. There is some delay between eating and registering what has been eaten. This is an important concept to understand.

This mechanism, which tells us when we have had enough food, is very delicately balanced. As we grow and mother dictates what we eat and when, this mechanism is constantly overridden. Instead of the child knowing and directing when he should eat, time and social factors dictate the feeding schedule so the innate control is taken over.

When he is not hungry and leaves some food he is told not to waste food, but to finish what is on the plate. Meal times often develop into 'battlegrounds' where food is the ammunition for both sides rather than nourishment for the body. Whatever his needs, he is told he should have three meals a day.

So as adults we may have lost the ability or willpower to eat when required and stop when we have had enough. The perfect balance of this device is seen in wild animals, they eat when hungry and stop – leaving part of the carcass if they are carnivorous – when they have had enough. That is why we don't see fat animals, except ones where humans have been involved in their feeding.

One of the main aims of weight control is to remove the layers of miscontrol which have superseded the one nature provided, and to get back to our natural individual mechanisms for starting and stopping eating.

As the baby grows the value of food is represented in a multitude of ways. It is a link with the mother – with survival. From the mother's side it is a sign of *love*: she gives food, gives herself, gives love. And so food takes on a different perspective from the original need for survival, to supply the body with nourishment to build growing tissues.

Food becomes a handy convenience to deal with many aspects of life. It is handy because it is available in many forms, varieties, tastes and it is convenient because it is easily acquired, readily accessible and acceptable as the 'currency' of the culture.

'Poor dear, you've fallen over, have a sweetie and it won't hurt so much.'

'You have a cold. Have something to eat and you'll get better quickly.'

'You are feeling low, here, have a piece of cake, that will brighten you up.'

'You look tired – here, have a good cup of soup and you'll have more energy.'

'I'm so sad your boyfriend didn't turn up. Never mind, come and have a cup of tea and a biscuit and you'll soon forget about him.'

And so it goes on and on, food forever satisfying needs which are not fulfilled in other areas: food the comforter, food the pacifier, food the healer, food the carrier of love.

So in the back of the mind a tape is switched on: 'Food will make *it* better', '*it*' covering the spectrum of negative emotions we go through during our growing years.

The fact is food does *NOT* make '*it*' better. With overweight people food makes it worse because as well as not solving the problem it adds another. The 'food will make it better' tape, plays whenever things go wrong and instead of seeking a solution to the problem or an acceptance of it, the refrigerator is consulted as having the answer to all things. Self-hypnosis can be used to change the tape to 'food will *not* make it better' (see diagram 15).

As the person (let's say a woman) grows and becomes overweight, the excess fat becomes involved in her lifestyle. She learns to use it for comfort, to hide behind, to punish herself, to gain attention, to punish others, as an excuse for failure and so it becomes part of her way of dealing with life.

So as the years pass a pattern is formed. On the one hand desperate attempts are made to lose weight – diets, calorie counting, etc., – and on the other hand there is a fear of losing weight because it provides such a resource to deal with problems.

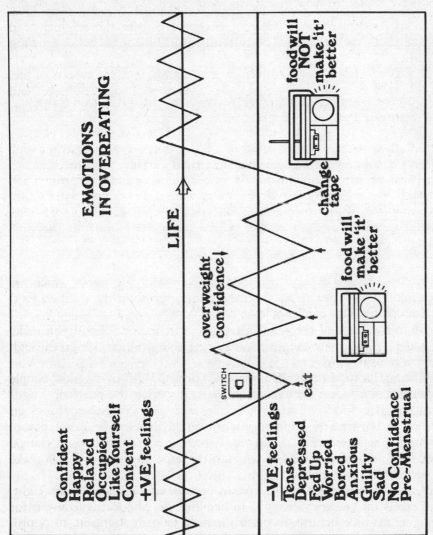

Diagram 15 Emotions in over-eating

HEALTH ASPECTS OF OBESITY

As well as the psychological effects of being overweght, there are many physical problems caused or exacerbated by excess fat. The harmful symptoms are related to how much overweight people are; the more fat the greater the problem.

Statisticians realise these harmful effects and as a result insurance policies are 'loaded' if the client is overweight. A range of normal values has been determined depending on age, sex and height. Problems occur when the weight is outside this range, but the *worry* of being a few pounds overweight probably causes more trouble than the actual weight does.

In order to simplify the medical hazards I have listed them according to the body systems affected. To appreciate the body's point of view I suggest, when next in a supermarket, you count the number of bags of sugar equivalent to your excess weight (if there are enough in the shop). Hold the sugar and walk around with it for two minutes (if the store detective accosts you tell him you are under doctor's orders) and appreciate what your body is carrying around all day.

THE CARDIOVASCULAR SYSTEM

If you can imagine a second-hand car driving around with fifty bricks on the roof, you may get an idea of the strain excess fat puts on the heart and blood vessels. The car engine is forced to perform much harder than it was built for and so wear and tear on all the parts is increased.

So it is with the heart; it needs to pump blood for one and a half bodies when it was not constructed to do so. The strain involved in increasing the work of the heart, which beats approximately 120,000 times a day, is shown in angina, heart attacks, palpitations. If you are a stone overweight hold fourteen pounds of sugar and squat down and stand up twenty times. Then put the sugar down, do the same thing and notice the difference. Your poor heart is doing that 120,000 times a day, 365 days a year, so it's no wonder that in many cases it gives up. How would you feel towards the person who forced you to carry that sugar with you wherever you go? Perhaps that is how the heart feels towards its overweight boss.

High blood pressure is helped dramatically in most cases by losing excess weight. It is the first thing cardiologists advise before using chemical therapy. The complications of high blood pressure are strokes (cerebral haemorrhage) or heart attacks.

RESPIRATORY SYSTEM

The diaphragm moving up and down is responsible for breathing at rest. The pot belly restricts this movement and limits the breathing capacity. A common reason for seeking help for obesity is shortness of breath. 'I didn't realize what my fat was doing to me until I tried to run for a bus and puffed like an asthmatic Pekinese' or 'I walked up some stairs and I couldn't speak for five minutes I was so out of breath.'

It is such a pleasure to see these people, after they have lost weight, come running up the stairs, beaming, to prove their fitness.

People with chest diseases – emphysema, bronchitis, asthma and chronic smokers – are much more limited if they are overweight. The extra weight may be the straw that breaks the camel's back and causes death from respiratory failure.

THE JOINTS

The joints of the spine, hip, knee and ankle all bear the brunt of the extra weight. Damage to the cartilage of the joint and increased 'wear and tear' all result from the heavier load they carry. Experiments testing the internal pressure in the hip joint showed that, for every stone overweight, the joint had an increased load of two stone due to the concentration of forces internally. Hence every pound lost results in a sigh of relief from the joint equal to two pounds – that's 2 to 1, which are good odds for any gambler.

Operations are much more difficult and the complications are increased for the obese. Surgery becomes a nightmare to the patient, surgeon, anaesthetist and nursing staff. Firstly, it is more difficult to diagnose some conditions if a thick layer of fat is between the palpating hand of the doctor and the diseased organ. This is especially so in abdominal or gynaecological conditions. Secondly, as breathing is restricted, anaesthetic problems and risks are increased both during the operation and post operatively.

Next the surgeon has practical difficulties because of the thick layers of yellow fat limiting his access. Wound healing is impaired, time for recovery prolonged, surgical complications more likely.

The poor nurse in the ward who has to supervise post operative recovery has an increased chance of injuring her back lifting and turning fat patients. So, all in all, you can see how harmful being overweight is, not only to the proud owner of all that reserve fat, but also to those who may become involved.

As time goes by and the dislike of the extra fat becomes more intense – especially when the warm weather arrives – other feelings join the pattern. A dislike of oneself, a loss of confidence, a feeling of inferiority, a depressed feeling, all add impetus to the pathway which ends up at the refrigerator.

Other people try to help – friends, husbands, partners, but it has the reverse effect. Criticism is met with anger and food, no comment is taken as not caring, praise taken as sarcasm and so further eating occurs whatever attitude is taken. It is a pattern which repeats itself as the years go by.

I would like to list some of the characteristics of the chronically obese person. These are naturally not specific for any one person but apply to the vast majority of overweight people I have seen. I hope there are no moral judgements involved in the attitude towards obesity. In my opinion it is a condition which causes an immense amount of suffering and pain and is badly understood by the medical profession and all those who have not been overweight.

The overweight person seeking medical help for the problem has some of the following characteristics:

The person is usually female.

She will have been overweight for some years.

Her weight problem started either when she was quite young, after the birth of a child or after severe emotional strain.

Either one or both parents were overweight.

Her mother thought or talked a lot about food and insisted she eat everything on the plate. 'Think of the poor children starving in India', was a common phrase at dinner time when food was left.

She has tried many diets and weight reduction programmes.

She has constantly lost weight and put it on again.

She feels depressed, has a lack of confidence due to the excess weight.

Trying on clothes that once fitted, or new clothes which are a size larger than the previous ones, is often the reason to seek help.

She feels people don't understand her problem, her husband (boyfriend) is no help, and whatever he says makes things worse.

Her visits to doctors are generally of no help and she is told it is *her* problem, to eat less.

She is a 'nice' person who would rather say 'yes' to avoid conflict than 'no' if she means no.

She tries to please people and be liked. She doesn't want to argue and has difficulty standing up for her rights.

She doesn't have self confidence as a rule and has even less when more over-weight.

She may have periods of 'bingeing', where she seems to stuff food into her mouth with no control and feels really guilty afterwards.

She eats quickly.

She doesn't do enough exercise and regards her overweight body as 'the enemy'.

She eats because she is fed up, bored, tired, depressed, anxious, lonely or upset.

She spends very little time on herself, most of her time is spent on the family, house, friends, charities.

She feels 'it's not fair' that she has a weight problem, when others can eat what they like and stay as thin as a rake.

She weighs herself constantly and talks about weight, diets, the latest fads whenever the opportunity arises.

She has been involved in weight reducing groups such as Weight Watchers many times and felt a comfort from being associated with others with similar problems.

She buys food with the excuse that it's for her husband and children but eats it herself.

She mistakenly believes that rushing around being very busy will help lose weight.

Her mind is constantly occupied with the worry of being overweight.

As she gets older the worry becomes more of a panic that she will be a fat old lady with no hope of being slim.

She would do *anything* to lose weight and feel better.

She may prefer the company of people fatter than herself as it helps her to feel thinner.

Whenever she starts on a diet she has a good excuse (like eating something she shouldn't) for breaking it. Or she may be always *about* to start a diet. Her initial commitment is strong but fades rapidly.

She has trouble refusing food offered her, with the excuse that it is bad manners to refuse food.

She knows more about calories and diets than the doctor she visits.

The eating pattern goes haywire before a period when a craving for sweet things occurs.

The extra weight feels like a prison which restricts her from going out.

She refuses to go swimming due to the embarrassment of wearing a swimming costume.

Phrases using 'eating words' are a part of her vocabulary – 'I'm fed up', 'With all my worries I've got such a lot on my plate', 'I can't get my teeth into the problem'.

There may be some foods she refuses to buy or keep in the house, 'fear foods' in case she gets out of control.

So you can see weight is not an isolated problem but ties in a multitude of difficulties and deficiencies. Sometimes there is an underlying guilt feeling related to childhood experiences, perhaps a sexual misadventure brings about the mistaken belief that punishment is necessary. This punishment continues long after the incident is forgotten. *Guilt* is one cause of obesity.

Comfort eating is another cause. 'Things are lousy so I can at least comfort myself by eating.' This starts in childhood and becomes an un-recognised pattern when adulthood is reached, a habit ingrained.

If you must have comfort, buying small presents (not food) for yourself, may provide the desired comfort without the price of weight.

Difficulty in being assertive can be a cause of obesity. If speaking your mind is a frightening experience then eating and being fat may provide an alternative.

Society's insistence that 'being slim is being successful' implies that anyone overweight is abnormal, an inferior citizen. This is an artificial criterion of how we should look, and attempting to fit into this concept may cause more worry than benefit.

Sometimes in a relationship the extra weight has multiple functions. It is a focal point for tension and arguments. It is an avenue for excuses. If the relationship is breaking down but the female partner fears leaving, then obesity may be used as an excuse for not leaving: 'If I was slimmer I would leave and find another man, but as I'm fat no-one else would have me, so I'd better stay.'

It may be used to embarrass and punish the partner, part of whose belief is 'He should like me as I am, I'm not going to lose weight just because he likes me when I'm slim.'

There are many incorrect lessons which we learn in childhood about eating which cause a lot of problems.

'You must have three good meals a day.'
'You must not drink with your food.'
'You must finish what is on the plate.'
'You must not eat before bedtime.'

There is often a gross misconception about *why* people eat. Many people eat because it is the time of day to eat or someone else is eating, or they have a feeling they label as 'hunger', which may be anything from anxiety to indigestion.

So you may now begin to understand the enormity (no pun intended) of the problem. So many factors are involved it's no wonder that the weight reduction industry is as gross as it is.

I would like to discuss a few points about weight reduction which may be helpful. I offer no guarantees of success, but I suggest if you follow the advice you will have a much greater chance of losing weight and staying slimmer.

The basic aim is to eat the correct amount of food *for your body* and to stop when you have had enough. It is important to have suitable exercise and other ways besides eating of dealing with the stresses of life.

I am going to list the factors involved and the changes you may need to make. Obviously many of the things I mention will not apply to you, but if you have a weight problem the *only way* you can deal with it is by making a change in some aspect of your life. If you are not prepared to make any changes, learning to accept your obesity may be the only choice for you.

1. *Diets* are seldom successful. A diet implies a temporary change of eating pattern with associated weight loss, followed by returning to the original pattern and accompanying weight gain.
2. *Eating pattern*
   Examine why you eat, how you eat, what you eat.

WHY YOU EAT

I would like you to consider yourself as a *mind* and a *body*. (See Chapter 22) *Eating is often done for the mind*, as previously discussed, when in fact it is to provide nourishment for your body.

If you are overweight it means your body does *not need* food, you are eating for your mind and your poor body is carrying the can. Whenever you put something to your lips ask yourself, 'Does my body need this?' If the answer is 'no', don't eat it. You will say, 'But I'm always hungry.' Hunger is a feeling provided by nature to prevent you dying of starvation. What you are feeling is a habit or false hunger, because you have been eating excessively for so long.

This habit hunger may be pain, discomfort or rumbling but it is not hunger. It is not the message to eat. It may be a message about anger, loneliness, boredom, tension, none of which are resolved by food. You may have been misinterpreting this message from your body for ages.

It is similar to driving a car and the fuel gauge registers empty. You go to a petrol station and fill the tank. After a few minutes driving, the gauge again registers empty and you pull into the next station but, in putting petrol into an already full tank, it spills on the ground.

The problem is the faulty gauge, not the need of the car. So it is with the body. The appetite control centre which hasn't worked properly for years is not letting you know when you have had enough. Its wishes have been overridden since birth by other people's directions.

If the answer to why you eat is boredom, depression, tension, loneliness, then find a more suitable solution than food.

HOW YOU EAT

The most common problem with the eating pattern is that overweight people *eat too quickly*. There is not enough time for the food to be digested and to reach the appetite control centre. So over-eating occurs. I remember having a meal and then being asked if I'd like some cheese. I really felt like it and so I answered yes. I was then called to the 'phone and when I returned I realised I couldn't possibly eat the cheese. In my absence there was time for my appetite control centre to register that I'd had enough.

Eating slowly is one of the most important things to do if you have a weight problem. Eat from a small plate as we do have a habit of finishing whatever is in front of us. If a large plate of food is given to us we will eat it all even while we protest that it is too much.

Eat in relaxed surroundings. If you have small children, feed them first, as getting up and down all the time hinders the digestion.

Decide what amount of food is right for you, don't let others decide. I know this may be difficult but you wouldn't buy a pair of shoes in a shop and leave without trying them on. So it is with the food requirement. If you eat everything that is given to you it is like taking the shoes which the shop assistant chose for you.

Learn to eat when your body needs it and to stop when you have had enough.

WHAT YOU EAT

Some foods will put on more weight for you. You will know them better from experience than anyone else. Avoid or limit these. I know you will say 'but I love them'. Unfortunately you have a choice – enjoy these foods or enjoy being slimmer.

There are many books by eminent dieticians advising on foods. I do not wish to enter this debate. There are obvious foods and drinks which have so many calories it would be foolish to eat them except in minimal amounts.

Some people tell me, 'I'm fat because I just love food, I can't resist it.' I'm sure it's true that some people really do live to eat rather than eating to live. Unfortunately the side effect of obesity follows this desire. Just as someone who loves to drive at 100 m.p.h., has a greater risk of accidents than someone who drives at 40 m.p.h. If they are prepared to take the risks and the complications then I don't feel they should hinder their desire, but they must accept that they will be overweight. It would be nice if we could have it both ways but, from my experience, 'life ain't like that.'

EXERCISE

Obesity is the result of an imbalance between food eaten and the metabolism which converts the food to energy. It is like having a fire with too much coal, to reduce the amount of coal either put less on the fire or increase the flame.

There are many factors influencing the metabolism and one is our attitude to our bodies. We have only one body and it has to last us a long time so it is advisable to look after it. Just as we service a car to ensure it works efficiently so, to get the best from our body, we should spend some time each day looking after it.

I believe it is important to spend at least ten minutes a day doing exercise. Any form of exercise may be appropriate, but the type will vary with the person. It's not a lot to ask for your body. Swimming, jogging, exercising to a record, skipping, brisk walking are all suitable. Include exercise in your daily routine – use the stairs not the lift, park the car some distance from the restaurant, get off the bus and walk some way to and from work. If it is possible to walk rather than using the car, do so. It is important to get into the habit of spending time on your body just as you spend time brushing your teeth to prevent decay.

THE MIND

This plays a vital role in either maintaining obesity or ensuring weight loss. As previously stated we often eat for our mind and use food to deal with emotional problems.

I believe that *worrying* about weight reduces the metabolism, hence less weight loss occurs. If you can *stop weighing* and stop worrying you are on the way to losing weight. People who get on and off the scales daily create a worry-eat pattern. I suggest you weigh yourself once every two weeks or not at all and just use your clothes as a guide to your weight.

Spending time on yourself each day is very important and this is where hypnosis may be useful. Allowing fifteen minutes a day *'just for yourself'* and doing self-hypnosis to relax and acquire a calmer attitude to the day's problems, is an essential part in losing weight and keeping slim.

Using hypnosis to understand previous emotions such as guilt, self-pity, anger, which may be involved in the weight problem is important to prevent the return of extra weight when future problems arise.

Use self-hypnosis to replace the old, incorrect tape in the mind 'that eating will make it better' with a new, more up-to-date, more appropriate one : 'eating will *not* make it better.'

Using self-hypnosis to build confidence and willpower, making a commitment to eat correctly and do exercise each day, provides an extra weapon in 'the battle of the bulge'.

The daily routine of self-hypnosis acts as a substitute for food in lowering tension, comforting and allowing you to feel better able to cope with daily difficulties.

Self-hypnosis is useful in helping you accept yourself, be youself, like yourself and so enable your outdated attitudes involving food such as 'I'm no good, I'm fat and useless, I may as well continue eating', to be dispensed with.

Using self-hypnosis to develop a positive attitude will improve the metabolism. I make this statement not with scientific evidence, but in observing many people who are able to deal with their weight problem much more easily when they stop thinking badly of themselves.

During self-hypnosis a positive image of the 'future you', slim, confident and happier, may be of use in enabling you to overcome the discomforts of not eating what you like, when you like.

Self-hypnosis may be useful in decoding the message the body is giving, both with the 'hunger' feelings and with the message the excess weight is trying to give. It may help you to understand how you became obese and how the obesity is continually being maintained. Self-hypnosis is also useful in diminishing the craving for sweet things pre-menstrually and the relaxation can lessen pre-menstrual tension.

Continuation of the eating directions we learnt when we were young forms a habit pattern. This pattern controls our eating without the conscious mind questioning when, where, how or why. It's as if we set our stomach on automatic pilot and pour into it whatever the habit dictates. Food offered is food eaten and once this habit gains control it is difficult to change.

Changing this incorrect eating habit is what causes all the pain and discussion about why 'we can't resist food'. The previous habit of eating may oppose how we 'ought' to eat and the old habit generally wins the tug of war.

Hypnosis may play a role in adding weight to your new resolution in this tug of war. In a trance, feeding in information to alter the pattern may reinforce the willpower. Using statements such as 'excess food is poisonous to your body, you can use willpower shown in other areas to direct you away from the fridge, you owe it to your body to look after it' or any other phrase or statement which will help you alter the pattern, will have more influence if repeated in a trance. This is because the habit is being maintained by unconscious forces.

Another way of helping to overcome the habit pattern of eating is to regard obesity as a disease similar to diabetes.

Diabetes is a disease of metabolism in which the pancreas produces less insulin, and sugar is not metabolised properly. The diabetic patient, if not aware of this, becomes very sick and may die in a diabetic coma when the blood sugar level is very high. So diabetics need to regard themselves as different from others, and eat according to a special diet with limited carbohydrate intake. They may see others eating sweet things with no problem, feel annoyed, envious and may develop the 'it's not fair' attitude, but if they stray from the diet they may end up in hospital in a coma. So bitter experience dictates their behaviour and most learn to lead a full and enjoyable life within these limitations.

We could regard people with long term obesity as having a similar metabolic disorder where, instead of a diabetic coma, obesity results if the eating pattern is not suitable for their specific metabolism. Obese people notice others eating sweet things with no problem but, unlike the diabetic don't realise that they are different, and need to conform to their own eating pattern to prevent obesity. They too can branch out and eat what they would like but they are reminded of their inevitable downfall when a mirror is next passed.

People who have conquered their obesity are like diabetics under control; they maximise their enjoyment and minimise the discomfort thrust upon them by their individual metabolic problems.

TABLETS

There are many tablets on the market to help weight loss. Some appetite suppressants, if prescribed by a doctor, may be useful in helping reduce the desire for food. Routine medical control of their use is essential and after a suitable period of time the tablets are stopped to prevent dependence.

In my experience over many years there have been negligible problems with the careful prescribing of appetite suppressants as an adjunct to all the other aspects of weight control. The tablets by themselves, without a relearning programme of eating habits, exercise and altered attitude, I feel are of very limited value and any weight that is lost will return when the tablets are stopped.

Another factor in maintaining weight loss is regular supervision by a qualified person. The fact that you will be seen by someone and admonished for failure and praised for success plays a great role in 'helping you stay on the straight and narrow'.

To summarise what is an immense subject, I would suggest that to lose weight and maintain the loss a *change* in your present habits is necessary. Correction of faults in your eating pattern, your exercise programme and your mental attitude is important, as well as patience and persistence. The race you are running is a marathon, not a sprint race, so keep in mind the necessary attitude required to complete it. At times you will fail and it is important to recognise this as a temporary failure, not an excuse to 'give up' and go back to the old, incorrect eating pattern.

It is a struggle, but I can assure you the benefits are worth it. There is a great difference between being overweight and unhappy (if being overweight causes you to feel unhappy), and losing weight and gaining confidence and optimism.

My suggestion is to analyse some of your incorrect attitudes and habits, start a plan of action and tackle it on a day to day basis. Make a commitment for twenty-four hours only and if some mistakes occur, learn from them to reinforce the next day's commitment; don't give up just because you've gone off the rails; use these mistakes to reinforce your commitment.

There may be people who are jolly and fat; I have not met too many. I have met many fat people who underneath are very unhappy and very keen to shed their excess weight and thus gain more self-confidence and self-esteem.

26 Self-confidence

Serve and obey.
MOTTO OF HABERDASHERS' ASKE'S GIRLS'
SCHOOL

Man's main task in life is to give birth to himself.
ERICH FROMM,
AMERICAN PSYCHOLOGIST

What do you think of yourself? How would you honestly fill in a form requesting your self-assessment? Would you feel that you may be boasting if you complimented yourself? Maybe you feel being humble and shy is an endearing quality. The motto of the Haberdashers' School certainly wouldn't lead to a swollen head.

In my experience one of the most important factors relating to problems people have is their low opinion of themselves. They continually limit themselves because of their poor self-esteem. If you keep under-estimating your abilities, feelings, thoughts, then you automatically magnify any problems which come on the scene.

Thinking to yourself, 'I'm really no good, I can't do this, or say that, I'm going to fail, what will people think?' is a very eroding internal dialogue. One of the main attributes of hypnosis is its ability to build up confidence.

I believe that in any hypnotic session, for whatever problem, confidence building should be incorporated. Just as a pinch of salt or some spices in cooking may make all the difference, so it is with self-confidence. Many doctors have their own ways of building confidence and I'd like to tell you a few.

The aim of confidence building in hypnosis is to use the confidence *you have* but don't realise you have. It is not to add any outside strengths. You have your own somewhere. Because of factors in the past, this confidence has been buried under a heap of negativity, guilt and self-criticism. The aim of self-hypnosis is, like a treasure hunt, to uncover the 'gold' hidden in the back of your mind. Due to lack of confidence the average man is considerably below average.

In the 1920s Emil Coué, a Belgian pharmacist, used the words, 'Every day in every way I'm getting better and better.' These were repeated fifteen times in the form of a chant, morning and night. This is basically using a positive attitude to overcome any negative tendencies.

The late Dr Milton Erickson – the father of American hypnosis – told stories about situations and people and hidden in the stories were messages of confidence. In these metaphors he informed the patient of his special and unique qualities. For example, if he was talking about a garden lawn he may say, 'In a lawn there are millions of blades of grass. Do you know each blade of grass is a different shade of green, yet together they make up this lovely expanse of green lawn', thus illustrating in an indirect way the individuality of the person in front of him.

The late Dr John Hartland – perhaps he could be called the father of modern British hypnosis – used what he called an 'ego strengthening technique'. This consisted of many phrases used to bolster the self-image of the person concerned who was directed to accept himself 'warts and all' as someone special. Any thoughts, feelings or actions were his and he should feel proud of them. He encouraged people to take off their 'dark glasses of negativity' and face the light of day.

Mr Geoff Graham is a therapist who uses a 'rebirthing' technique where clients are retaken through their birth and view it from an adult point of view. He uses a unique confidence builder:

G.G: How would you feel if you were in a marathon race against 5 million others? What chances do you think you would have of winning?

CLIENT: None at all.

G.G: How would you feel if you won?

CLIENT: I would feel fantastic but that would never happen to me.

G.G: It already has.

CLIENT: What do you mean?

G.G: Just what I say. You have already competed against at least 5 million others in a marathon race and won.

CLIENT: I don't understand.

G.G: Well, you were the sperm that won the race to the ovum and you should feel very proud and pleased with yourself.

Along the road of life our confidence and feelings of self-respect are eroded by guilt and other people's criticism. Due to situations that occur we learn to dislike and distrust ourselves. As these thoughts and feelings become part of us, our abilities are lessened and every failure reinforces this false belief.

In diagrams 16A (page 209) and 16B (page 210) a comparison between two theoretical upbringings illustrates how confidence can be made or destroyed.

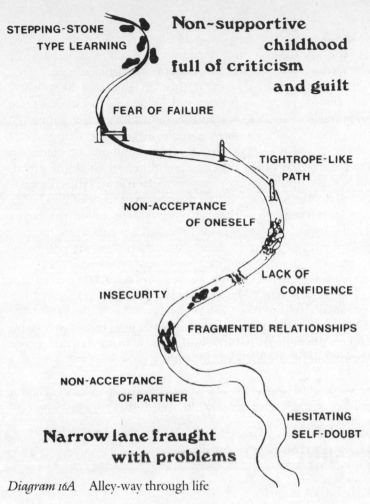

STEPPING-STONE
TYPE LEARNING

Non~supportive
childhood
full of criticism
and guilt

FEAR OF FAILURE

TIGHTROPE-LIKE
PATH

NON-ACCEPTANCE
OF ONESELF

LACK OF
CONFIDENCE

INSECURITY

FRAGMENTED RELATIONSHIPS

NON-ACCEPTANCE
OF PARTNER

Narrow lane fraught
with problems

HESITATING
SELF-DOUBT

Diagram 16A   Alley-way through life

Using self-hypnosis, old out-of-date opinions may be discarded and newer, more accurate, ones used to replace them. Going into a trance and reviewing the positive aspects of the day, small things that you have done that you can be proud of, will gradually rebuild your own, more appropriate, image of yourself. When you notice negative self-talk, tell yourself it is from the past and no longer true.

The aim is to learn to feel good about yourself, learn to like yourself, even love yourself. To realise that you *are* special, in spite of what you or anyone else thought, is a great start and a great weapon to deal with life's problems.

As you learn this, in your own way and your own time, you will find yourself becoming more assertive, standing up for yourself, not apologising all the time.

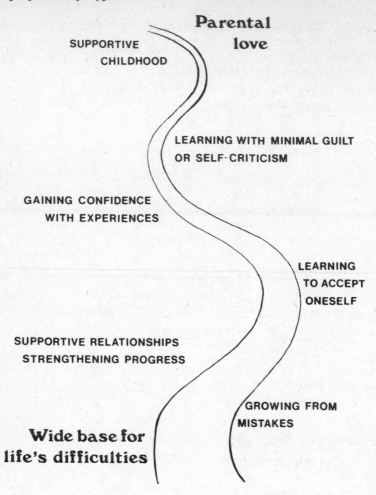

Diagram 16b   Free-way through life

Many people become confused between being assertive and being aggressive. They are two completely different attitudes. If a parent was aggressive the child often tells himself, 'I never want to be like that' and he assumes the completely reverse position. Any attempt to encourage him to stand on his own two feet is seen as behaving like Dad and so he avoids it at all costs.

Learning to like yourself, feeling comfortable about yourself – your thoughts, feelings and actions, provides you with a freeway along which you can cruise and of which you can feel justifiably proud, because you built it yourself.

In America a program to encourage children to feel unique and special has been started. The children have their fingerprints taken and are told no-one else has the same pattern. They are very special and can feel proud and confident about this. The program is called 'I.M. Thumbody', and this is printed on a badge for them to wear.

An important thought to carry with you at all times is: Don't compromise yourself, you're all you've got.

27 Phobias

Let me assert my firm belief that the only thing we need
to fear is fear itself.
FRANKLIN D. ROOSEVELT

I will show you fear in a handful of dust.
T.S. ELLIOT, *The Wasteland*.

The definition of a phobia is 'an extreme, abnormal fear'. How does
this exaggerated response to a situation come about? Sometimes the reasons are known, but most of the time there is no conscious awareness
of the cause. Treatment may be directed to find out 'why', or to deal
with the situation as it is in the present.

The fact that the phobic person is 'out of control' could be interpreted
as being 'in the control' of the unconscious. There may be a protective
or punishing aspect to this behaviour and hypnosis is often the treatment
of choice, to enable control to be restored to the conscious mind.

Almost any aspect of life may become fearful as T.S.Eliot so aptly
claims, and people who have one exaggerated fear that is prominent
often have many others that are not so obvious.

Some common phobias are a fear of insects, heights, spaces (open
or closed), crowds, aeroplanes, dentists, swimming, the dark, cats, cancer,
death and so on. In fact it is possible to have an irrational fear (a phobia)
about almost anything. As hypnosis has a relaxing component it may
be used in various ways to minimise the fear.

In self-hypnosis imagining the feared object or situation at an immense
distance, whilst feeling comfortable, provides a start to treatment. Being
in control and allowing the situation or object to approach at such a
rate that comfort can be maintained, helps 'desensitise' the fear.

The time taken for this 'desensitisation' depends on the individual,
and it is important not to proceed too rapidly and cause a panic situation.
When, in a trance, the object or situation becomes close and the person
feels at ease, it is time to proceed to a reality situation.

Imagine you have a phobia of cats. This can be dealt with by imagining a cat at a distance and gradually bringing it closer in the mind with an associated calm feeling. When, in time, it is possible to imagine the cat on your lap, then proceed to use a real cat at a distance.

Choose a friend who has a cat (preferably not vicious). Arrange for the cat to be in the next room with the doors closed. Achieve the relaxed feeling recalled from the trance state. Gradually, with you in control of the cat's position and coupling thoughts of the cat with calm thoughts, arrange for it to be brought closer little by little. Having a calm scene in the mind, such as a garden or beach, helps to diminish the fear caused by the presence of the cat.

Suzie had an irrational fear of swimming. She was forty-years-old and would never go to a pool. If her family went to the beach she would sit on the sand all day and swelter. All attempts to persuade her to go in the water failed and she had resigned herself to always being 'hot and bothered' at the beach, until someone suggested hypnosis.

Any conscious suggestion to her that it was safe to go in the water was met with strong resistance. I showed her how to relax and go into a trance and I asked her to practise this at home to gain some calmness when thinking about the sea.

When she returned she said she couldn't relax as the thought of the sea prevented her. I tried to help her imagine the water in the distance then her slowly walking down to it, but as soon as she got her feet wet she became very scared and opened her eyes.

We decided to explore the cause of her fear, and in a trance she recalled that when she was four-years-old she was swept out to sea by a strong current. She was terrified and swallowed a lot of water. She was rescued in a few seconds by her father, but it must have seemed like hours to her. I explained that this had happened a long time ago and that now she was older she could look after herself. I asked her to do self-hypnosis at home and to explain to the four-year-old 'in her mind' that she didn't need to be so frightened of water.

Over a period of weeks she managed to control her unnatural fear and now goes for a dip in the sea, but she is still not too happy about taking her feet off the sand and always stays near the shore. Those few seconds of terror all those years ago have left an indelible mark on her mind.

Tom is a forty-five-year-old businessman who has lost promotion due to his *fear of flying*. He has not flown since he was seven and always goes on holiday by car or boat even when it is very inconvenient.

He had another phobia which was fear of the underground train so I decided to see if we could deal with this first. We discussed why these fears may have arisen in childhood, but he had been through so many unhappy experiences that there did not seem to be one specific cause for his fears.

I taught him self-hypnosis and encouraged him to update his uncon-scious mind so that he was no longer reliant on childhood fears for safety.

After a few sessions, when he felt comfortable, we went to the local tube station and spent some time going up and down the escalators. If he felt frightened we would stay at the top until he calmed down.

Next we sat on a stationary train and got off before the doors closed. We did this a few times, then he put himself in a light trance and we travelled one stop. He got out, said he felt safe and so we travelled completely around the Circle Line with him becoming more confident with each stop.

Some weeks later we went through the process of imagining a flight – preparation, take off, landing, until he felt comfortable about making a journey. I told him to choose a short flight and let me know how it went.

A week later he rang me to ask if I would accompany him on the flight. He was going to Manchester and back. I told him it would be very inconvenient for me to take off so much time but perhaps if he was going to Paris I could see my way clear to join him. He agreed to that and we met at Heathrow at 10 a.m. He was very nervous so we had a cup of coffee to discuss 'tactics'. I said we would buy the tickets on the condition that he could get a refund if we didn't fly.

At the booking desk this was agreed to and I asked the time of the next flight to Paris. 'In twenty minutes, sir, but I wouldn't go on that 'plane – it's very narrow and if you have trouble on the flight it's difficult to get out.'

That's just what Tom needed. He went as white as a sheet and rushed to the toilet. I thanked the gentleman for his help and waited for Tom to emerge.

Some cups of coffee later and after lots of discussion and cajoling, we went onto the 'plane and, apart from some white knuckles gripping the arm rest, all went well.

We had lunch in Paris and Tom was in good spirits. Looking out of the window on the way back he said, 'There's nothing to it, why didn't I do this years ago?'

I, too, was very happy after a most unusual consultation, resulting in my going home with some French bread sticks and paté for dinner.

Frightening situations in childhood may leave an indelible mark in the back of the mind, suggesting the necessity for lifelong protection. As the child grows into an adult this protection is no longer necessary, but the fear remains with the same intensity as in the original incident. The child that is frightened holds onto the original terror as a warning to get away and this terror continues to recur in future non-threatening situations.

Jackie, aged thirty, had a fear of open spaces (*agoraphobia*) for ten years. Whenever she went to a park or a beach she panicked and had to leave. It first happened when she found herself on a wide open plateau while on holiday; she felt a terrible panic and rushed to a clump of bushes and hid in them until someone took her away in their car. A completely illogical reaction to a harmless situation – how could she possibly make sense of this terrible feeling which just took over?

Since the first incident the panic feeling had occurred on hundreds of occasions. She trembled, sweated, her pulse raced and she had the feeling, 'I must get out of here'. She tried many forms of help – tablets, acupuncture, psychotherapy, meditation and received some benefit but the condition recurred some time after treatment had stopped.

She had grown up in a house full of tension. Her father was an alcoholic and was constantly frightening her mother or any of the four children who were within reach. All the family knew to keep away from Dad when he'd been drinking. Jackie soon developed a protective cunning by hiding in all sorts of places when Dad was on the rampage, and stayed there until he collapsed on the floor in a drunken stupor. Then the family would come out of hiding, like mice when the cat is asleep.

Perhaps this held the secret for her fear of open spaces. Maybe to young Jackie the need for a place to hide was life-saving, and her adult panic of open spaces was really the child inside behaving as she did twenty-five years before.

As we talked about this possibility I noticed a glimmer of hope cross her face and I explained that I would like to teach her self-hypnosis to get in touch with the young, frightened Jackie and tell her she doesn't need to be frightened anymore.

Self-hypnosis can be very useful in communicating with the 'problem child' inside. The adult's difficulty can be viewed as if the child inside is retaining the feeling which was appropriate to a previous situation. Becoming a 'new parent' to that child by supporting, understanding, educating and helping it, will allow the feeling to be dispensed with as unnecessary.

Jackie was a deep subject and readily went into a trance to talk to the young Jackie and to explain to her that things are often reversed in adulthood. Open spaces are much safer than dark alleys and hiding places, and her need to fear them was no longer a problem.

As she talked to herself she cried a lot and talked about her fears that her father may hurt her, that he didn't love her, that she must have been a very bad girl for such terrible things to happen to her. With patience, time and understanding, the older Jackie reassured the young one by supporting her, listening to her and allowing her to be herself. She talked about the fact that there was no need to be frightened of father as he now lived in another country and wouldn't hurt her.

After being in a trance for half an hour she opened her tear-stained eyes and said, 'I think she is going to need a lot of convincing', then closed her eyes to rest after what must have been a most upsetting ordeal.

I explained that she should spend twenty minutes a day with young Jackie talking, listening, understanding and letting her know it was going to be all right. She made a commitment to provide the little girl with the support she had never had. I also asked her to go to a park and use the message of panic as a message from young Jackie. When she felt the panic she was to talk to young Jackie as one talks to a frightened puppy, soothing, pacifying and explaining things to her, using the feelings as an avenue of communication.

It took some weeks before the panic attacks began to subside. Many other problems in her life became evident as her visits continued and as she sorted them out the agoraphobia became less and less. She spent time communicating with young Jackie and found it helped her confidence in many different ways; gradually, in her own time, she allowed the past to slip into the past where it belonged. She carried inside her a much happier and more peaceful little girl than she had previously.

If a situation can be interpreted positively or negatively, a frightened person will always choose the worst outcome as most likely. This is a form of self-protection and so it is very difficult to offer positive logical alternatives for a phobic person who is in constant fear. That is why hypnosis, in dealing with the unconscious and avoiding the conscious logical mind, is an easier, safer, more successful approach to the problem.

POSSIBILITIES AND PROBABILITIES

During our daily life we automatically divide events into two categories – possibilities and probabilities. Walking down the street we may be aware of the *possibility* of a brick falling on our head but we don't dwell on that catastrophe as if it were a *probability*.

We concern ourselves with happenings which have a likelihood of occurring and take steps to deal with those. If it is cloudy we may take an umbrella when we go to work (except in England where an umbrella is always a necessity). We allow time for a traffic jam on the way to the airport to meet a 'plane. These are all probabilities and require us to be concerned about their occurrence.

A person who has a phobia has somehow allowed *possibilities* to get into the *probability* compartment of the mind. Associated fears and worries are involved in a most unlikely event occurring. A fear of flying may involve excessive concern about the 'plane crashing. The rare possibility has become confused with a probability.

One way of helping such a person is to guide their thoughts in a more appropriate direction. As the unnatural fears continue to dominate his mind he is directed to say to himself, 'Yes, it is a possibility that such and such will happen and I should worry proportionately but the probability is that it will not happen.'

These thoughts are directed to the unconscious mind during hypnosis, helping to bring logic into an illogical situation. Just reassuring the phobic person on a conscious level is unlikely to achieve the desired result.

Tony, a forty-five-year-old architect, had an unreal fear of dying. He worried about this most of the day and tossed and turned at night fearful of dying in his sleep. His home life and work were greatly affected by his 'death phobia'. He had consulted many doctors and been prescribed sedatives, which helped slightly for a short time.

Four years previously he had been involved in a car accident and was nearly killed. This triggered off and magnified the possibility of him dying and he had ruminated on this thought ever since.

I talked to him about dying and reassured him that indeed he *would* die and that was certain. *When* he would die was a matter of debate – the probability was that he would *not* die today but there was a remote possibility by some accident that he may die today. He should be less concerned about the one in a million chance of a freak accident and more concerned about the likelihood of living. I directed him to spend a suitable amount of time being concerned about each of the two eventualities.

We discussed the pity of wasting his life worrying about death with the likelihood that when eventually he was about to die he would be concerned with living.

Using hypnosis I directed similar logic to his unconscious mind and using post-hypnotic suggestion asked him to continue worrying a minute amount about dying and use the rest of his energy with the problems of living. When his fear occurred during the day he was to recognise it as being acceptable but magnified.

Over the next few months he gradually apportioned more of his time to living and became more involved in his work and home life. Strangely when he heard about death via the television or news it seemed to improve his attitude towards living. There were many occasions where he dropped back into the old routine, but fortunately lifted himself out by talking to himself about possibilities and probabilities.

28 Smoking

Giving up smoking is easy. I've done it hundreds of times.

A cigarette is a tube with a fire on
one end and a fool on the other!

'To smoke or not to smoke?' that is the burning question. I wonder how much time, thought, money, energy, discussion and research is carried out each year about smoking, its effects and how to promote or stop it.

It's as if a battle is continually being waged between those that benefit from smoking and those that wish to reduce its harmful effects. This battle is carried on in executive suites, laboratories and households.

How can such a small innocuous object cause so much intensity of feeling and expenditure of money? How come the smokers and non-smokers hold such positive views about their beliefs?

In a social gathering if someone realises I use hypnosis in my medical practice two questions invariably follow.

'Does hypnosis work?' A question I find quite extraordinary having spent ten years using it and promoting its benefits. I compare it to asking a chauffeur if he can really drive. The next question is 'Can you make me stop smoking?' as if I have been waiting for this opportunity to test my skills.

I would like to discuss the use of hypnosis in helping people to stop smoking under various headings, explaining methods, success rate and likelihood of it being a suitable form of therapy. The discussion takes the form of a smoker's first consultation.

I. WHEN DID IT START?

Smoking usually starts when teenagers try to be grown up. The cigarette is the symbol of adulthood. 'Keeping up with the mates' is a force which overcomes the taste, nausea and coughing spasms which accompany the first cigarettes.

Parents' smoking may set the standard for children to follow. The habit sets in after a period of time and then no conscious thought is involved in the ritual of 'lighting up a fag'. An automatic response occurs in what was originally a deliberate act. Many so called benefits are attributed to the nicotine, but most of these derive from *the belief* rather than the chemical.

'Cigarettes make me relax, feel more confident, give me something to do with my hands, help me to think better' are all comments in praise of the 'weed'.

There are many reasons for initially giving a cigarette this false power:

'I started smoking when studying for exams sixteen years ago and as I passed the exams I attributed my success to smoking.'

'I started smoking when I was writing essays; I'd say to myself, I'll have a break from work and have a smoke. I associated the pleasant rest period with smoking and have continued that belief since.'

'I started smoking because I was nervous. The ritual of lighting up gave me something to do and I felt better. I am no longer nervous but the habit continues.'

So it goes on, starting for a reason (perhaps false) and continuing long after that reason has vanished.

II. THE INDIVIDUAL HISTORY

This gives an important assessment of the likelihood of success in stopping smoking.

a) 'Have you given up before and for how long?' If someone has given up previously for three months or more, this is a positive indication of the willpower required. If they have tried numerous times and only stopped for a few days at a time, the motivation this time will need to be very strong for success.

b) 'Does your partner smoke?' People whose partners continue to smoke may relapse quicker than those whose partners have given up or are non-smokers.

c) 'Why do you want to stop smoking?' If the reason is because someone else wants you to, the chances of success are minimal. Doing it for *yourself* is the necessary motivation.

In my experience concern about health is more powerful than financial reasons.

d) 'Do you have children at home?' Often this provides a stronger incentive to stop.

e) 'How many cigarettes do you enjoy?' Most people enjoy five to six cigarettes during the day irrespective of how many they smoke. They have their 'favourite fags' – after coffee, first thing in the morning, after dinner, etc. If you smoke thirty a day and enjoy each one you are unlikely to give them up.

THE FIRST CHALLENGE

When people ring to book an appointment to stop smoking, I ask them to cut down as much as they can for the twenty-four hours prior to the visit. This gives me an indication of their motivation and willpower. If someone stops completely for twenty-four hours it's a very good sign. If they say 'It didn't do any good, I smoked the same number as usual' it is obvious that they are not providing much of *their* energy towards stopping and are relying on hypnosis being the magic cure. I can assure you this is not the case.

THE ATTITUDE

'Let's get started Doc. I've had my last cigarette and I'm ready to be a non-smoker.'

'I'm still smoking and I really like it; I'm anxious about how I will be without a cigarette but I want you to stop my desire.'

These are two different attitudes – one taking responsibility and requiring help, the other giving their problem to someone else to solve.

HYPNOTISABILITY

The capacity to be hypnotised is an important factor if hypnosis is to be used. The majority (85 per cent) of people are capable of using hypnosis.

Even people who are non-hypnotisable may benefit from the 'pep talk' the doctor gives – which can provide an altered attitude. Paying money to stop often helps, too.

EXPECTATIONS

I discuss at length the intended way of stopping with the person concerned. It is important to *stop*, not just to cut down the number smoked. We work out a programme about how this is to be done. Some people prefer to reduce by a certain number a day or week, others feel better if they don't smoke after leaving my office.

When the 'plan of action' is decided upon, I spend some time explaining hypnosis and correcting any false ideas or fears that are present.

I believe it is most important that each person is recognised as an individual, with a uniqueness about his strengths and weaknesses, his views and expectations. A 'set routine' for smokers may help some but will fail with many. There are some clinics where a pre-recorded tape is used and there is no personal interaction. A man came to see me after being to such a place. He related how he had seen an advertisement claiming great success with stopping smoking. He went to the clinic and was met by the receptionist who requested £50, which he paid. He was then shown into a room and told to lie down on a couch. The lady left the room and a tape recording was played about stopping smoking. He was so furious that as he left he 'lit up' to deal with his anger.

FALSE BELIEFS

There are many false assumptions made which the smoker continues to tell himself to legitimise his habit. These need to be discussed and corrected. 'Smoking relaxes me.' This may or may not be true. It is hard to imagine how nicotine, a stimulant, can relax, but the *belief that it does* will certainly create a relaxed feeling, so an alternative way of relaxing, using self-hypnosis, should be provided.

'Smoking helps me to feel confident.' If the smoker believes this then using confidence-building techniques during the self-hypnosis may replace the role of the cigarette. Sometimes smoking is a form of self-punishment for previous guilt. 'I'll smoke myself to death', is the unconscious message. Discussing this and bringing it to conscious recognition may enable it to be dealt with.

DANGER TIMES

There are some times in the day when the smoking urge is very great. Each individual will know these times – on the 'phone, with a drink, at parties, after coffee, etc. These should be recognised so that 'being warned is being armed'.

FORBIDDEN TIMES

There are some times or places where smoking is *not* done. These show the capability of stopping and can be used to advantage. In a non-smoking section of a train, in church, in bed, in the bath, with mother-in-law, when underwater diving, etc. The knowledge that you *can* stop for some time, may be the basis of building the confidence to stop for longer and longer periods.

THE SELF-HYPNOTIC TECHNIQUE

There are a multitude of hypnotic techniques used to help people stop smoking. There are aversive attitudes where the cigarette is directed to taste like camel dung (whatever that tastes like), there are directive techniques where people are ordered to stop, with dire consequences if they do not. I am not in agreement with these directions as I feel people should be encouraged to use a positive attitude in the direction of becoming a non-smoker.

Dr Herbert Spiegel, an American psychiatrist, is a leader in this field and has done much research and many follow-up studies to determine how effective his method is. He uses one session of forty-five minutes, teaches his clients to use self-hypnosis and directs them to use this technique in a positive way.

He explains that the mind and body are two separate components and as the mind controls the body it is important for it to do so in a direction which leads towards health rather than away from it.

He teaches a rapid induction technique which takes only a few seconds and as the client drifts into a trance they repeat three sayings to themselves to diminish the urge to smoke. The sayings are:

1.   For my body smoking is a poison,
2.   I need my body to live,
3.   I owe my body this respect and protection.

In a very brief time 'the message' gets through and the client comes out of the trance. This can be done in public places in such a way that others are not aware of what is happening. He explains that people going to a pet shop wouldn't buy pet food for their dog if it had on the label, 'this food will poison your dog' and he suggests you should look after your body at least as well as your dog. The point is to direct your thoughts in a positive way, 'Yes I'll respect my body', rather than taking the negative approach 'I won't smoke'.

I will now relate an approach I use which involves relaxation and an altered attitude. I will recount the words as they were used in a session with someone who had come to see me for the first time. The session was taped and the tape given to the patient to play twice a day at home. After a few days he was asked to see if he could achieve the same relaxation without the tape, and was to be seen one or two more times for reinforcement, depending on how he was going.

Good. Allow yourself to get comfortable. Look up as high as you can, strain your eyes – that's right. Take a deep breath in. Hold it.
Slowly let the air out and allow your eyes to close.
Allow a drifting, floating feeling to develop in your body with each breath out.

In your own time and in your own way, feel yourself floating down, time is insignificant, don't *try*, just allow it to happen, all the way down.
(After about half a minute)
Now use your imagination to walk ten steps into a garden, a lovely garden of your own creation, counting from 1–10 for each step.
Feel comfortable and secure there.
Notice the trees, flowers, shrubs, notice the warmth, the sounds, the smells.
Perhaps you can see and hear the birds.
It is very calm and relaxing, peaceful and isolated.
Feel the fresh air as you breathe it.
Imagine how clean and fresh it is for your lungs and your body.
Enjoy each breath and know you are using your body the way it should be used, the way it was made to be used.
(Half a minute silence)
Now I want you to imagine how nature would be if all the things in the garden began smoking. Notice the smoky haze in the air, the brown nicotine discolouration of the flowers, petals and leaves.
The smell of the flowers like a full ashtray.
Look in the trees, notice the birds with cigarettes dangling from their beaks.
Notice how they all sound like crows – no more beautiful birdsong, coughing instead.
Notice the grass is brown and littered with cigarette butts.
Notice how unnatural nature looks smoking. You are part of nature.
You are as natural as the birds or the flowers.
To your lungs you are acting as harmfully as the birds and the flowers would be if they smoked.
Enjoy the garden as a *smoke-free zone*, allow your lungs to be like the garden, to enjoy the natural air provided for them, without poisoning it with smoke.
Spend the next few minutes enjoying becoming part of nature in that garden and make a decision – a commitment – a resolution to keep it that way for the next twenty-four hours. Each day spend some time enjoying the smoke-free garden zone in your mind, pay respect to your body which needs this protection to look after you for the rest of your life.
When that commitment for the next twenty-four hours is agreed upon, then slowly leave the garden by counting from 10 to 1, keeping that good feeling of making a step in the right direction and come out of the trance in your own way and your own time.

> 'You won't object if I smoke?'
> 'Certainly not – if you don't object if I'm sick.'
> SIR THOMAS BEECHAM, REPLYING TO A WOMAN
> IN A NON-SMOKING RAILWAY COMPARTMENT.

THE ENEMY

There are many forces directing people to keep smoking. Friends offer cigarettes (they never did before) when they learn you are giving up 'the weed'. 'Go on! One won't hurt you!' as they wave the packet under your nose. It is a strange phenomenon and occurs also with obese people on diets and alcoholics trying to dry out. Perhaps it's jealousy; anyway, be forewarned.

Advertising does its utmost to point out how masculine (or feminine) you are to smoke a certain brand. Advertisements on billboards, cars, sporting grounds, magazines, all promote wonderful successes in all spheres of life if you smoke their brand.

An interesting example of reframing is that of the cigarette advertisement which has as its only reference to smoking the government's health warning.

SUCCESS RATE

There is great difficulty in assessing the success of any therapy for stopping smoking. Unless a long term follow up is made, it is possible to have exaggerated statistics which are far from reality. People who stop after treatment may well go back to smoking three months later and the therapist will still count that as a success, because he has no information to contradict this. Dr Spiegel in America has a meticulous system to follow-up his patients and his figures show an overall 40 per cent success rate over a period of years. This rate varies for different groups within this study. It was shown that the highest success rate was amongst people who are highly hypnotisable and are involved in loving relationships. Somehow this factor provided an increase in the willpower required to keep to the original commitment.

> I feel so much better in every way since I stopped smoking. My taste buds work properly, I breathe easier and I just feel good about myself having broken a habit I loathed.

Giving up smoking is a very difficult task for some people; this is illustrated by a woman with arterial disease who was referred to me by her physician.

He had told her that if she didn't stop smoking the chance of her legs requiring amputation was very high. If she stopped, the arterial disease may not progress and she may save her legs.

She continued to smoke thirty a day. I saw her on four occasions and no matter what I did or said she continued to smoke her legs away. I believe she was even smoking before they took her to the operating theatre.

It's hard to understand but true; this woman preferred cigarettes to her legs.

So it's really up to you; it's your body and your decision not to put the cigarette between your lips and set light to one end. Is the burning question to remain on your lips? – Will you maintain an unhealthy habit or relearn an old habit – that of being a non-smoker?

29 Dentistry

There was a door to which I found no key;
There was a veil through which I might not see.
OMAR KHAYYAM

To most patients and many dentists, hypnosis is an enigma and a mystery. It owes its stormy history partly to the lack of a scientific explanation, even though no special skill is required to produce this altered state of awareness.

This chapter will discuss the use of hypnosis in dentistry and show how once this art has been learnt, work on the teeth can become acceptable, even enjoyable.

It has always been known that the teeth are the strongest and most durable part of the body. Given an unrefined diet, the biting surfaces wear slowly enough to last a lifetime and the forecast for the teeth of a Roman legionnaire or a sailor on the 'Mary Rose' was invariably good.

This pattern changed completely when cane sugar was introduced into the diet. With a crystal refined to 99 per cent purity, a decay–abscess–loss sequence was started which became established for many generations. The desire for sweetness was satisfied at a terrible cost, not only in pain and suffering, but early loss by extraction of the very component which should be the last to succumb to the ageing process. By contrast, compared to the natural teeth, a complete set of artificial dentures has an efficiency of something less than 1 per cent.

Today dentistry has reached a stage where the restoration of a decayed tooth is certain and long-lasting, where extractions are exceptional, where the skill of the dentist is matched by the excellence of his equipment and where the patient can expect to be treated with sympathy, kindness and understanding.

These advances in technology are all in vain if the patient refuses to visit the dentist due to fear. A dentist waiting by his modern dental chair, new high speed drill at the ready, local anaesthetic drawn up, a nurse waiting to be of assistance, are all of no use if the patient is cowering in the waiting room unable to move.

A normal fear of dentistry is very common and has some justification. Unnatural fear, where teeth rot and fall out due to lack of treatment, is a failure of great magnitude and an unnecessary loss of face (no pun intended) for the rest of the patient's life.

Usually children are not frightened on their first visit to the dentist; the imprint of anxiety is stamped on the mind by an actual experience involving pain, blood or an intolerant dentist. It may have been the suffocating experience of an anaesthetic mask being forced over the small face of a screaming child.

These images and memories remain in the back of the mind and act as a protective device to prevent a repeat performance. Unfortunately the knowledge of improved conditions, techniques and equipment does not reach this part of the mind. If not an actual experience, then one related by a well known and trusted person, may create the fear. These tales, exaggerated, harrowing and told in an over-enthusiastic way, can instill a terror of entering 'the bloody battle' with the dentist which can last for years. Any attempts at enlightening these frightened people with correct facts are seen as a ruse to be lured into a threatening situation.

These stories or experiences may remain dormant and forgotten in the back of the mind until a dental situation triggers off the defence mechanism of fear. The fight or flight mechanism (see Stress) which occurs, serves the purpose of keeping the person away from the dental surgery.

If this reaction occurs when the patient is in the dental chair, and he punches the dentist or runs away with the mouth gag dangling from his mouth, no useful purpose is served.

The fear that people feel is shown in many ways, some more subtle than others – delay in making the appointment, changing the appointment time, arriving late, taking too long to remove an overcoat, frequent and prolonged rinsing and asking innumerable questions to delay the inevitable.

Once the mouth is open and the dentist is 'in', further examples of anxiety are demonstrated by gagging, retching or vomiting, sweating, palpitations and overbreathing, perhaps even fainting.

This is where hypnosis plays a major role in converting a terrifying and unsuccessful dental appointment into a relaxed, acceptable situation. Compare the change in the following scenes and you will be able to appreciate the benefits of hypnosis, both to the patient and dentist.

Steve is terrified of the dentist. He had a bad experience with a rough dentist when he was young and has avoided dentists for twenty years. His teeth are in a foul condition, with many cavities and decay requiring urgent attention to save them. He has repeated bouts of toothache which he accepts to avoid having any dental treatment. Things get so bad – the pain, bad breath and difficulty in eating – that he forces himself to visit the local dentist, having a tot of whisky first, for Dutch courage.

He sits in the waiting room, his heart pounding, his imagination running wild, hoping against hope that the dentist has been called away and that he will be sent home.

No such luck. His name is called and he stiffly marches into the dental surgery, eyes staring, turning this way and that to notice every aspect of the chamber of horrors. He sits in the chair, grips the armrests tightly and awaits the outcome.

He hears as if from a distance! 'Open please' and feels the sweat pouring down the back of his neck. He opens as widely as he can, but the tension is such that the dentist cannot examine his mouth properly.

'Relax a little, I'm not going to hurt you.' Steve only hears the word 'hurt' and tenses even more, screwing up his eyes in anticipation of the pain that will follow.

After some minutes of trying, the dentist puts his instruments down with a clatter and announces 'I can't do anything. You're so tense it's as if you're the English goalie trying to stop a vital goal in the World Cup. I can't see or do anything; you'll have to learn to relax.'

Steve breathes a sigh of relief as escape now seems possible. He opens his eyes and closes his mouth to listen to the lecture about the state of his mouth and the need to repair some of the damage.

He is told he can learn to relax through hypnosis, and with or without the aid of relaxing drugs have the dental work done with a minimum of discomfort. He realises that he can't continue with the bad breath and pain so he undertakes to learn to relax.

After a few weeks practice he returns (after a tot of whisky) to the dental rooms, sits in the waiting room practising his self-hypnosis and waits to be called.

He is still nervous as he settles into the dental chair but is reassured nothing will happen until *he* is ready. He goes through the routine, assisted by the dentist, of relaxing and imagining a calm scene. When he is ready he indicates by nodding his head and gently local anaesthetic is injected and the dental work performed with a minimum of fuss.

You may feel this is a glib story which has been romanticised to make it sound good. It is not so, and daily these scenes are occurring which convert a nightmare into a daydream. But there are many more scenes where the fear and fighting continue due to lack of knowledge of the inaccessibility of this form of therapy.

A description of dental treatment with the patient in the altered state of hypnosis may be:

His eyes are closed, his breathing is slow, shallow and steady. His pulse is regular and firm. The muscles are relaxed, so much so that an arm lifted would feel heavy and limp and drop like a rag doll's. Suggestions are acted upon slowly and positively and without criticism. The patient appears to be 'miles away' and yet is willing to 'surface' to do as the dentist asks. The mouth and jaw muscles are relaxed allowing access to any tooth required.

Why then if this is available to the population are there so many people prepared to let their teeth rot rather than face the dentist? Is it the lack of education of the general public? Are there too few dentists practising and promoting hypnosis? Is there a general disbelief about the effectiveness of hypnosis or is the fear such that it won't even allow the thought of a dentist to be entertained?

Of the many attitudes prevalent in the community I will list a few which help to keep patient and dentist apart.

1. 'I'm sure no-one can hypnotise me.'
2. 'I'm scared of what I may say when he gets me under.'
3. 'I don't believe in mind over matter.'
4. 'I'm scared of what he may find when he looks in my mouth.'
5. 'I can't forget what happened when I went to the dentist when I was young.'
6. 'How do I know it will work?'
7. 'I'm too nervous to relax, I can never relax, it's not me.'

Other limiting factors are the number of dentists competent and interested enough to spend the extra time involved, and the lack of information available to people about dentists who do use hypnosis.

The specific uses of hypnosis in dentistry involve:

1. Reducing the fear of pain and dentistry itself.
2. Reducing the discomfort of dental work by allowing the local anaesthetic to be more effective or even unnecessary.
3. Allowing better relaxation for access to the mouth.
4. Preventing gagging or retching.
5. Reducing bleeding following extractions.
6. Allowing the dentist to have first class operating conditions.

Modern dental treatment has the advantage of a feather-like drill, quick-acting local anaesthetics, sedative drugs if required, efficient filling materials. These are all used to the best advantage if the patient is relaxed.

If teeth and gums are not cared for they deteriorate and extractions may become necessary. The fear of dentistry is now generally unwarranted and the choice is between learning to relax or having false teeth that are 1% as efficient as normal teeth.

To find out which dentists utilise hypnosis in their practice contact the societies listed at the end of the book.

30 Sleep

Care-charmer sleep, son of the sable Night,
Brother to Death, in silent darkness born:
Relieve my anguish and restore the light,
With dark forgetting of my care return.
DANTE, *Sonnets to Delia*

'Do you sleep well?' is a question asked in a medical interview. The answer tells a lot about the patient.

'Like a log; as soon as my head hits the pillow I'm away.' This, as a rule, indicates the person is dealing reasonably well with the stresses of life.

'I toss and turn all night, my bed looks like a battleground', may mean inner turmoil relating to past or present events.

'I wake at 2 a.m. and can't get back to sleep', may be a sign of depression.

'I'm dead tired when I go to bed and I sleep for a couple of hours then wake up alert and can't get off to sleep', may indicate many unconscious factors playing a role in making certain he doesn't sleep.

To those who enjoy a good night's sleep its pleasure goes unnoticed; to those who struggle to obtain its benefits the long night is never-ending. Many curses, blessings, potions, pills and charms have all been directed to Hypnos the God of Sleep.

Hypnosis was coined as a word when it was believed that an hypnotic trance was similar to sleep. It is not, but hypnosis has proved very useful in helping treat insomnia.

Modern science has much research data about sleep patterns and problems. Sleep laboratories study people whilst they are asleep and monitor various physiological aspects of their mind and body. We now know a great deal more about the 'Brother of Death' and treatment varies considerably depending upon the specific problem encountered during the night.

I would like to discuss some important aspects of sleep problems in order to explain how hypnosis plays a role in their solution.

1. Some people sleep all night but wake up tired and unrefreshed. This is because they do not reach a suitable *depth* of sleep and remain in a light sleep which does not allow the mind and body to benefit from the rest. This may be due to worry and anxiety from past or present events. The conscious mind does not 'let go' enough for the person to drift into a deeper state of sleep.

    Hypnosis is useful in these situations either to uncover the past experiences causing the anxiety, or to provide a way of 'turning off and relaxing' so that the tranquil state of self-hypnosis will lead to a natural sleep of suitable depth.

2. We often fail to estimate the length of time we sleep. In hospital many patients claimed they 'haven't slept a wink', but have been observed by the night nurse to have snored for many hours and don't even wake whilst having their blood pressure taken. I was always amused to observe nurses waking up patients to give them their sleeping tablets!

3. *Trying* to go to sleep is the best way of staying awake. Due to the need for a good night's rest, if we don't sleep after half an hour of going to bed, a pattern may be set up which directs us to *try* to go to sleep. 'I must go to sleep or I'll be no good at the office tomorrow' directs the mind to be alert and worry and guides it in the opposite direction to turning off.

    Hypnosis as a 'being' state rather than a 'trying' one, can lead into a natural sleep. Using muscle relaxation followed by self-hypnosis, a tranquil, peaceful scene may be encountered and all thoughts of 'trying' fade into the distance.

    A sleep tape made for the individual person can provide a suitable background to allow sleep to occur. This is played in bed as the basis of self-hypnosis. Often patients complain they never hear the end of the tape as they have dozed off.

4. Sleep the Brother of Death. As children we may have said the prayer:

    > Now I lay me down to sleep,
    > Pray dear God my soul to keep,
    > If I should die before I wake,
    > Pray dear God my soul to take.

    What a terrifying prayer for children to repeat before going to bed. The association between death and sleep is obvious, and has been remarked upon by poets since time immemorial. There is fear in many people's mind – either consciously or unconsciously – that they may not wake up in the morning and hence by staying awake they stay alive.

    Many years ago I saw a Jewish patient who had not slept well for twenty years. He had used every sort of sleeping tablet with no real effect. His problem started soon after the War when he had been captured by the Russians and sent to Siberia.

He stayed in an enormous tent in the snow and there were a number of braziers with fires to warm the tent. Hundreds of men lived in the tents and many died each night due to the freezing conditions.

He had always stayed close to the fire and knew if he fell asleep he would be dragged away so someone else could take his place. For many months he made sure he stayed in a very light sleep at night to remain alive.

After the War his unconscious still had the message 'don't sleep or you'll die' and it was only after a number of hypnotic sessions that it went off duty and allowed him to sleep normally.

5. Sometimes insomnia may be a form of punishment for some real or imagined guilt. Hence the saying 'the sleep of the innocent'. Using hypnosis to uncover the past experience and bring it to consciousness may allow it to be reassessed and a 'reprieve' obtained.

6. 'Don't sleep on the job' may be taken literally by the unconscious mind. Someone striving to achieve in business or other aspects of his life may, at some level, believe that staying awake will help him do better in his work. This, of course, is not logical and is not in the conscious awareness of the insomniac. He tosses and turns at night ruminating about the activities of yesterday and tomorrow. He is very tired but as soon as his head touches the pillow, as if by magic he becomes very alert.

The more he worries, 'I'll be tired tomorrow at work', the more sleep disappears over the horizon. The voice in the back of his mind saying 'Sleep is an activity of the slothful' keeps him awake.

Using hypnosis to explain that sleep at night is not laziness and does not mean failure, often helps in achieving an inner peace which leads to a sound, restful sleep.

7. Past failures at going to sleep often awaken a self-fulfilling prophecy of 'I know I won't sleep again tonight'. Each night is a separate entity and lack of sleep one night has no relevance to the following night's pattern. Worrying about staying awake will most likely create that unenvied state. Using self-hypnosis as a routine at bed time provides an avenue to direct the mind, which does not involve worry and ruminations about previous failures. The very act of muscle relaxation and drifting into an altered state provides a restful bed where sleep can occur.

8. Sleeping tablets (hypnotics) are prescribed in their millions as a way of dealing with sleep problems. In many cases they provide a suitable night's rest but often the sleep is not of the depth required, and the

'sleeper' wakes tired and groggy. They tend to have a habit-forming quality and may not produce a sleep pattern that is similar to natural sleep. Many people have great difficulty in trying to stop them.

If self-hypnosis can be learnt it removes any dependence on drugs, bolsters self-confidence and provides a natural sleep where the sleeper wakes rested and refreshed in the morning.

The relaxing aspect of self-hypnosis lessens any tension or worry which may be involved in the person's lifestyle or in his 'trying' to go to sleep. Many patients following a session of hypnosis in my surgery say, 'If I'd stayed in the trance a few more minutes I would have gone to sleep.' The trance state is so similar to the twilight state just before going to sleep that it directs the mind towards the tranquillity of sleep rather than to the alertness of the waking state.

Remaining in a trance state, even if sleep does not follow, provides the mind and body with many of their restful requirements. So if an hypnotic tape is played in bed and the person stays in a trance for some hours, he will 'wake' rested and refreshed on most occasions.

We all have the ability to sleep. We have 'unlearned' that ability due to some experience or experiences in the past. Relearning our ability to sleep may not require the sledgehammer tactics of nightly sleeping tablets with all their inherent defects. Perhaps learning to use your own resources to relax would be a more useful gateway to the land of Nod.

PART SEVEN

Some Queries about Hypnosis

31 *Answering Questions, Questioning Answers*

If we can really understand the problem to answer will
come out of it, because the answer is not separate from
the problem.
KRISHNAMURTI

It is time we gave up looking for questions and began
looking for answers.
G.K. CHESTERTON

Question 1

Can anyone be hypnotised?

Answer

There is a wide variety of opinions on this subject and many misconceptions exist, so I will give a broad outline of present day knowledge.

Being hypnotised *is in no way* related to being weak. In fact quite the reverse is true. Mentally defective people cannot be hypnotised as their concentration span is so limited. Schizophrenics cannot achieve a trance state. People who are more determined, able to use their imagination and are motivated are more likely to go into a trance.

There have been many scales devised to determine the hypnotisability of people. These scales involve noting the reaction to induction procedures and suggestions.

In general the results of these scales show the reaction that people can be divided into three arbitrary groups

Group I 10–15 per cent of the population are very hypnotisable. These are called deep subjects and are often the subjects of stage hypnosis. These people could have an operation using hypnosis as the anaesthetic, they can regress back to an early age, and do not remember being in a trance.

Group II 70 per cent of the population experience a trance state in a medium way. They feel the daydream-like state, can use hypnosis to benefit them in many ways but also may be aware of their surroundings during a trance.

Group III 10–15 per cent have a minimal trance capacity and may not be able to experience any of the trance phenomena such as arm levitation, altered sensation. They may feel relaxed but know what is happening all the time and remain in the conscious controlled state.

There are a great many factors which influence the ability to go into a trance and the foremost one is confidence and trust in the therapist. The unconscious mind is not going to allow itself to be exposed or influenced by someone it does not feel secure with.

Many people seek hypnosis but due to the insensitiveness of the therapist achieve no response. They then say (or are told) they cannot be hypnotised. With another, more competent, sympathetic therapist they easily achieve a trance state.

Motivation is also an important factor in enhancing the likelihood of being hypnotised. Fear, resistance, not wanting to change, will all prevent the 'letting go' that is necessary.

This trance capacity – the ability to go into a trance – is part of your make-up, just as your height and the colour of your eyes. Consciously trying to be more able to experience hypnosis has no influence. The ability remains constant throughout life.

In order to discover your trance capacity, either seek a competent therapist and ask to be taught, or practise some of the self-hypnosis inductions in this book, or listen to the tape (see page 252).

Question 2

What is the likelihood of staying in a trance and not coming out of it?

> Experience is the comb life brings you after you have lost your hair.
> JUDITH STERN

Answer

There are many stories about thus happening. I have never actually heard of it happening. It certainly hasn't happened with me or with anyone I know in medical hypnosis. So the answer is that there is no likelihood of it happening during therapy with a competent therapist. If the therapist should die of a heart attack while the patient is in a trance, the patient will wake up in his own time.

Sometimes people enjoy the relaxation of a trance state so much that, when directed to open their eyes, they remain in a trance for a few minutes more before doing so. Sometimes at a conscious or unconscious level, due to antagonism towards the therapist, the eyes may remain closed for some time after being requested to open them.

I have read of an occasion when this happened and the therapist said, 'Mrs Jones, I see you enjoy remaining in a trance; please stay in that state; I just remind you my fees are £30 an hour and I will continue to charge you at that rate.' She came out of the trance 10p later!

Question 3

Will I say things I don't wish to under hypnosis?

> Words fluttered from him like swallows leaving a barn at daylight.
> O. HENRY

Answer

Many therapists do not require the patient to talk in hypnosis at all. Some use ideomotor signalling (the use of finger movement to indicate 'yes' or 'no'), to communicate with the unconscious mind.

Generally the unconscious is very protective and will allow only as much communication in a trance as can be dealt with by the conscious mind. If 'dark secrets' are revealed, the discussion following proves useful in dispelling fears that were remaining dormant.

Most frequently memories that are causing problems are released slowly and only at a pace that is comfortable for the person concerned. These 'dark secrets' may be causing problems in the back of the mind and being able to release them provides comfort and relief over a period of time.

It is important that a sensitive and competent therapist is involved, so extra pressure to talk is not used. This is why stage hypnosis is frowned upon. A sensitive person who has a high hypnotic capacity may perform on stage in a way that causes future problems. In therapeutic hypnosis where the aim is to help, not entertain, these things should not occur.

There is often a fear that you will be commanded to say or do things you do not wish to. This does not occur in medical hypnosis. The resistance of the unconscious mind to perform acts which are against its nature is so great, that if you are in a trance you will come out spontaneously or avoid the command. A sensitive, competent therapist would not use such a technique when trying to help a patient deal with problems.

Question 4

Is hypnosis available on the National Health Service?

> Time is the great physician.
> BENJAMIN DISRAELI

Answer

Because it takes time, most General Practitioners are unable or unwilling to use hypnosis as a means of treatment. There are some who make time during the week and see an occasional patient on the NHS. Most hypnosis within the medical or dental professions is done by private practitioners. Referral by your GP is most important so continuity of therapy is maintained and your medical history is then available to the therapist practising hypnosis.

Lists of doctors, dentists and psychologists practising hypnosis are available from the societies mentioned at the back of the book.

Question 5

How would I or the hypnotist know if I was in a trance?

> Anyone who isn't confused really doesn't understand the situation.
> EDWARD B. MURROW,
> AMERICAN BROADCASTER

Answer

There are many signs of being in a trance but none are infallible. The hypnotist will be looking for signs of muscular relaxation, response to directions (such as arm levitation), immobility, calm breathing, lack of response to noises.

The person being hypnotised may feel a 'parallel awareness' – being in the room and elsewhere and altered sensations such as tingling, heaviness, warmth. A feeling of 'not caring', a daydream-type experience with deep relaxation. He may have visualisations of being somewhere else, such as in a garden or on the beach and actually feel he *is* there. He may suspend judgement about the illogical experiences he is having. Time takes on a different perspective and often people who have been in a trance for an hour feel it was only for a few minutes. The person has a relaxed feeling of nearly dropping off to sleep and, after coming out of the trance, needs time to re-orientate themselves to the room.

One aspect of hypnosis is that the patient is often unaware of being in a trance. This is where a Catch 22 situation exists. Incompetent therapists, worried about failing, will often tell people they were hypnotised (in an altered state) when they were not. When the patient denies it the therapist explains that this is part of the trance.

If you are hypnotised you will be aware of the daydream-like quality, the tranquillity and relaxation; you may have thoughts you haven't had for a long time or you may have altered sensations, different perspectives on things.

Question 6

How do I know if the hypnotherapist is competent?

> All genuine knowledge results from direct experience.
> MAO-TSE-TUNG

Answer

Hypnosis is a tool in the hands of a therapist, not a treatment. It is difficult to discern competence from incompetence in any sphere of medicine. How do you know if the surgeon who is going to operate on you is competent? Mainly by trusting the hospital employing him or the General Practitioner referring you.

Choosing a therapist who belongs to a society and who is a trained doctor, dentist or psychologist, will provide you with an important guideline, but it is no guarantee. As in many spheres of adult life, you need to take some responsibility for your choice and if you don't feel comfortable with the person you have chosen it may be better not to return to him.

Anyone can advertise in magazines as a hypnotherapist with or without training. Just as you would prefer your car to be fixed by a trained mechanic rather than someone just 'having a go', so you need to find a competent, fully trained hypnotist. There are a number of hypnosis societies (listed at the end of the book) who provide training and supervision of therapists.

In the end it is up to you to use your sensitivity and experience to decide if the therapist is suitable for you. You need to have a good rapport to trust him and be able to let him know your feelings and queries, and to notice an improvement as time goes on.

I have great confidence in people knowing what is best for them. When I had just started practising hypnosis and lacked a great many qualities, since gained through years of experience, many people did not return for their next appointment. I couldn't understand why, and I believed the fault was theirs. Looking back on it, I now see how wise they were; they assessed my competence and understanding very quickly and followed their feelings.

The number of visits required varies greatly depending on the patient, the condition and the therapist. In general, hypnosis is not a prolonged form of treatment. Psychoanalysis may go on for years but the benefit of self-hypnosis is that the control is handed over to the patient. Most conditions should be suitably helped by ten sessions, many by five to ten sessions. Some hypnotherapists only see people for one or two sessions and if they are not helped in this time suggest an alternative form of therapy.

Question 7

Is age regression something that everyone can experience in a trance?

> What is an adult? A child blown up by age.
> SIMONE DE BEAUVOIR

Answer

Age regression – going back to an earlier age – is a phenomenon occurring in people with a high trance capacity; that is, 10 per cent of the population who are 'deep subjects'. This abiity to go back in time and actually feel as if they are there, may occur spontaneously or by direction from the therapist.

If a previous experience, remaining in the unconscious, is causing problems in the present, it may be useful to go back and look at it from today's point ov view. Using 'uncovering techniques' which question the unconscious, the patient is actually *in* the experience and can discuss it with or without the emotional involvement.

By this method, fear, pain, guilt or anger which has been 'locked away' for so long can be released with great relief, and by bringing them to the surface can be seen in their true light.

In the regressed state the patient talks and acts as if he were that age. The language, vocabulary and mannerisms are all appropriate to the age that he has regressed to.

An American therapist regressing a patient to an earlier age realised he had lost contact with the patient. His questions were not being understood. He checked his notes and realised that the man had been born in Germany before moving to America. He called in a German-speaking secretary who asked the regressed patient some questions in German. The man, who was now at the age of a twelve year old, understood and answered in German. He had really gone back to being twelve at which time he had not learnt English so he couldn't understand the therapist.

Many therapists have utilised regression to the birth experience and to previous lives. In their hands this provides a very useful way of helping the patient and so is of great benefit. As I have only had minimal experience in this area and have a very open mind towards it, I will not enter a prolonged discussion on the subject.

Question 8

What is meant by post-hypnotic suggestion?

> The future is not what it was.
> BERNARD LEVIN

Answer

A most important component of hypnosis is termed post-hypnotic suggestion. This means that a suggestion made by the therapist (or by yourself in self-hypnosis) will be carried out at some later date.

In stage hypnosis people are directed to behave in a certain manner when they return to their seats or at some future time. The performer does not remember the direction but carries it out as if by some inner compulsion however logical or illogical it may be.

In one hypnotic session in a dental surgery a client was told that after he left the room he would return and ask for his umbrella (which he didn't possess). The embarrassed client returned some minutes later saying, 'I've come for my umbrella, but I know I didn't bring one.' He was displaying the contradiction between his logical mind and the post-hypnotic suggestion present in his unconscious mind.

This ability may prove very useful to overcome problems and avoid resistance. Suggesting to someone they will have confidence and act assertively will be met with a great deal of resistance if discussed on a conscious level. If presented during a trance in either a direct or indirect way, it becomes much more acceptable and may be carried out without the logical, conscious mind interfering.

I saw an overweight patient who binged on chocolates each day. She couldn't resist going into the sweet shop and buying four bars of chocolate a day. Any discussion on a conscious level was met with arguments about it being out of her control. In a trance I suggested how nice it would be to realise she had arrived home each night and forgotten to go into the sweet shop. She had no recall of what I said to her and reported some weeks later at how amazed she was that she had passed the sweet shop each night, but was so involved with her thoughts that she was on the bus home before she realised she hadn't bought the chocolate.

This aspect of hypnosis is used to a greater or lesser extent in most hypnotic sessions. Suggestions of confidence, well-being, overcoming phobias, etc. all have some post-hypnotic suggestion involved which enables the trance state to be so useful. In self-hypnosis the same effect is reached by putting the intended suggestion to yourself when you are in a trance. For example, someone lacking confidence may say to themselves, 'Tomorrow I am going to be more assertive, stand up for myself, not be so concerned or frightened.' These words and thoughts drift through as suggestions to be carried out the next day.

The time for the suggestions to be carried out varies, depending on the situation. One therapist, with tongue in cheek, told me how a man had rung him to say he had made the necessary change for which he had sought therapy. The 'phone call came eighteen years after the therapy and my friend stated it was due to post-hypnotic suggestion.

Question 9

Is hypnosis useful in the treatment of asthma?

> In a study of 173 asthmatic patients it was shown that 82 per cent became much better or were cured using hypnotherapy.
> DR G. MAHER LOUGHMAN,
> LONDON PHYSICIAN 1970

Answer

Asthma is a chronic disease of the lungs where the bronchial tubes become narrower, causing a wheeze (difficulty in breathing out) and is due to many factors. The severity of the condition may vary from being mild to causing death from lack of oxygen.

The cause may be allergy, stress, infection or unknown. It comes in the form of asthmatic 'attacks', where the patient struggles for breath and needs assistance in the form of tablets, injections or inhalers which relieve the spasm and allow the free flow of air to the lungs.

It is well known that some asthmatics develop an attack when they realise they have left their spray at home. This indicates the role of anxiety in the disease. This anxiety releases chemicals which cause spasm in the smooth muscle around the bronchi resulting in the wheeze.

Treatment of asthma with hypnosis should only be carried out with the support and co-operation of the treating physician. It is imperative that no therapist should use hypnosis to try and treat asthma without the knowledge and associated treatment by the patient's General Practitioner.

Dr Maher Loughman, an authority in this field, has been using hypnosis to help asthmatics for more than twenty years, with results showing improvement in 80 per cent of the people treated. With most of these people their drug treatment was stopped or significantly reduced.

He suggests that using hypnosis and auto-hypnosis (auto-hypnosis is a form of self-hypnosis where the therapist's words are repeated following a post-hypnotic suggestion during the original hypnotic session) to produce relaxation and calmness from stress, provides a basic state which allows the asthma to diminish. Practising auto-hypnosis daily allows body chemicals to circulate to prevent spasm of the bronchi and reduce attacks. As the fear of an attack is reduced and confidence builds up, the patient begins to have control over his breathing.

The time taken for this to occur varies from three months to a year and constant daily practice is required to alter the internal mechanisms of the body. Continued use of bronchodilators, if necessary, proceeds until dependence on them becomes less. As the body begins to produce its own chemicals the reliance on manufactured ones becomes unnecessary.

I must repeat that it is most important that if you suffer from asthma you only have hypnosis with your general Practitioner's knowledge and agreement and only use a therapist who is trained in the problems and difficulties of asthma.

Question 10

What are the dangers of hypnosis?

Fear born of ignorance is worse than fear born of knowledge.
DR CHARLES HILL

Answer

Hypnosis may be compared to wine. If it is drunk with a meal it has many pleasant and beneficial effects. If it is abused, problems can occur. The problems with hypnosis are solely related to the therapist concerned. As I have said, hypnosis is a tool and may be misused.

In competent hands hypnosis is much safer than most forms of drug therapy. There are minimal side effects. The dangers occur when ill-trained people practise the use of hypnosis for their own benefit or for entertainment. As the mind is extremely sensitive, it needs the greatest of respect. The therapist should understand the specific strengths and weaknesses of the client and adjust the therapy accordingly.

There are occasional stories of problems occurring after hypnosis but these mainly happen with untrained people practising without the necessary care or concern for their client.

As with any form of therapy it is not possible to guarantee the outcome, but as hypnosis is using the patient's own resources, a built-in safety device is present.

The dangers of self-hypnosis are negligible, just as any form of meditation. The resultant relaxation, insight and increased suggestibility present no problems.

Stories of mishaps following stage hypnosis often have their humorous side as well as pointing out the dangers of such situations. One woman was admitted to a Glasgow hospital in a 'trance' state after she had been hypnotised at a club. She was under the impression that she was a cuckoo. Another was told, during a stage performance, that his 'belly button' had been stolen and he complained to a policeman.

There is such a vast difference between such a situation and the seeking of help from a qualified person that I don't feel the fear of these dangers should play any role except to guide you to a competent therapist.

In self-hypnosis you will automatically grade the exploring and learning that can occur and so can proceed at your own pace.

32 Medical Attitudes towards Hypnosis

Physician Heal Thyself
MOTTO OF BRITISH HOLISTIC MEDICAL
ASSOCIATION

I went to my doctor and asked for something for persistent
wind. He gave me a kite!
LES DAWSON, COMEDIAN

In six years of medical training I received very little education about
the mind. There were three or four lectures from a psychiatrist, but
as they were not relevant to exams many students did not attend.

We had one lecture on hypnosis and even fewer students attended.
Those who did hoped for a stage performance where one of their friends
might 'quack like a duck'. But it was a monologue about the importance
of the mind in disease and was forgotten very quickly.

We were much more involved in essential things like the anatomy
of the facial nerve as it continues a tortuous path through the skull,
as this might appear on the exam paper.

Later on during fifteen years of general practice I realised that more
than 50 per cent of the patients I saw had psychological components
to their illness, either stress related conditions, or illnesses which could
have been helped had my knowledge of the mind been improved.

Of the many thousands of patients whom I failed to help due to this
lack of education, I only recall one where my knowledge of the anatomy
of the facial nerve was of value.

Patients who had no demonstrable organic disease were labelled as
neurotics, and given sedatives or a lecture. I often told them there was
nothing I could do to help. They were misunderstood and were allowed
to struggle on with their problems unaided, with the added fear that
'the doctor couldn't find anything wrong so I must be imagining it.'

That was twenty years ago and, although change is occurring very slowly, this attitude is still prevalent amongst many doctors. The lack of education about the mind, its problems and strengths, leave many doctors unable to help people whose psychological problems play a large part in their illness.

During my medical training I was directed, either by inference or actual comment, to believe that alternative medicines were wrong and we, the doctors, were right. We were not allowed to refer patients to acupuncturists, homeopaths or chiropractors. Thankfully this has changed considerably and respect is now being shown to a number of these complementary areas.

Hypnosis seems to fall into a strange area of its own. It still has an aspect of mumbo jumbo and is often only utilised at the insistence of the patient. Although the number of doctors attending training courses in hypnosis is increasing, it is still a drop in the ocean.

The medical view may be described as:

1. Diagnose the disease.
2. Treat the disease.
3. If no known disease is diagnosed 'fix' the symptoms.

For many illnesses this is very satisfactory and the patient is cured and returned to health. For many other illnesses it is not satisfactory and the patient returns again and again with the symptoms and the doctor attempts to 'fix' them with a prescription.

The results are that doctors prescribe tablets to many patients in order to minimise the symptoms. The number of patients attending the doctor is large so the time for each patient is only a few minutes. There is no time to talk or listen and many of the psychological components of the illness are missed and the symptoms continue.

Instead of the symptom being assessed as part of the whole person, it is treated as an entity itself. The basic contract between patient and doctor may be stated, 'Doctor, here is my problem, will you please fix it for me.' The doctor, realising he has a waiting room full of patients, may choose the quickest way of 'fixing' it with a prescription.

In some conditions this transaction may result in a healthy patient, but in many situations the problem is the patient's responsibility and no-one can 'fix' it for them.

An understanding that the doctor may play a role as teacher, to help the patient deal with his own problem in a more effective way, is a completely different transaction. These situations become a necessary alternative after repeated visits to the doctor over months and years have not managed to 'fix' the problem.

Let us take a hypothetical case as an example. Mrs Smith has an itchy rash on her arms and legs. She goes to the doctor and he prescribes a cream. The cream works temporarily but the rash returns. Over the next six months repeated prescriptions are given for different creams and different strengths, sedative tablets may be added, all with limited benefit.

Mrs Smith may then be referred to a skin specialist at the hospital, tests taken and further creams or tablets prescribed. By this time she realises she has a chronic skin condition and is losing faith in ever being without it.

Perhaps it may be reasonable to look at what role Mrs Smith is playing in her skin condition. Looking at her skin as part of the whole person and learning more about herself, may be a useful attitude. I don't suggest she needs psychoanalysis but perhaps the mind is playing a major part in her problem and creams will not be the answer.

I do not want to portray hypnosis as the answer to everyone's problems. I maintain it is a useful tool to be used alongside other forms of medicine and if the doctor's treatment is not working, then trying something different *may* be more effective.

Why do doctors relegate hypnosis to the end of the list of treatments provided? The following points may be relevant.

1. As there is minimal training for hypnosis it is not considered as a form of therapy when the patient attends.
2. Hypnosis is still viewed as hocus pocus by many doctors.
3. A common attitude is that 'one must not meddle with the mind.'
4. There are many false ideas, misunderstandings and stories about hypnosis which are believed by doctors and these need to be corrected. I recently was asked in a lecture to doctors, 'Isn't it true that hypnosis drains the willpower and should be avoided?' With this archaic and false attitude, it is understandable why many in the medical profession give hypnosis such a wide berth.
5. One of the main reasons for avoiding its use is the lack of time doctors have with each patient. As so many minutes are allocated to each patient, it is understandable that with a full waiting room the doctor does not have time to listen and help teach patients to deal with their complaints.

'I just don't have the time to spend using hypnosis' is the most common reason given by general practictioners for prescribing sedatives, etc. I have no answer to that problem, but it reminds me of a joke about a drunk looking for something under the street light. When questioned what he was doing he said, 'I'm looking for my wallet.'

'Where did you lose it?'
'Over there in the dark.'
'Then why aren't you looking over there?'
'It's easier to see here under the light.'

I believe it is very difficult to make time to spend with patients, but if that is what is required to help their illnesses, then it is no use prescribing in the light to avoid time in the dark.

For me it is very difficult to write this section which raises points of criticism of the medical profession. It is very hard to generalise about doctors and very easy to be critical. I have had many many experiences with doctors who have very closed minds and as the mind is like an umbrella – 'it works better when it's open' – it is very difficult for these doctors to understand the role of complementary forms of medicine.

In my enthusiasm I may have painted a picture of hypnosis being a cure all; I can assure you it is not.

In the hands of a doctor with an open mind and an educated attitude towards the patient and disease it has proved to be very useful.

At a lecture about stress and alternative therapies one speaker said, 'There are not orthodox doctors and alternative doctors – there are good and bad doctors. Good doctors have a knowledge, an open mind, as to the various therapies available and choose the most appropriate one for the specific patient. A bad doctor has a closed mind and does not allow his patients to receive the benefits of other forms of therapy.'

I feel, in order to increase doctors' awareness of the various forms of complementary therapies available, pressure may need to come from you, the patients. Due to our 'blinkered' education as doctors it is hard for us to 'see in the dark'. Perhaps if you shine the torch a little, it might be easier for the light of knowledge to be spread more quickly.

If a patient turns out to be really ill after all, it is always possible to look grave and at the same time say, 'You realise I suppose, that twenty-five years ago you'd have been dead.'
STEPHEN POTTER, *One-Upmanship*

33 Conclusion

No improvement in the health care system will be
effective unless the citizen assumes responsibility for his
own well-being.
PROFESSOR GINZBURG
COLUMBIA UNIVERSITY

How does one write a conclusion to a book that is a conclusion in itself?
Perhaps by my making a few important points you may refer back to
the relevant chapters to refresh your mind.

1. You already possess all that is necessary to improve the quality
   of your life.
2. Self-hypnosis is *one* way of gaining access to the abilities required.
3. You are already limiting your resources by self-imposed restrictions, relating to past experiences.
4. Learning to be flexible, taking risks and being positive, will all
   be useful ways of improving your situation.
5. Spending time on yourself, for yourself, is an essential component
   of feeling better.
6. 'Being' not 'trying' is an appropriate attitude towards the time
   you spend on yourself.
7. Be yourself, not what others – past, present or future – believe
   you should be.
8. Take responsibility for your situation, attitude, illness.
9. Learn to understand the messages your body is giving you in the
   form of symptoms. Use self-hypnosis to achieve this.
10. You only have one life here. Self-hypnosis is one way of increasing
    your capacity to enjoy it. It is up to you to make use of this
    natural talent.

Best of luck.

Self-hypnosis Tape

If you wish to learn more about self-hypnosis and how it may be helpful for you, an audio cassette is available. This cassette will enable you to listen to Dr Roet teaching you to use self-hypnosis. By listening to the tape you will be able to assess your ability at going into a trance.

One side of the tape is about *relaxation* and provides a basis to allow yourself to experience deep relaxation using visual imagery of being in a tranquil garden, learning from the plants and flowers growing there.

The other side describes a method of gaining *self confidence* and a positive attitude. It explores the use of altering some negative attitudes you already hold and replacing them with more up-to-date, optimistic ones.

This tape may be purchased by contacting:

In the UK   Sound Partnership
             Dorset Lodge
             8 Dorset Square
             London NW1

             Telephone: 01-723 4253

In Australia Equinox Media
             PO Box 95
             Moreland Post Office
             Moreland
             Victoria 3058

             Telephone: AH 3872518

Suggested Reading

HYPNOSIS

Barnett, Edgar A. *Unlock your mind and be free*, Junica Publishing, Ontario, 1982
Le Cron, Leslie. *The complete guide to hypnosis*, Harper & Row, New York, 1971
Meares, Ainslie. *Relief without drugs*, Fontana, 1979
Spiegel, Dr Herbert. *The inner source – exploring hypnosis*, Holt, Reinhart & Winston, New York, 1984

STRESS

Montgomery, Bob, and Evans, Lynette. *You and stress*, Thomas Nelson (Aust.), Melbourne, 1984

DREAMS

Delaney, Gayle. *Living your dreams*, Harper & Row, New York, 1971

HEALTH

Cousins, Norman. *Anatomy of an illness*, Bantam Books, 1981
Harrison, John. *Love your disease – it's keeping you healthy*, Angus & Robertson, 1984

PAIN

Peck, Connie. *Controlling chronic pain*, Fontana, 1985

Suggested reading

PHOBIAS

Weekes, Claire. *Simple treatment of agoraphobia*, Angus & Robertson, 1976
  Peace from nervous suffering, Angus & Robertson, 1972

CONFIDENCE

Cohen, Herb. *You can negotiate anything*, Angus & Robertson, 1983
Dixon, Ann. *A woman in your own right*, Quartet Books, 1982

The following bookshops usually stock these books; they can be ordered if not in stock.

In the UK

Changes Bookshop,
242 Belsize Road,
London NW6

Tel. 01-328 5161

In Australia

Readings Bookshop,
384 Lygon Street,
Carlton,
Victoria 3053

Tel. 3476085

List of Hypnosis Societies

In the UK

British Society for Medical and Dental Hypnosis,
42 Links Road,
Ashstead,
Surrey KT21 2HJ

Tel. Ashtead 73522

British Society for Experimental and Clinical Hypnosis,
Dr Michael Heap (Sec.),
PO Box 133,
Canterbury,
Kent

British Holistic Medical Association,
179 Gloucester Place,
London NW1 6 DX

In Australia

Australian Society for Clinical and Experimental Hypnosis,
Royal Melbourne Hospital,
Royal Parade,
Parkville,
Victoria

Tel. 3475269

Branches in all other States

The Australian Society of Hypnosis,
PO Box 366,
Glenleg,
South Australia 5045